Flashgun Casey, Crime Photographer
From the Pulps to Radio and Beyond

Also By

J. Randolph Cox
> TAD-Schrift: Twenty Years of Mystery Fandom in The Armchair Detective, Editor, 1987
> H. G. Wells: A Reference Guide (with William J. Scheick), 1989
> Man of Magic and Mystery: A Guide to the Work of Walter B. Gibson, 1989
> Masters of Mystery and Detective Fiction: An Annotated Bibliography, 1989
> The Dime Novel Companion: A Source Book, 2000
> Dime Novel Round-Up, Editor, 1994–Present

David S. Siegel
> The Witch's Tale, Editor, 1998
> The Used Book Lover's Guides Series, 1993–Present
> A Resource Guide to the Golden Age of Radio, 2005 (forthcoming)

Flashgun Casey, Crime Photographer
From the Pulps to Radio and Beyond

By

J. Randolph Cox and David S. Siegel

With an Introduction by William F. Nolan

Book Hunter Press
Yorktown Heights, New York

Flashgun Casey, Crime Photographer: From the Pulps to Radio and Beyond
by J. Randolph Cox and David S. Siegel. © Copyright 2005 Book Hunter Press.

RETURN ENGAGEMENT by George Harmon Coxe.
First Published in *Black Mask*.
Copyright 1934 by Pro-Distributors Publishing Company, Inc.
Copyright renewed © 1962 by George Harmon Coxe.
Reprinted by permission of Brandt and Hochman Literary Agents, Inc.

"Hanged by the Neck" and "the White Monster" by Alonzo Deen Cole. Copyright The Estate of Alonzo Deen Cole. Reprinted with permission of Sharon Cole Hudson.

Radio's Golden Years Casey Illustration. *Radio's Golden Years: A Visual Guide to the Shows and the Stars* by Frank Bresee and Bobb Lynes. © Copyright 1998 by Frank Bresee and Bobb Lynes. Reprinted with permission from Bobb Lynes.

All rights reserved. No part may be reproduced or transmitted in any form or by any means, electronic or mechanical, including photocopying, recording or by an information and retrieval system, without permission in writing from the publisher or the appropriate copyright holder.

Cover by Alice Pfeifer. www.alicepfeifer.com

Photograph restoration by Amanda Osborne. www.odd-designs.com

Printed and bound in the United States of America

Library of Congress Catalog Card Number: 2005928221

ISBN 978-1-59393-429-3

Book Hunter Press
PO Box 193
Yorktown Heights, NY 10598
(914) 245-6608
www.bookhunterpress.com/radio
bookhunterpress@verizon.net

Dedication

The authors dedicate this volume to the memories of George Harmon Coxe and Alonzo Deen Cole, each a genius in his own right.

Coxe, the creator and literary father of *Casey*, who as few other writers can claim, invented a character whose many adventures in various media venues went on to enjoy a life of his own.

Cole, whose skill as a writer of radio scripts nurtured *Casey's* reputation for over a decade in the medium in which the vast majority of *Casey* fans continue to recall his adventures today.

Acknowledgments

The authors wish to express their sincerest appreciation to Brandt and Hochman Literary Agents, Inc. for permission to reprint the very first appearance of Casey in print in *Black Mask*, March 1934.

They also are grateful to Sharon Cole Hudson, daughter of Alonzo Deen Cole, who preserved her dad's papers, notes and scripts and who so generously shared these valuable treasures with the authors, granting them permission to reprint the two original scripts included in this volume.

The authors would also like to express their appreciation for the work of Susan Siegel, our editor, without whose tireless, imaginative and creative efforts over the past six months this book would not have been possible.

Others who provided valuable assistance in the form of research, advice and insight and who deserve our everlasting appreciation include:

John Behrens, CBS Audience Services, Dick Bertel, Frank Bresee, Art Chimes, James O. Cox, Jim Cox, Janet Coxe Davis, Demetrius Driscoll, Ray Faiola, Director, CBS Audience Services, Tom Fagan, Jack French, J. David Goldin, Leigh Goldin, Beinecke Rare Book & Manuscript Library, Yale University, Gordon Gregsen, Michael Henry, Deidre A. Johnson, Brian KenKnight, Kristine Krueger, Center For Motion Picture Study, Sidney Lumet, Bobb Lynes, F. Gwynplaine MacIntyre, Bob Mott, William F. Nolan, Michael Ogden, Duane Olson, Ken Roberts, Ron Sayles, Karl Schadow, Charles Schlessiger, Jean Renee Schneider, Lysna Scriven-Marzani, Samuel French, Inc., Charles Shibuk, Ivan Shreve, Nathaniel Simpkins and Nina Turner.

Table of Contents

Preface (DSS)	1
Introduction (WFN)	3
1. The Literary Life of George Harmon Coxe (JRC)	5
2. Memories of a Mystery Writer's Daughter (JCD)	23
3. Recollections of My Father (SCH)	27
4. Casey at *Black Mask* (JRC)	29
5. "Return Engagement," A Flashgun Casey Short Story (GHC)	45
6. Casey at the Movies (JRC)	61
7. Casey on the Radio (DSS)	69
8. Radio Log (DSS)	95
9. "Hanged by the Neck" and "The White Monster" Casey Radio Scripts (ADC)	109
10. Casey at Alfred A. Knopf (JRC)	151
11. Casey on Television (DSS)	169
12. Television Log (DSS)	183
13. Casey in the Comics (JRC)	193
14. Casey on the Stage (DSS)	199
15. About the Authors	203

Author Key: ADC=Alonzo Deen Cole, DSS=David S. Siegel, GHC=George Harmon Coxe, JCD=Janet Coxe Davis, JRC=J. Randolph Cox, SCH=Sharon Cole Hudson, WFN=William F. Nolan

Preface

If you are a fan of vintage detective fiction heroes like Sam Spade or Philip Marlowe, Jack "Flashgun" Casey should appeal to you.

If you are a fan of film noir or the less sophisticated B film series that thrived in the 1930s and 1940s focusing on detectives like the Saint, Charlie Chan, the Falcon and others, you should feel equally at home with this volume.

If you listened to radio during its Golden Age, or, more recently discovered tapes of the old radio detectives like Pam and Jerry (Mr. and Mrs.) North, Nick Carter, Philo Vance or Jack, Doc and Reggie of *I Love A Mystery* fame, or if you remember watching early television pay homage to the exploits of Sergeant Joe Friday, Peter Gunn, Cannon and Perry Mason, you'll recognize that the common themes that connect these pulp style detectives to their movie, radio and television counterparts are also illustrated in the many lives led by Jack "Flashgun" Casey.

The authors, each of whom confesses to being a fan of the old pulps, the B movies, the Golden Age of Radio and the other guilty pleasures that chronicled the long and distinguished career of the news photographer created by George Harmon Coxe, have laid out for the reader a long overdue portrait of this enduring media crime fiction hero.

The genius that is associated with a writer whose character has managed to survive in so many different media venues certainly suggests that he be recognized along with similar penman like Leslie Charteris, Earl Derr Biggers and Erle Stanley Gardner, creators respectively of Simon Templar, Charlie Chan and Perry Mason. While the authors acknowledge that the reputations of the aforementioned trio may outshine their own nominee, the fact that Conan Doyle created an even greater hero than the three authors rolled into one does not lessen their importance any more than their success should lessen the importance of Flashgun Casey.

Read on and discover for yourself how the pulp character who *Black Mask* editor Shaw initially thought not worthy of a series went on to enjoy a popularity that grew far beyond either the editor's or the writer's wildest imagination.

Introduction

By the spring of 1934, a pivotal new talent was being showcased in the *Mask*: George Harmon Coxe, dubbed "the professional's professional." For Shaw, Coxe created one of crime fiction's most colorful and enduring characters: photographer Jack "Flashgun" Casey, who appeared in 24 issues of *Black Mask*, into 1943.

Coxe was asked where he got the idea of making a series hero out of a crime photographer. "In those days, everybody else seemed to be writing about tough reporters and hard-nosed private detectives," he told an interviewer. "I was an amateur photographer myself, and I'd worked on papers, and knew a lot of news photographers. Seemed a natural idea to use one as a pulp hero. And it worked out very well."

Indeed it did. Coxe sold Casey not only to magazines, but the character was featured on radio (for nearly a decade), in films, in six published books and, finally, on television. There was even a Flash Casey comic book. Coxe went on to create a second crime photog, Kent Murdock (in many respects, a Casey clone), who starred in 21 novels. Obviously, here was an author who knew how to take maximum advantage of a saleable idea.

Ironically, when Joe Shaw purchased the first Casey story, he told Coxe (who wanted to write more about the character) that the *Mask* didn't need any new series characters; the magazine was "overloaded." However, after reading the second Casey tale, Shaw changed his mind. "Okay, George, I was wrong," he admitted. "Go ahead, send me more."

George Harmon Coxe was born in Olean, New York, in April 1901. Educated at Purdue and Cornell, he worked in a lumber camp and an automobile factory, then switched to reporting for various papers in New York, Florida and California.

Discovering that he possessed "a way with words," Coxe turned his attention to the pulps in 1922. ("I wrote everything — sports stories, love stories, sea stories — whatever I could sell. But mostly I wrote crime fiction.") When he created Flash Casey for the *Mask* in 1934, he knew that he had struck gold. There was immediate, positive reader response.

Jack Casey originally worked for *The Boston Globe*. Unlike most magazine heroes, he didn't carry a gun (although he kept a loaded .38 in his desk drawer, next to the office whiskey bottle). One critic described him as "six foot one...a large, rumpled man with a rugged face and unkempt shaggy hair...When angered, he's as mean as a hungry bear." In keeping with *Black Mask* tradition, Casey was a "tough, aggressive photographer whose greatest thrill was snapping an exclusive picture even if he had to risk his neck to get it."

As Coxe wrote more about him through the years, Casey mellowed, losing much of his hard edge. The author, gradually emphasized his character's emotional side, but there was nothing mellow or emotional about Casey's early adventures in the *Mask*. Consider this, from "Hot Delivery" (July 1934):

> Casey dropped behind the desk as the automatic roared. He scrambled around the side on hands and knees. Flip screamed in pain, fired again. Then Casey straightened, leaped forward. Flip was trying to get out of the chair. Blinded, he waved the gun wildly, one hand closed to his blackened, charred face...He was nearly erect when Casey hit him. Flip went over backwards with the chair. Casey landed on top, his hand on the automatic. He wrenched it free, struck once, twice. Crushing, violent blows. Flip's body did not move after that, probably would never move.

From 1936 to 1938, Coxe worked for M-G-M, then wrote for the slick paper magazines from the 1940s through the 1960s. He enjoyed vacations in the Caribbean with his wife and two children, but never slowed his prodigious production. Month by month along the way, Coxe turned out one novel after another, running up a total of 63 published books into 1975. In 1964, the Mystery Writers of America proclaimed him an official Grand Master, an honor he certainly deserved, marking a career of mythic dimension.

George Harmon Coxe died in late January 1984. He was 82. Now out of print and largely forgotten, Flashgun Casey died with him.[*]

(Excerpted from "Behind the Black Mask," which appeared in the November 2004 issue of *Firsts* magazine.)

---

[*] While the authors of this volume respect and admire the views of William F. Nolan who so generously allowed us to reprint his wonderful article on *Casey*, we respectfully take issue with what we view as Mr. Nolan's premature burial of our hero. To us and to countless fans of Old Time Radio of all ages, Flashgun Casey is still very much with us. And, who knows, perhaps the publication of this volume will result in an interest in the revival or reprinting of those wonderful *Black Mask* Casey adventures.

1
The Literary Life of George Harmon Coxe

Introduction

Tuesday, August 10, 1971. This writer, accompanied by his brother James, who had served as driver from Minnesota, arrived in Old Lyme, Connecticut. We stopped at a drugstore to make a telephone call to a number that had been included in a letter from mystery writer George Harmon Coxe. In a few minutes a car pulled up and a tall, slender man in his early seventies stepped out and introduced himself. It was easier to find the house by following Coxe in his car than to do it on our own. In a few minutes we were at the house, called "Deepledge" on Coxe's stationery, and this writer was unpacking his equipment: notebooks and pencils and a large reel-to-reel tape recorder.

We were made to feel welcome. Mrs. Coxe suggested that James might like to visit the local country club while her husband and I were talking, but James declined. He had been behind the wheel of the car for so long that just sitting still for a time felt good. The previous stop had been at the Beinecke Library at Yale University in New Haven for a session with the treasures in the George Harmon Coxe Collection there. Some of the findings prompted questions that would be answered in the next few hours.

The mystery writer took the researcher to a room in the basement where there was a collection of many issues of the pulp magazines to which he had contributed. This writer spent a profitable hour or so taking notes from every magazine in sight before going upstairs for the next phase of the afternoon, a taped interview with George Harmon Coxe. The tape recorder was set up in Coxe's study, a pine-paneled, book-lined room with sporting prints on the walls along with the originals of Arthur Rodman Bowker's illustrations from 1930s issues of *Black Mask* magazine.

The following biographical sketch is based on that interview along with personal correspondence and other sources. An earlier version appeared in issues of

The Armchair Detective in 1973. At the end of the formal interview Coxe signed some books and sat for photographs taken by James Cox. Then Coxe, this writer and his brother moved to the living room for a welcome glass of Scotch before the Minnesotans drove off in search of the next stop and a motel.

Growing Up

George Harmon Coxe was born April 23, 1901, in Olean, New York, but grew up in Elmira, which was also the home of Frederic Dannay, one of the writers of the Ellery Queen stories. There is no record that they ever met before they had embarked on their chosen careers as writers. There is also no record of just when Coxe decided to become a writer. His first career choice was mechanical engineering and it was with that goal in mind that he entered Purdue University in 1919. At Purdue he was on the freshman relay swimming team and continued playing tenor banjo, a skill he had acquired in high school.

The next year he transferred to Cornell where he continued to play banjo with a dance band to such an extent that he was asked by the administration to leave since the music seemed to interfere with his studies. In 1922, he published a somewhat fanciful account of his musical experiences in an article in *The American Boy*, "Playing One's Way Through College." It was signed, as were most of his early efforts, George H. Coxe, Jr. That same year he had sold two short stories to Street & Smith's *Detective Story Magazine*. At the time, he didn't expect anyone to take either of them seriously. They were published a year apart in 1922 and 1923. These were not his earliest publications, however. Even before writing the article for *The American Boy* or the stories for the Street & Smith pulps, he had written some articles for *Popular Mechanics* as a way of practicing his self-taught skills as a writer.

After college, Coxe worked in a lumber camp and in an automobile factory and then went to the West Coast. It seems axiomatic that writers experience a series of widely differing jobs designed to supply them with a background from which to write. The jobs that came Coxe's way must have helped in that respect. On the West Coast he worked for newspapers in Santa Monica (the *Outlook* in 1922), in Pasadena and in Los Angeles (the *Express*). As he told it in a 1944 article for *The Delta of Sigma Nu*, his fraternity magazine, he returned East as "promotion manager for the now defunct *Miami Tribune* and the equally defunct *New York Commercial*, which used to be down on Park Row. I did a little advertising work for the *Elmira Star-Gazette*, and finally wound up in Cambridge, Massachusetts, with an advertising outfit." This was the Barta Press. He also worked for the Utica, New York *Observer Dispatch*. Contrary to what has been written about Coxe's early newspaper experience, he was never a reporter.

The Reference Librarian and the Mystery Writer (J. Randolph Cox
and George Harman Coxe), Old Lyme, CT, August 10, 1971.

A Writer is Born

It was at the Barta Press that he met his future wife, Elizabeth Fowler. They were married in 1929. He stayed on at Barta for five years from 1927 to 1932 before deciding to become a full time writer. In a column for the 1968 *Mystery Writers of America Annual* Coxe waxed nostalgic in his account of those years of struggle. He didn't know any other writers, editors, agents or publishers; he was on his own mailing stories out and getting them back almost by return mail. Finally he began to see notes of encouragement on some of the rejection slips, notes signed by the initials "R. A." This turned out to be Robert Arthur, assistant to Howard Bloomfield, editor of *Detective Fiction Weekly*.

When he was able to afford it, Coxe went to New York City from Cape Cod, where he and Elizabeth were living with their daughter Janet, and called on Robert Arthur at the Munsey Building and took him to a modest lunch. At lunch, Arthur gave Coxe the names of two or three agents whom he queried about his stories. Sydney Sanders asked to be shown some samples and placed three stories with Street & Smith's *Top Notch*, the magazine that had been founded by Gilbert Patten, the creator of Frank Merriwell. The semi-monthly magazine published Coxe's three stories in quick succession in the issues for July 15, August 15, and September 1, 1932. The titles were: "Special Delivery," "No Work, No Pay" and "Stop Sign." The next month his son George Harmon Coxe III was born.

That same year, Coxe sold the first of several stories ("Bad Medicine") to another Street & Smith magazine, *Complete Stories*, which was to publish more George Harmon Coxe stories than any other magazine with the exception of *Black Mask* and *The American Magazine*. The following year he made at least 23 sales to Clayton's *Clues*, *Argosy*, *Dime Mystery Book*, *Dime Detective*, *Detective Fiction Weekly*, *Detective Story Magazine*, and (of course) *Complete Stories*. He also sold a suspense-adventure story to *The Open Road for Boys*.

Coxe's agent, Sydney Sanders, also represented Raymond Chandler at one time. In later years, both writers changed to Brandt and Brandt.

The question of why George Harmon Coxe turned to writing as a career is less easily explained than why he chose to specialize in mystery fiction. So many of the early stories he wrote for what he liked to call the "smooth paper" magazines (as opposed to the pulps) were not mysteries at all, but light romances, sea stories and straight adventure stories. He wrote what each magazine wanted.

How to Write Mysteries

When asked in the 1971 interview for *The Armchair Detective* why he chose the mystery as the field in which to do most of his work, Coxe replied that the only thing he could think of was that when he was young he read mysteries and that influenced his choice. He read Sherlock Holmes as a boy and S. S. Van Dine in the 1920s; everyone read Van Dine in the 1920s. Coxe's fellow resident of Elmira, Frederic Dannay, based Ellery Queen on Philo Vance. When Coxe began to write for a living his mind seemed to formulate mysteries more than any other plot type.

While he admitted that he didn't read mysteries much as an adult, he felt that crime was a universal subject and that thinking up something that had a twist or a gimmick to it was easier than writing successful love stories. Whatever the reason, he figured he'd rather be a pretty good mystery story writer than a half-baked novelist that no one ever heard of. He may have had the right sort of mind to begin with, one that worked out believable stories in which logic, or something akin to logic, played a key role. Coxe never used esoteric means for murder in any of his books or stories, but had his characters stabbed or bludgeoned or shot because he felt that was the way most murders were done in the real world. He may have used poison a few times, but the simple methods seemed better to him.

Along with teaching himself how to write fiction, Coxe developed some theories about the structure of the mystery story that he set down in a series of articles for *The Writer*, a magazine of practical advice for would-be writers. He was careful to make the main character real to himself so that he could then focus on the mystery as his starting point and work out the rest of the story from that. Since the focus of a mystery was that someone had to be killed, the rest was simply a matter of explaining who, why and how.

Once Coxe began writing novels in 1934, he made outlines of his stories with a list of the characters, with thumbnail sketches of them, which he found handy as reference tools throughout the writing of the actual book. He needed to pace himself so that he wouldn't run out of story when he was only halfway through the publisher's requested number of words.

He learned that characters were what were important in a mystery, because they were what the reader remembered and not the plot twists or even the clever ideas. With proper attention to characters, he could overcome plot ideas that were sometimes not as brilliant as he had thought they were at the beginning of the book.

For a period of time he kept a notebook in which he listed his stories, where they had been sold and how much he had been paid for them. In 1978, he sent me a photocopy of five pages from his notebook for 1934. He had recorded information on 37 short stories and novelettes and summed up the year in economic terms: Words Written — 408,200 plus Novel 68,000. Stories sold – 33.

Earned — $4,168.69, Exclusive of 10% commission (Money Received). Approximate Words Sold — 335,000. That $4,168.69, he estimated, would have been close to the equivalent of nearly $20,000 in 1978. In 2005 that 1934 income would be equal to $60,000.

The Pulp Years

Even in his earliest stories for the pulps, Coxe made use of bits of suspense and twists of plot to hold the reader's attention. His two stories from the 1920s may have been written almost as jokes, but they exhibited an attention to detail and an unassuming style characteristic of his later work. There were facts ignored by the crooks that tripped them up and Coxe handled the dialogue easily and well. In the stories of the 1930s there were basic themes, situations and characters used again and again. These were not marks of a lazy writer, but of one who had to write fast in order to make a living. Writing in order to live, and writing for transient magazine publication, tended to foster a certain reliance on salable formulas. A writer might not be opposed to stylistic experiments or to creating characters that were more than two-dimensional, but there was usually insufficient time to worry about such matters. The market demanded a good story and the writer wanted to produce one satisfactory enough to sell before he moved on to the next one.

Coxe told many of his earliest stories from the point of view of the crook, not the detective, and laid trails that involved the forgotten details that helped to trip him up. These were details overlooked in an otherwise foolproof scheme: a bit of extra information, a changed timetable, or a color-blind crook. They weren't exclusive to his stories, but he used them with a considerable amount of skill.

In 1933 Coxe decided to expand his horizons a bit and see if he couldn't sell a story to *Black Mask*, perhaps the most important crime fiction pulp of them all. Since he had taught himself to write fiction he found he could study the market and determine just what sort of stories the editor at *Black Mask* wanted. With a combination of perseverance, skill and luck, his first story was accepted and one might say, the rest was history. In all, he wrote and sold 25 stories, short stories and novelettes to *Black Mask*. In addition, he wrote two novels that were published as serials in the magazine, so that he appeared in 31 issues between 1934 and 1942. Most of the stories were about a news photographer named Jack (Flashgun) Casey, but two years after the first Casey story appeared, Coxe wrote four stories about Paul Baron.

Baron was not a character who was easy to categorize. He was a cop turned plainclothes detective, framed for a bond theft and murder, who found he needed to be tough to survive and clear his name. An inheritance gave him some money of his own and because he looked good in formal wear he fit in with socialite Janet Grainger's set. He moved easily between her glittery world and the edge of the underworld. After leaving the force, Baron never became an official private detective but stood on the fringes of the underworld, trusted by neither cop nor crook. After four stories, Coxe abandoned the character. Perhaps he ran out of situations in which to place him. Perhaps he was looking ahead to new horizons.

Themes and Variations

After writing several stories told from the point of view of the crook, or would-be crook, Coxe began to use detectives as characters in more than just the final scene. These characters, who were as often as not police officers when they were not plainclothes detectives, came to dominate his stories. Magazine editors may have had something to do with this shift in emphasis because some editors demanded certain types of characters for their publications.

Coxe never set out to be a "hard boiled" writer, although he wrote some of his best stories for *Black Mask*. He wrote what the market demanded and saw *Black Mask* as a bridge between straight pulp writing and the smooth paper market, the market that was often referred to in the trade papers as the "slick" market. If the stories had to be tough to sell, Coxe made them tough.

He told most of his stories in third person, a form he found had greater advantages than first person. Interestingly enough, one of his few examples of using first person was frequently reprinted. This was "Invited Witness," from *Dime Mystery Book Magazine*, August 1933. The detective was Jack Wolfe, alias The Wolf, and was about as close to being an avenger detective story as any Coxe ever wrote.

One of his recurring themes was the plight of the misfit, the loner or the underdog. If the misfit was unable to carry on, perhaps because of death, someone needed to return his possessions to his family. If he survived, as in "Easy Money" (*Complete Stories*, July 1, 1934), he did so against some of the most insurmountable odds. These characters had to prove their worth, no matter what. They were not the detectives, but the victims of the crimes. In the course of the story they were required to display courage or some other unsuspected quality.

The private detective in Coxe's fictional world was often someone who had been on the police force, like Tom Flagg in "Special Messenger" (*Complete Stories*, November 1, 1933). For one reason or another these men had quit the force to apply their skill in the private sector. It was a good way to explain how the hero learned his trade, something many writers ignored. Often the detective was teamed with someone from a different background. Coxe wrote a series of stories about Sgt. J. H. "Dutch" Kramer whose partner was Ted Clarke, a millionaire playboy.

In his early days, the nearest Coxe came to writing a story in the Sherlock Holmes tradition was "Touch System" (*Complete Stories*, January 1, 1934), about criminologist Tom Farnham and his "Watson," Charley, the lawyer. Like Holmes, Farnham set out deliberately to train himself to be a detective. Many of Coxe's later detectives worked toward the solution in a case with an equal sense of confidence.

Even though Coxe never graduated from college, college was obviously an important part of his background and he transferred his set of values to many of his heroes. Those characters were often well educated, were either in college or had been to college. The bodyguards for rich men, even gangsters, might be former college football players. Often, as with Dutch Kramer and Ted Clarke, the clash between cultures was a source of humor in the stories.

Books and Movies

While Coxe was never as prolific a writer for the pulps as Max Brand or Erle Stanley Gardner, he wrote enough to make a comfortable living. One year he recalled writing 32 stories, mostly novelettes, and selling all but one. He knew editors, such as the one at *Complete Stories*, who would buy almost everything he sent them. If the move to writing for *Black Mask* was considered a bridge to writing for smooth paper magazines, it was also a bridge to writing full-length novels and screenplays. It was Casey who paved the way for both.

In 1934, Coxe and his family were living on the island of St. Vincent, British West Indies, when he began work on his first novel. He decided to continue his winning streak writing about a newspaper photographer, but he didn't think Casey was right for that first novel. Instead, he created a new character, Kent Murdock, a sophisticated photographer for the Boston *Courier-Herald* (later called just the *Courier*). Murdock would be more at ease in situations where Casey might not know whether to take off his hat or leave it on. Murdock would know people on several levels of society and that could open up possibilities for a greater variety of plots and situations. Murdock even had a wife, Joyce, who seemed to fade from the scene after several books.

The first novel was called *Murder with Pictures* and the publisher was Alfred A. Knopf, but that was not the first place the manuscript was sent. As Coxe's agent, Sydney Sanders sent the manuscript to Little, Brown who turned it down. Sanders then sent it to Farrar and Rinehart who also turned it down. Then Coxe got lucky. The next publisher to receive the manuscript was Knopf and it seemed there were two people there who read *Black* Mask and were Casey fans. Knopf accepted the manuscript, but asked for some revisions.

The editor at Knopf thought the story began more like a straight novel than a mystery. He suggested Coxe add a paragraph or two to make it clear to the reader that this book was really a mystery novel. Coxe was glad to oblige and in only a day or two wrote a new first chapter. In this revision he borrowed a gimmick from *The Front Page*, by Ben Hecht and Charles MacArthur (or perhaps the 1931 movie version), and crafted a scene in which a group of reporters and photographers were waiting outside a courtroom for the verdict in a high profile case. It made it possible for him to introduce his new hero in a highly dramatic way. Knopf accepted the book and published it in 1935. In addition, Knopf took every book Coxe wrote for the next 40 years and never turned one down or asked for a rewrite.

Coxe had a second Murdock novel in mind by the time the first was accepted and *The Barotique Mystery,* published in 1936, was actually set on the island of St. Vincent. That decision began a long-running arrangement where Coxe might write a novel set in the same exotic location where he was living. Sometimes the novels were about Kent Murdock, but sometimes they weren't.

By the time Coxe wrote the third Murdock novel, *The Camera Clue*, he had developed a relationship with *The American Magazine* in which he would write two versions of the same story, one to be published as a novelette in the smooth paper magazine and the other to be published in cloth covers by Knopf. The arrangement came about as a matter of simple necessity. Coxe found that ideas were the things that bothered him the most rather than the actual writing. If he could make the same idea work in two sales, all the better, so he would plan the story in two versions, a 20,000 word novelette for *The American* and a 70,000 word novel for Knopf.

It was Henry La Cossit, fiction editor of *The American,* who came to Coxe's new agent, Carl Brandt, to ask if his client would write a novelette for the magazine. This was the period when the magazine was beginning a regular feature of publishing a short mystery novel in each issue. Coxe and La Cossit had lunch and Coxe went home to write a novelette. Nothing had been said about the subject matter so he wrote a Casey novelette. La Cossit turned it down, but two years later he made the same offer. This time Coxe was shrewd and refused to write anything on speculation. The editor agreed that he would have to approve the idea first, Coxe would then write the story and that would be a sale. That turned out to be the situation between Coxe and *The American* for years to come when he worked with five different editors. The Casey novelette, "Casey Comes to Town," didn't go to waste however and Coxe quickly sold it to *Black Mask* where it appeared in 1942 under the title "Murder in the Red."

Usually the novelette for *The American* appeared first, followed by the novel, but the situation was reversed with *The Camera Clue*. Coxe wrote the novel and then cut his own text for the novelette. At least he had control over his text and title that time. This was not always the case. The name of the newspaper for which Murdock worked became the *Times-Clarion* in the *American* novelettes, a name Coxe told me was something he would never have used.

Coxe's next two novels for Knopf, *Murder for the Asking* (1939) and *The Lady is Afraid* (1940), were not about Kent Murdock at all, but Maxfield Chauncey Hale, an extension of the playboy-turned-detective that Coxe had last used in the Kramer and Clarke stories for the pulps. Hale began his life in manuscript under the more prosaic name of Rolf Barr. He was an interesting character, but Coxe appeared to tire of him and his novel for 1941, *No Time to Kill*, was a non-series entry. He returned to his old friend Casey for his next book, *Silent Are the Dead*. Before that happened there was something of a hiatus in his career when he became a scriptwriter in Hollywood.

In 1935 or 1936 Coxe sold a Casey story, "Women Are Trouble," to M-G-M. The film was released in 1936. About the same time he sold two Casey stories to Grand National and his first Murdock novel to Paramount. The films based on these stories will be discussed in a later chapter. The sale to M-G-M led indirectly to his working for the studio. He worked as a contract writer from 1936 to 1938, fixing up other people's scripts, and on one occasion he received a screenplay credit. This was in 1938 for *Arsene Lupin Returns*, with Melvyn Douglas as the gentleman thief. Coxe shared screen credit with James Kevin McGuinness and Howard Emmett Rogers at a time when everyone had three names. Frank S. Nugent in *The New York Times* considered the screenplay made Lupin more English than French, but that the film was "fairer than most in its presentation of clues."

The War Years

In 1939 Coxe bought some land in Old Lyme, Connecticut, and built a house. Apart from that year in St. Vincent, he had lived in Falmouth, Massachusetts, as the return address on his early manuscripts attested, but felt he needed something closer to New York City where his agent and his publisher had their offices. He once described his Connecticut home as a farm, but said that depended on your definition of "farm" since this one had no livestock and no crops, except a victory garden, a woodlot and some apple trees that the bugs usually got to before anyone else. He had a comfortable study that served as his office for reading, thinking and actual writing. He enjoyed it so much he sent a photograph of the house to Raymond Chandler in California.

The books and the magazine stories kept coming. He concentrated more and more on the smooth paper market and less and less on the pulps. In a letter to Raymond Chandler in 1940, Coxe expressed his concern over the war in Europe and his stories began to reflect this. He wrote a number of magazine stories about people who were somehow connected with the military, including the Coast Guard. Perhaps he felt he could do his bit for the war effort through his fiction. Later he was one of a group of writers sent to the Pacific by the War Office to serve as a war correspondent for three or four months. Coxe was given the rank of captain and there is a photo of him in his correspondent gear, looking much like Ernie Pyle, on the jacket of his 1945 novel *Woman at Bay*. It may have been about that time that he spent two years writing scripts for a radio series called *The Commandos*. He was sent scripts that the regular staff writers had written and he rewrote them as he saw fit and returned them, often the same afternoon. *The Commandos* was a sustaining series on CBS, which meant it was not sponsored commercially. In 1943, Coxe was instrumental in launching *Casey, Crime Photographer* as a radio series on CBS, although he didn't write the scripts after working on the first one with Ashley Buck. The series lasted about a decade.

Some of Coxe's books during the war years also reflected the war. By 1945, he enlisted Kent Murdock in the army as a captain for the period covered by *The Jade Venus*. Two years later in *The Fifth Key*, Murdock was out of the army, home from Italy, and covering a radio show called *Sob Sister* about a girl reporter and a photographer. The background of the novel revealed much about the workings of the radio industry, something Coxe would have known about first hand from his experience with *Casey* on the radio.

Even though Coxe was not writing new Casey stories, four of the *Black Mask* novelettes were collected as *Flash Casey—Detective* by Avon Publishing Co. and published in paper covers in the Murder Mystery Monthly series in 1946.

During this period Coxe also began writing novels set in the Caribbean. The first of these was *Assignment in Guiana*, written and published in 1942. The planning had begun as far back as 1934 while *Murder with Pictures* was being written. Coxe had made notes and taken pictures while he was looking for an inexpensive cottage on the beach in which to write his first novel. In 1942, he resurrected those notes and photos and wrote the novel that appeared first as a six-part serial in *Argosy*, one of the better general fiction pulps. In the story, Lane Morgan is a young Boston architect summoned to Georgetown at the request of his uncle Johnny Hammond, only to find him murdered. From the moment Morgan's ship docks and he experiences the heat simmering up from the water and the wharves and the shade which doesn't bring coolness and he learns to sleep under mosquito netting, the architect is on his guard in a bewildering sequence of events. Isaac Anderson gave the novel a positive review in the *New York Times Book Review*, saying "the author gives us mystery, adventure, romance and a bit of international intrigue, all intricately interconnected in such a way as to afford thrilling entertainment as a momentary respite from the horrors of war."

Coxe's next story with a Caribbean setting was *Murder in Havana*, a novel of espionage, followed a few years later by his last wartime Caribbean novel, *Woman at Bay*. This involved the search for the manuscript to the memoirs of a Vichy collaborationist named Armand Sevigny. After that, Coxe returned to chronicling the adventures of Kent Murdock.

But what may be Coxe's finest short story was not a mystery and was not concerned with the war. This was his first sale to the *Saturday Evening Post*, "See How They Run," published in 1941. The plot had most of the elements that readers expected in a *Post* story: a guy, a girl, a conflict to be overcome — but the situation was unusual: Johnny Burke takes his father's place in the annual Boston Marathon and learns just what kept his father returning to the event for twenty years. Perhaps the most impressive aspect of the story remains the vividness with which Coxe portrayed the feelings of a man who had to run the full twenty-six miles and three hundred and eighty-five yards.

The author's third major series, after Casey and Murdock, was about medical examiner Paul Standish. Created for *Cosmopolitan* in 1942 and continued in *Liberty*, *Mystery Book Magazine*, and *The American Magazine*, Dr. Standish was also the hero of a 1948 CBS radio series starring Gary Merrill. Coxe was one of three writers who worked on the scripts.

The Standish series was obviously one in which its author took a good deal of pride, and rightly so. Coxe made certain the medical background was as authentic as the newspaper background in the Casey and Murdock series. Several of the short stories appeared in anthologies, some more than once. Even the earliest ones with their somewhat dated references to the Second World War remain good stories.

In the middle of the decade, Coxe went back to M-G-M, this time for a finite period of time — six weeks guaranteed, expenses out and back. If they didn't like what he had done in that time, that was to be the end of it, but if they liked his work he would stay until the picture was done. At the end of six weeks he had a treatment that they liked very much, so he stayed to work on the screenplay. The film was *The Hidden Eye* with Edward Arnold as Baynard Kendrick's blind detective, Captain Duncan Maclain. Coxe shared screen credit with Harry Ruskin and the film was released in 1945. One reviewer called it "a fast-moving, entertaining mystery."

Because it was still wartime, Coxe had a little trouble getting decent accommodations to return to Old Lyme, but he knew his children were growing up and felt he had been gone long enough. The person he spoke to in the transportation office at M-G-M said they couldn't get him a sleeper on a train for ten days to two weeks. Coxe reminded them that he was on the payroll until they got him out. They got him out in two days.

Coxe's novels began appearing in paperback editions from Dell Publishing Co. during the war years. *Four Frightened Women* was the first to appear and was issued in March 1943. It was also the initial title in Dell's famous "mapback" series where each book had a distinctive map of the location of the story on the back cover. Seven years later, the same novel was adapted to comic book format and published in digest size as "A Kent Murdock Murder Mystery Told in Pictures." Dell had plans for a series of these "told in pictures" books, but only two ever appeared. Apparently the reading public was not ready for graphic novels on the newsstand.

That wasn't the only illustrated book signed with the name George Harmon Coxe. Perhaps the most unusual book in Coxe's long list of publications was *Peril Afloat*, 1938, a reprint of one of his novelettes from *Thrilling Detective*. The publisher was Saalfield of Akron, Ohio, and included Coxe's story in its "Little Big Book" series. This was similar to Whitman's "Big Little Book" series in which each book had facing pages with an illustration and story text.

Acclaim in the Post War Years

The next two decades found Coxe writing as usual, turning out dependable work in novels and magazine stories. Sometimes it was a Kent Murdock novel, sometimes a Caribbean thriller, occasionally a novel about a new character, as though the author wanted to try out another variation on a theme. Such a character was detective Sam Crombie. He appeared in only two novels, *The Frightened Fiancée* from 1950, and *The Impetuous Mistress* in 1958, but he made his presence felt both times. Crombie was a big man of considerable bulk inside a seersucker suit and Panama hat. He was solid rather than fat, his voice hearty and hoarse, a distinctive figure rather than a caricature. Seen mostly through the eyes of the other characters, the glimpses of Crombie were all the more valuable for being brief. He was something of a blend of William Jennings Bryan and Clarence Darrow. Interestingly, the first title was set in the country near Old Lyme. (Remember, a writer should write about what he knows.) Anthony Boucher found both novels filled with fresh approaches to classic themes.

In the 1960s, Coxe revived Casey in three novels for Knopf; these will be discussed in a later chapter in this book.

Coxe had always been active in his professional organization, the Mystery Writers of America, and had served on its Board of Directors in 1946–1948 and 1969–1970. On February 13, 1952, he was elected president of the national group. Seven years later, in June 1959, he was elected president again to fill the unexpired term of Raymond Chandler who died March 26, 1959. The Board had nominated Lawrence G. Blochman, Dorothy Salisbury Davis and Coxe as candidates to fill the vacated office; all three were past national presidents. Blochman and Davis withdrew their names, leaving George Harmon Coxe who officially took office following a ballot of the active MWA members.

The Mystery Writers of America was founded in New York City in 1945 by a small number of American mystery and crime writers. The headquarters were in New York City and every year since 1947 the organization presented awards to professional writers for their distinguished achievements in the preceding year. The awards became known as the "Edgars" named for Edgar Allan Poe, considered to have been the first American writer of detective fiction. The most prestigious and coveted award was that of Grand Master, which recognized not only important contributions to the field over the recipient's lifetime but also consistently high-quality work. In 1964, George Harmon Coxe received the Grand Master Award and the ceramic bust of Edgar Allan Poe in recognition of his achievement.

He brought Dr. Standish back for a single novel, *The Ring of Truth*, in 1966, and concluded the sixth decade of the twentieth century by writing the twenty-first and last of the novels about Kent Murdock, *An Easy Way To Go* in 1969. The genesis of the final Murdock story was a novelette, "Speak No Evil," which was published in *The American Magazine* in 1947, but not expanded into a book for twenty-two years.

Sunset

Most years George Harmon Coxe published at least two novels each year. Some years he edited an anthology of short mystery fiction for the MWA. In 1966 he decided his tax situation was such that it would be best if he published only one novel annually. The next decade he published only six novels, three of them featuring Jack Fenner, the private detective friend of Kent Murdock, while the other three were non-series books. *Double Identity*, 1970, *Woman with a Gun*, 1971, and *The Inside Man*, 1974, returned to South America and the Caribbean. A mistaken identity, a double murder, and a skyjacking for a $450,000 ransom served to drive the plots of the three novels. Before working on *Woman with a Gun,* Coxe returned to St. Vincent and looked up his old cottage, now a small inn, and used it as the background for the novel.

Fenner was too interesting a character to remain in the shadow of Kent Murdock. He was described differently over the years as though he were aging. He was a neat dresser without being fancy, wore a worn gray topcoat and a battered felt hat. Once he grumbled that while Murdock could look neat in anything he wore, he (Fenner) always looked as if he was wearing his uncle's suit. At one time Fenner had an office on Shaw Street. By the time he emerged in his own series in *Fenner* (1971), he shared a suite of offices with attorney Frank Quinn on the third floor of a four-storied building around the corner from Boylston.

In a tough spot, Fenner could still remain cool enough to deliver a lecture on the differences between television and real detectives — if only to stall for time — when asked why he didn't carry a gun. *No Place for Murd*er, from 1975, was Fenner's last case and George Harmon Coxe's last novel. It ended on a poignant note as Fenner was trying to decide who to call after the case was wrapped up and what music they would listen to: "Oldies with Art Tatum and Herman Chittison; with Bobby Hackett and Jack Teagarden. Maybe a couple of new ones with Ruby Braff and Hank Jones, or Dick Hyman. Maybe Yank Lawson's group or Count Basie on 'Sweet Lorraine'." Fenner finally decided to call the client because "it was always gratifying to be able to report good news to a client; to know you had done a proper job and really earned your fee."

The final scenes and pages of *No Place for Murder* may be read with greater significance when the reader is made aware that it was intended to mark Coxe's fortieth year with Knopf as well as the retirement from writing of its author. Coxe sent a copy to this writer with the inscription: "Here's the latest—and possibly the last. Hope it measures up."*

It isn't certain just when Coxe began to think about retirement from writing mystery novels. Ideas were coming more slowly. He continued to clip articles from magazines like *Time* looking for ideas for short stories even though he hadn't written a short story for years. His mother was perhaps his staunchest fan and her death in February 1972 at the age of 95 may have made him stop

---

* Because this writer had written at such length about him for *The Armchair Detective* Coxe dedicated one of the Fenner novels, *The Silent Witness*, to me. He was surprised that *The Armchair Detective* articles were published without their author receiving any monetary remuneration and hoped the dedication would compensate for that. Then someone in the compositors' room at Knopf spelled my name "J. Randolphe Cox" and changed part of the dedication to read "The Complete Librarian" instead of "The Complete Bibliographer." Letters of apology from both the author and someone at Knopf arrived at about the same time as an inscribed copy of the book.

and think. Ever since *Murder with Pictures* he had sent her a copy of each new novel so that she was one of the few who had a complete set of his books.

In a letter to this writer in 1978 Coxe said there were several reasons why he decided to call it quits after selling 62 novels to Knopf without a rejection. One was the memory of James M. Cain "who did all those good things and then could not be accepted by Knopf even after getting a chance to fix a manuscript; who could sell to the next publisher only after agreeing to let some other man rewrite his stuff; and finally could not sell at all." When asked about copies of his manuscripts that hadn't been sent to the Beinecke Library for the Coxe collection, he revealed that he had torn up every original short story after he had a clean copy. He thought he had perhaps 25 carbons, but no originals and the same was true of the novels. The 25 or so full length manuscripts at Yale were all there were, the others having been destroyed. How was he to know that anyone would ever want his material?

But the author was not completely put out to pasture. In 1976, Coxe was asked by Herbert Ruhm for permission to include a Casey story in a book on *Black Mask* and the arrangement for "Once Around the Clock" to make another appearance between covers was made. The book was *The Hard-Boiled Detective: Stories from Black Mask Magazine, 1920–1951* published by Random House in 1977. He was also asked by Otto Penzler to write a 2000–2500 word piece on Casey for a collection of "biographies" of characters in detective fiction. Coxe thought about it for a while and then went back to the typewriter and wrote a biography of Casey. His method was to use part fiction, part fact and it worked. The result was included in the collection called *The Great Detectives*, published by Little, Brown in 1978.

He also had an idea for an anthology of some of his short fiction, perhaps a Casey novelette as well as a *Collier's* novelette, the last one they had bought from him. In between he wanted to include some non-mystery shorts from the *Post*, *Collier's*, *The American*, *Liberty* and *Cosmopolitan* to have something on the library shelf to prove that while Coxe was known for his mystery novels he had the ability to write stories on a variety of subjects. Unfortunately, nothing came of this project.

In retrospect, he wondered if he had been right in creating a new character for his first novel instead of using Casey. In a 1972 letter he told me: "I was selling Caseys then but thought my hero in the first book should be a bit more polished and suave than Casey, quite possibly a mistake since fans I knew always told me Casey was the better character, or at least I handled him better."

George Harmon Coxe went into his twilight years knowing that there had been thousands of readers who enjoyed what he had written. Then, on Monday,

January 30, 1984, at the age of 82, years of heavy cigarette and pipe smoking caught up with him and he died of cancer of the esophagus. He was survived by his wife, Elizabeth, and his daughter, Janet Davis. He was buried the following Sunday at the Duck River Cemetery in Old Lyme, Connecticut.

Legacy

Coxe was called "the professional's professional" by critic Anthony Boucher and "a master of the art of the detective novel" by Yale professor William Lyon Phelps. Erle Stanley Gardner referred to his books as "uniformly entertaining, gripping, and exciting." These were phrases to gladden a publicist's heart and were concise enough to fit on a book jacket or in a newspaper advertisement. He was the first to use a photographer in the role of detective. But the real legacy was the unspoken one from the readers. Thousands of them simply enjoyed his characters, especially the secondary ones like Fenner whenever he appeared in the Murdock novels or Logan in the Casey stories.

Some readers appreciated him as a straightforward storyteller with few sub-plots, little concern for societal relevance and no extraneous love stories, extensive exposition or recapitulation of events. His readers became involved with the characters from the first page and continued to read to find out what would happen next. Things happened to Coxe's characters and there was a good use of dramatic conflict told in a deceptively simple formal style. The structure of a Coxe story was a simple one: someone had something worth stealing, someone else was after that treasure and the hero had to work toward the resolution of the situation taking the reader with him.

Newer readers have come across his world of fiction almost by accident when they found some of his books on a library shelf or bought some of them at a Friends of the Library book sale. One such reader recognized characteristics Coxe had in common with Erle Stanley Gardner, whom she had read, and trusted the newly discovered author not to disappoint her. After awhile she found there were mysteries within mysteries as major characters in one book didn't appear in each book in the same series and she went back to read them again in order of publication to learn for example, just what had happened to Joyce Murdock, Kent Murdock's wife.

For this reader, and many like her, Coxe's books were a great escape and she found a certain amount of pleasure and comfort in the predictable situations and familiar personalities of the characters. She enjoyed revisiting the exotic settings of the Caribbean novels and becoming reacquainted with characters like Kent Murdock and Jack Casey. In short, she found the novels a good, old-fashioned read.

2
Memories of a Mystery Writer's Daughter

Somebody asked me the other day when I was first aware of what my father did for a living and did I realize that his vocation differed from that of other dads. It had to be when we lived Old Lyme, Connecticut (I was in the 5th grade). Dad worked at home in his study; other fathers went off to work. I had a younger brother named George and mother had to keep the two of us quiet around the house. We couldn't have other kids over to play because that would be too noisy. Many were the bellows that came out of dad's study when he was working.

Dad was born in Olean, New York, and grew up in Elmira. I was told that when dad finished high school, his father (George Harmon Coxe, Sr.) told him that he was on his own and not to expect any help from him. Dad, who was named for his father, went to Purdue for a year as he thought he wanted to be an engineer, but after working very hard on an engineering drawing and having it ruined by having something spilled on it, he decided that engineering wasn't for him, so he went to Cornell.

I think dad would have been in the Class of '23 at Cornell and in order to pay his tuition he played in a band. I know he played piano, banjo and guitar, but which one he played in the band, I'm not certain. While there, he was a member of the *Sigma Nu* fraternity. He didn't graduate from Cornell. Playing in a band at night kept him from attending his early classes and the Dean "suggested" that perhaps he had better leave the institution. He felt very strongly about Cornell, kept in touch with some of his classmates, and followed the Cornell sports teams very closely.

Dad never worked as a reporter to my knowledge, but he did work for newspapers across the country in the circulation department. He would hire the young men who had the delivery routes, be there when the papers were dropped off and get them off on their routes. From what he told me, he was very good at organizing these departments.

At some point he ended up in Boston working for the Barta Press, selling advertising. That was when he met my mother who was from West Roxbury, a suburb of Boston. She had graduated from Connecticut College in New London, CT, and was working as a salesgirl at Jordan Marsh. They were married May 18, 1929, and I came along September 28, 1930, with my brother on October 17, 1932.

The way I understand it, dad asked mother if she would mind being poor for a while because he wanted to try his hand at writing. She said okay and we went to live in Cotuit on Cape Cod in one of Grampa's summer cottages. My grandfather, Robert T. Fowler, Sr., was in real estate and had done some developing on the Cape, so I think we lived there rent free. I think there was a space heater in the kitchen and upstairs in a bedroom where dad was working. From what I have been able to determine, dad taught himself how to write fiction. He seems to have read magazines on the subject and assembled scrapbooks with articles he clipped to illustrate different aspects of a story. His first sales were not fiction, though, but articles for *Popular Mechanics*. As far as I know, these have not been identified. I have been told that he made $400 that first year.

We lived in St. Vincent, British West Indies, in 1934–1935. I remember only a few things about that time but came across some pictures and memorabilia the other day that reminded me of many of the social events organized by the colony's British residents: polo and cricket matches, teas, etc. (As I recall, I went to some kind of nursery school.) It's my theory that the island's reasonable living expenses provided a good environment for dad to write his first book, *Murder with Pictures*, which was later made into a movie.

In 1936 and 1938 we were in Santa Monica. Dad was working for M-G-M as a scriptwriter. I remember going to Franklin School and Roosevelt School. One time we lived around the corner from Shirley Temple's brother. Mother would sometimes go to Hollywood to pick up dad and I saw Clark Gable in his roadster. We used to drive to Pasadena on Sundays. It was a fairly long drive out into the country in those days.

The house in Old Lyme was built in 1939–1940. Dad bought the land during the 1938 hurricane and we were all at my grandparents' home in Falmouth on the Cape when that one hit. We didn't know whether dad was alive or dead. I think Old Lyme was chosen because mother had been at Connecticut College and it was halfway between Boston (where her family was) and New York (where dad's agent and publisher were). There was a dutch door on one side of the living room, which led to our apple orchard. I understand that an office was to have been built off the living room for dad's study so he could work in peace, but it never came to be.

The house in Hilton Head was built in 1961-1962. Mother and dad used to go away almost every winter to get out of the cold in Old Lyme. They went to Barbados several years and then to Gulfport, MS. While there dad came across an article about Hilton Head in a golf magazine and so it became their winter home. Because my mother's health was not good in later years, I would fly to either Hilton Head or Old Lyme, help him close up one house, drive with him to the other house, open that house, stock the larder and then fly back to my own home. We made quite a few of those trips together and now I wish I'd had a tape recorder. He had some fascinating stories to tell about Hollywood and the people he knew there.

Dad wrote wherever he was until he went into retirement in 1975. He was extremely organized and his life was very structured, at least in Old Lyme. He got up at the same time every morning, ate the same breakfast and went into his study at the same time. He was out at 10:30am, for graham crackers and milk and back into the study. Out at noon (lunch was at 12:30) and then perhaps a short lie down in the study (especially as he got older) and then worked until 6:00pm. Dinner was at 6:30. You could set your watch by his schedule. He always said that even if he didn't write a word during the time in his study, he was always reading and thinking. He was very strict with us and I think there were lots of times his mind was on something he was writing.

In the early days (especially in 1934) he kept a notebook in which he wrote the title of each story, the number of words, where it was sold and what he received for it. Of course, the prices were in 1934 dollars, so they would be much more in today's dollars. He told me once that he used to write two books a year, but when he realized how much the IRS took he decided to only write one a year. I guess that was as he got older.

I don't know whether dad's love of jazz came before he was at Cornell or not, but it was always a part of my life growing up. One time dad took George and me to Eddie Condon's in New York City. I think I was 12 and George was 10. Dad was a great fan of Art Tatum, Teddy Wilson and the like and used to go and hear them when he was in the City. He discovered Herman Chittison, the Blue Note piano player, and wanted to give him a boost up so he had him hired for the Casey radio show. He (Chittison) visited my parents in Old Lyme along with other people from the show, including Staats Cotsworth, Johnny Dietz, John Gibson and their wives.

One of the neat perks of having a famous mystery writer for a father was meeting dad in the City and having dinner and going to a Mystery Writers of America Meeting. One person I seem to remember was Herb Brean. Mother and I came to the City to attend an annual MWA dinner and that was where I met Rex Stout. Having dinner with dad one night at Louis and Armand, on East 52nd Street, we saw John Cameron Swayze having dinner by himself nearby. Dad said "He probably thinks I am your sugar daddy."

Since dad wrote so much about photography, people ask about the extent of his interest and knowledge. Dad had a very good Leica and he had a darkroom in the basement of the house in Old Lyme where he did his own developing and printing. I think that's why he could write so knowledgeably about Casey. He took many pictures and notes of all the places he went so that when he came to write about a particular setting, he had a great deal of documentation in both categories.

Dad was an avid Giants fan in football and, of course, a Red Sox fan as were both George and myself. We used to listen to the games on the radio and plot all the action on charts we made. Dad also played some baseball for an American Legion team in Old Lyme and played quite a lot of golf. I know he played in California. He used to tell me about sand greens and must have been pretty good as we had quite a good looking martini set on the sideboard that he had won out there. He played in Old Lyme and Hilton Head even though in later years he would have to use a piece of sponge rubber with each hand to grip the golf club as his hands were so arthritic from pounding the keys of an old Remington typewriter.

He was pleased with the way each of us turned out (I graduated from Vassar and later worked at *Time, Inc.*), but he was very pleased when my brother graduated from Exeter and then went on to Cornell. He was George III on the dedication of one of dad's books, but on another one he was called Georgie. His story is the one tragedy in my dad's life. He was killed in a single car accident in July 1951 and that was the end of a very promising young man. My parents established the George Harmon Coxe Award in American Literature and Creative Writing in his memory at Cornell.

Over the years dad dedicated a number of his books to various people in his life, family and friends, writers and editors, business colleagues and his literary agents. Some of them are easily identified, I am certain, but a few of the names may seem obscure to those who don't know dad's history and the people with whom he came in contact. I'm sure he wanted to show some of these people how deeply he cared about them.

He died in 1984 after a long and profitable life as a writer of mysteries.

3
Recollections of My Father

From the age of seven till I was almost 14, I grew up with my parents in Newtown, Connecticut. My dad was in his 50's when I was born and I remember my friends thinking that he was my grandfather when they met him.

My father spent most of his time writing in the den of our home as he didn't have an office. So it was weird for me to have my father home all day as other kids' fathers went off to work all day. As I was an only child, I spent most of my time outside, playing with the cows in the pastures across from our house.

My parents did not socialize much, except for occasional trips to New York City for business. One thing I do remember very clearly was that my father was an avid reader who especially loved history.

By the time I was a teenager in the mid 1950s, the radio era was coming to an end so my father started writing scripts for television. He had a couple of things pending, but as the business moved to Los Angeles, my father, then in his mid 60's, decided to move the family to Glendale, California expecting to start anew with fresh hopes and dreams.

Those dreams didn't materialize, however, and instead of a new beginning, the move to the west coast marked the beginning of the end of his career.

Once in California, I remember that he wrote some scripts for the *Munsters* but I don't think they were ever used. Basically, once the radio thing dried up, his career was pretty much over. He kept writing but it was a steady downward slide.

Although money was tight in those days, my father could not bring himself to get a "normal job," even when we had very little money. Talk about ego; no bare bones job for him! He wouldn't even let my mother, 23 years his junior, get a job when we needed money.

With no work, no money and failing health, the downhill slide continued.

Despite his failing health, my father lived until 74, dying of a massive heart attack at home in the wee hours of the morning. I was 23 at the time and seven months pregnant with what would have been his first grandchild.

Two months later, when my son was born, he was given the family name "Deen" as his middle name.

My father is buried in a cemetery in Glendale.

4
Casey at Black Mask

Jack Casey was born in the pages of *Black Mask*, undoubtedly one of the most significant magazines of the pulp era. Here were found the stories of Dashiell Hammett, Raymond Chandler and other writers who defined the concept of hard-boiled detective fiction. While the character of Casey was not introduced in the very beginning of the first Casey story, "Return Engagement," March 1934,[*] once the cameraman made his entrance, it was difficult not to notice him. He was big, thick-chested, with a head of curly brown hair. Admittedly a prima-donna among cameramen, he could afford to be. Simply stated, he was the best and he knew it. While he had a short fuse, he also had guts. Any paper would gladly have hired him, but he preferred working for the Boston *Globe*, because he had such a good working relationship with Blaine, the city editor.

The description of Casey in the first story remained much the same throughout the other 20 stories, shorts and novelettes, published in *Black Mask* between 1934 and 1942. There were two novels serialized in the magazine in 1941 and 1943, but those will be covered in a later chapter. Six feet two, weighing between 210 and 220 pounds, sometimes Casey was described as having a washboard stomach, sometimes his hair had flecks of gray, but the description was consistent.

That description, or a variation on it, even turned up in the "biography" of Casey that George Harmon Coxe contributed to a book edited by Otto Penzler in 1978, *The Great Detectives*. This was a collection of biographical sketches of fictional detectives composed by their creators. The biography of Casey may have been the last professional writing that Coxe produced; he had retired from

---

[*] Other authors listed on the table of contents in the March 1934 issue were Paul Cain, Frederick Nebel, Erle Stanley Gardner, Roger Torrey, Nels Leroy Jorgensen, and Thomas Walsh.

writing novels with *No Place for Murder* in 1975, 62 novels and 40 years after his first novel, *Murder with Pictures*, was published. It was also the retirement from his 50-year career as a professional writer. That it was about Casey was appropriate for Casey had done a lot for his creator.

According to that account, Casey might never have been given the nickname of Flashgun, later reduced to Flash, had Coxe had his way. Apparently, someone on the staff of *Black Mask* came up with the name and it stuck.

After years of writing and selling short stories and novelettes to the pulp magazines, Coxe decided to try to crack one of the more difficult story markets, *Black Mask*. He knew how to tailor a story for a particular magazine so he studied editor Joe Shaw's publication and wrote a story to fit its style and plot demands. Surprisingly, he succeeded with his first offering. Something about that story clicked with the editor and "Return Engagement" was accepted. By the time Coxe heard the news, he was writing a second story about Casey and said so in a letter to Shaw. Shaw replied that the magazine wasn't looking for another series character, but on reading the second story, "Special Assignment," the editor changed his mind. History was made.

That first story may have seemed to be mostly about young Tom Wade, fresh from the small town and eager to make good in the big city, but on the fifth page Jack Casey made his bow and soon took over the story and the series.

In a 1971 interview, Coxe told the story of why he chose to make a photographer the hero of his stories, but he had told that story before. Perhaps the first occasion was in a 1941 issue of *Black Mask*. He created Casey, he said, to fill a void in the world of fictional detectives. While there had been many reporters who played sleuth in fiction, there were no photographers. Coxe felt that the photographer as hero had an advantage over the reporter.

Having worked in newspaper offices for four or five years in California, Florida and New York, Coxe thought he understood something of what reporters and photographers were like. The reporter in fiction was often a central character, even a romantic figure, but the photographer, if he showed up at all, was little more than an extra at the scene. This may have seemed natural enough. Photographers may not have been romantic figures, but they had to give as much as they got, and the pictures they took told the story more truly than the reporter's typewriter. Words could be shaded to convey a meaning shy of the truth, but, as Wendell Wilkie once said, "the photographer's lens always remains true." It was only fair, Coxe thought, that the guy with the camera be given his due.

The cameraman, Coxe believed, had a difficult job and he often had to stick his neck out to get his pictures. The cameraman of the 1930s was far removed from the paparazzi of today: there was no telescopic lens, no electronic flash, no rapid sequence shutter. In the beginning, Casey used a "spreadlight," an early version of flashbulb that was a narrow metal trough into which the photographer tapped magnesium powder. Both highly combustible and highly dangerous, magnesium powder was kept in a tightly sealed bottle. Beneath the trough there was a trigger and a sparking device much like a cigarette lighter. The light from this "flash-gun" was enough to illuminate the subject being photographed. The reporter could record what he saw in a notebook from a distance, but the photographer had to be right on the spot. This dangerous proximity suggested a number of story lines and plot twists to an enterprising young writer of fiction.

Thus, Jack Casey came into being and provided the vehicle by which George Harmon Coxe was able to lift himself above the usual pulp markets, *Thrilling Detective*, *Argosy*, *Complete Stories* and others to join the ranks of writers like Dashiell Hammett, Carroll John Daly, Erle Stanley Gardner, Frederick Nebel, Raoul Whitfield and Raymond Chandler in the pages of the prestigious *Black Mask*.

A Snapshot of Casey

Of all the characters in the series, Casey was undoubtedly the most rounded. Coxe portrayed him, warts and all, giving him a quick temper and a partiality for hard liquor. In the 1930s, most readers may not have noticed his drinking; it's only in today's society that this seems to stand out. There were several scenes throughout the series in which Casey was shown to be drinking or thinking about drinking or buying a drink for someone else. The opening sentence of "Mixed Drinks" read: "The Old-Fashioned slid gently across the bar and stopped an inch from Casey's hand." Another Old-Fashioned followed that first one toward the end of the scene. Of course, in that story, it was implied that Casey was able to hold his liquor in contrast to young Tom Wade. In "Murder Mixup" Casey opened his desk drawer and brought out a half-filled pint of whiskey and a glass.

Casey never seemed to be partial to one brand over another, as long as it was whiskey. When Slattery, the night city editor of the *Globe*, called him out of a sound sleep in "Special Assignment" to cover the Hub Oil Company fire in Belleville, he'd had a pint before going to sleep. Whether it was the pint or the half-hour of sleep, Casey had a headache that hadn't disappeared when Kimball showed up with his camera and equipment. Ever the gracious host, Casey offered the rewrite man a drink to warm him before he went home. Casey left the apartment right after that.

Judging from the number of women in the stories who called Casey by his first name and not one of his nicknames, the photographer seemed to lead a normal social life. According to his creator in that 1978 biography, Casey's tastes ran to "companionable youngish widows and divorcees without ulterior motives, whose needs were compatible with his own." Rose Nielsen in "Murder Mixup" might have been one of these, because their friendship went back several years.

None of Casey's automobiles was more than transportation for him, whether it was a roadster or a convertible. Much of the time the car Casey drove wasn't described at all, but in "Hot Delivery" his cream-colored roadster was distinctive enough for the gangsters to take advantage of that feature and force him to drive onto the grounds of the home of Lieutenant Governor Larrabee. In "Murder in the Red," the last of the *Black Mask* novelettes, whatever Casey drove was just sufficient to get him around Bayport, the defense plant town, and it wasn't an important enough prop in the story for a more detailed description.

Casey's own past was never spelled out in detail, but there were enough references so one could fill in the blanks. He was old enough to have served in the First World War, but too old to serve in the second. Having a trick knee didn't help either. It was in France in World War I that he learned how to use a handgun. According to the stories, Casey preferred a .38 automatic and he kept one in a drawer in his apartment and another in the office, but he also had a smaller gun, a .25, which he found useful to keep hidden when he needed to go undercover. He rarely resorted to either; his weapons of choice were his flash camera and his fists.

Even though *Black Mask* published detective stories, Casey was not really a detective. He was a cameraman, sometimes just called "a camera," who stumbled onto crimes, mysteries to be solved, in the course of his job, getting the best pictures for his paper before the other guys in town could get pictures for the rival papers. In "Casey—Detective," one of the stories in which he displayed some real detective work, he admitted that anyone could have taken the picture that was taken, but Casey's job was to get the picture that was hot. Coxe explained in 1978 that whenever he wrote Casey as a detective, *Black Mask* editor Joe Shaw reminded him to keep Casey unique. There were detectives of every kind in *Black Mask*, but only Casey carried a camera.

On two occasions, Casey found himself giving advice to young women who wanted to become reporters, Helen Draper in "Women Are Trouble" and Edith French in "Too Many Women." It was as though the story was too good to be told only once. Casey warned Helen against viewing the newspaper game as a romantic one. She'd lose her ideals eventually and not even have honest emotions to fall back on, and she wouldn't be above double-crossing someone who helped her out.

Casey had been double-crossed by rival newsperson Lyda Nugent in "Push-Over" so he knew what he was talking about. When he gave his advice speech to Edith French he was tougher on her than he had been with Helen Draper. He advised her to fool the other reporters into giving her tips so she could double-cross them, to forget about having a conscience and her illusions. He recommended she strive to be a wise-cracking, hard-boiled dame with all the angles in the book—and be a good reporter.

But in spite of that gruff, crabbing exterior, Casey couldn't help himself from helping the helpless and befriending the friendless. Just as he had taken young Tom Wade under his wing, he did the same with Helen and Edith. He still remembered what it was like to be young and enthusiastic and to take pictures as though it were the only thing that mattered.

In "Once Around the Clock," Casey took pity on the drunken ex-piano player, Lew Bronson, and helped Edith Roberts get him home. Part of his reason for helping Bronson was to help Edith who reminded him of past favors she had done for him.

Some of the best scenes Coxe ever wrote were at the beginning and ending of "Once Around the Clock" when Casey confided in Gus, the bartender at *Pinelli's*, that the life of a photographer wasn't easy. Yeah, yeah, said Gus . . . "but you eat it up." Yeah, yeah. Casey paid for two drinks with a dollar and didn't bother to collect the 20 cents change. It was another day and another dollar. "He picked up his plate-case and trudged away, a burly, imperturbable figure, absorbed in his thoughts that softened the lines of fatigue upon his face and left his dark eyes remote and faintly smiling. Behind him came the tinkle of two dimes in the glass beside the cash register reserved for tips . . ."

Supporting Characters

Coxe developed a cast of characters to support Casey in his quest for the perfect photo or the solution to the mystery. Some were seen in story after story while others made only the briefest of appearances.

First, of course, was Tom Wade, the young guy, wet behind the ears, fresh from the small town, eager to make good in the big city taking pictures. He clearly idolized Casey even to the point of cursing like the master.

The best account of Wade's character was in the first story, "Return Engagement," and it is tempting to speculate on what direction the series might have taken had Casey not arrived on the scene in the second act, so to speak.

The depth of characterization of Wade was remarkable for a section that covered only five pages in that issue of *Black Mask*. It was all there: the hesitation as Wade got his flash-gun ready to get a shot of Greek Joe, the mobster's reaction that knocked Wade off his feet, the cameraman's dismay when he discovered he'd lost his camera, his ingenuity as he talked the camera store proprietor into selling him one of the new candid cameras, and billing it to the *Globe*.

Wade's encounter with Blaine, the city editor, when he explained why his eight-year-old camera was in pieces formed the blueprint for a dozen encounters between any photographer and the older newsman. It was obvious that Wade, tired of covering routine and mundane stories like tree plantings, had gone out on a limb to get a picture of Greek Joe, a real scoop.

Wade had been in the city only six months, had never been away from his home town before, and his only newspaper experience had been on the small town daily. Enthusiasm and cockiness had taken him this far at the *Globe*, but he was still making only twenty-five a week as an odd job photographer. Wade's attempts to explain matters to Blaine cut no ice with the city editor, whose sarcasm had brought bigger men than him to their knees. Blaine explained coolly and logically what Wade should have done, and then he fired him.

That may have been the first time Wade was fired, but it wouldn't be the last. He turned out to be a pretty good cameraman, after all, with a knack for taking brilliant pictures. Casey stuck up for him throughout his career and was willing to have Wade along on any job. That was why, in "Special Assignment," when Wade was shot getting a picture of a gunfight and was taken to the hospital, the first person he asked for was Casey. The big photographer was surprised and even a bit emotional about it all.

Wade never really grew up. He may have been more confident after several months at the *Globe*, but he remained the same smooth-faced blue-eyed youth with a head of reddish hair under his faded hat, the same fresh kid from upstate. There was no better example then the time, in "Mixed Drinks," when he was obviously worried about something and paid several visits to Steve's bar and restaurant. On his second visit he drank two rickeys, a Scotch and soda and followed those with a Manhattan which, as he said, was "to get the taste out of his mouth." Casey was furious and castigated Steve, the bartender, for allowing Wade to drink so much when the kid didn't really know how to drink. When Casey finally caught up with Wade, he had to admit that, drunk or sober, the young cameraman could still come up with a good picture.

The story of the young man who came to the big city to break into camera work on a major newspaper was too good for Coxe not to revisit it from time to time. When he did so on at least two occasions for *Black Mask*, he switched the genders for the characters. In "Women Are Trouble," it was Helen Draper who felt the romantic tug of the printers' ink and wanted to be a reporter. In "Too Many Women," it was Edith French who was assigned by Blaine to work with Casey, with dramatic results.

Blaine was one of the characters whom readers probably wished Coxe had used more often. The city editor of the *Globe*, he was described in a precise thumbnail sketch in "Two Man Job" as "a tall, slender man, prematurely gray and dressed immaculately right down to the stiff collar. Astute, brilliant, both as a reporter and city editor, he was a politely sardonic driver." Because the managing editor of the paper was away so often, Blaine was really the man in charge and the man the photographers turned to for their assignments. He knew story values because, at heart, he was still a reporter.

The immaculate attire (in "Push-Over" he was described as wearing "an Oxford gray suit, the knot in his blue-and-white checkered cravat nestling perfectly at his stiff collar") was a way for Coxe to give him a distinct appearance. He worked hard, but his shirtsleeves were never rolled up, his tie was never askew, like the stereotypical city editor in fiction. That stiff collar was part of the typical attire of the 1930s.

Blaine's sarcasm was legendary. He dressed Wade down for not telling him ahead of time where he was going and what he was going to do, knowing full well the young man was impulsive, and for losing not only his camera, but also the pictures that should have graced the front page of the paper. On learning that Casey and Wade were working together (again, in "Push-Over"), he asked if they were "going to team up again and produce another of your masterpieces." But Casey could be sarcastic too, as when he cited the *Globe's* "kind, fatherly city editor" as the reason he continued to work at the paper.

The man from the police department, so necessary in a crime story, was Logan, Lieutenant Logan, with no first name ever given. Logan made his first appearance in "Mixed Drinks" and from the beginning Casey liked him. He nearly always called Casey by his first name and the photographer knew he was a straight shooter in his dealings with others as well as an expert pistol shot. Logan was someone who cared about the way he dressed and the impression he made on others. He always had a fresh handkerchief in the breast pocket of his suit and sometimes he even had a boutonniére in his button hole. In the 1930s, he was the sort who wore spats and a derby hat in the winter and got away with it because that was the sort of person and cop he was.

Logan saved Casey's life on more than one occasion, usually because, as in "Mixed Drinks," he shot first. Raymond Chandler once wrote that when all else failed to liven up a story, he would bring someone through a door into a room with a gun in his hand. Logan was a cop after Chandler's heart.

Logan made his last appearance in the short stories and novelettes in "Once Around the Clock." The case wasn't going too well and Casey was reminded of that when he called on Logan in his fourth floor office and found him with his feet on his desk and his hands behind his head. It was an uncharacteristic pose, but the two old friends were able to share their discomfort with the way things were progressing, or not progressing, for that matter. This malaise didn't last long and Casey was able to watch when Logan, Manahan and a couple of plainclothesmen arrested the guilty party and Casey could go back to *Pinelli's Grill* and down the glasses of Old Crow that Gus put in front of him and explain to himself just how the case had ended.

Other supporting characters came and went, described in broad brush strokes, just enough for them to be recognizable. Names like Captain Judson of the detective bureau and Sergeant Manahan represented the police, but the rest of the cast was made up of members of the staff at the *Globe* or the *Express:* MacGrath was the circulation manager at the *Globe* while another MacGrath was the managing editor at the *Express*, Kimball, the rewrite man ("short, round-faced, practically bald, with tired-looking eyes and a weary manner"), Slattery, night city editor, or Crandall, the lobster shift city editor. The "lobster shift" was the work shift on a newspaper that began at 4:00 a.m.; it was also known as the "tombstone shift," but Coxe never used that term. These were colorful terms for otherwise colorless men.

Coxe's descriptions of minor characters in specific stories included some interesting metaphors so beloved of writers of hard-boiled detective fiction. In "Push-Over," Scudder's eyes were "lacquered slits." Mallon, a reporter for the *Globe*, was described in "Hot Delivery" as "a back-slapper who spelled personality with a capital P." Mrs. Sam Jenny in "Women Are Trouble" was "a plump, faded blonde who looked as if an Ethel M. Dell novel and a box of chocolates constituted her idea of an exciting afternoon." In "Too Many Women," Stella Nissen was described as looking "like a girl who knew most of the answers."

Settings and Plots

At the beginning of the Casey series Coxe attempted to have his character frequent the same bar in every story. This was Steve's which was a restaurant according to the sign out front, but that was only for the license. Casey thought it should have read "Bar — by special appointment to the *Globe*." It was handy to reach after work; all you had to do was take the elevator from the city room, turn the corner (whether right or left was never indicated), and go three doors.

Steve's was the place where Casey, Wade and Blaine went for drinks at the end of "Murder Picture" to celebrate their leaving the *Globe* and going over to the *Express*. But they never seemed to return and if *Steve's* became their regular hangout we were never told about it.

Streets were described in thumbnail terms so you immediately knew where you were: Charles Street or Beacon Hill: by day, a busy thoroughfare, by night, strangely deserted. Hotels were delineated so you knew your way through the front doors into the lobbies and up the stairs. These were real places.

The plot of almost any Casey story could be summed up as a triple conflict: Casey was after a picture that represented a news story; the crooks didn't want him to get the picture; the police didn't want him to interfere. Coxe expressed it a little differently when he wrote that Casey got involved for personal reasons: "an attempt by some shady character to steal a negative others wanted; the occasional invasion of the paper's darkroom for a similar purpose, or the abuse of an associate; the interference in any manner by some hired hands, with or without a gun, as well as any attempt to damage his equipment. These were the things that prompted an immediate reaction sometimes more reckless than wise."

One of the pivotal episodes in the Casey series was "Murder Picture," *Black Mask*, January 1935. This was the occasion, mentioned already, when Casey left the *Globe* for a similar job with the *Express*. A brief summary may be in order.

> Casey's only good picture, taken at a raid at a racetrack, can't be used because the son of the new owner of the *Globe*, who is also the brother of the managing editor, is in the picture with his arm around a woman who isn't his wife.
>
> Managing editor J. H. Fessenden personally smashes Casey's plate and tears up the print and this makes Casey angry. Logan finds the body of a private detective named Grady in the men's room at the site of the raid and Casey's picture includes someone coming out of the room at the time the murder was committed. The killer wants the plate and only Casey, Wade and Logan know the plate has been smashed, but there is another print that is still intact.
>
> Wade goes to see the girl who was in the picture, Alma Henderson, and finds her dead in her apartment room in the Edgemere building. Things become more than a little confused when the word gets out that the police don't want that picture used in the paper and a shoot-out occurs as Casey and Wade escape some gunmen at the Henderson apartment.

At the end, with everything tied up, Casey learns that the original order to kill that picture came from someplace other than the police department. The picture is printed in the paper anyway, Casey is fired, tells Blaine off and starts to leave the office. When Blaine realizes what happened, he accompanies Casey and Wade to Fessenden's office to learn who really wanted the picture suppressed. This leads to the three of them resigning to begin a new career at the *Express*.

The adjustment to working for a different paper continues into the next story. In "Casey—Detective" the photographer is not certain he will like it at the *Express*. For one thing, he has difficulty adjusting to the management style of managing editor MacGrath. Casey discovers he can't fight MacGrath the way he could Blaine. MacGrath is simply too calm, understanding and logical. MacGrath informs Casey that since he hasn't given the *Express* any good pictures after joining the staff he may as well get drunk, relax and start all over again. This approach is something new for Casey, but he decides to follow MacGrath's advice. Being Casey, he soon stumbles onto a story and gets some pictures he can use as well as some he can't. One of the latter shows up the police in a bad light so that Casey tears up the picture rather than make the police look bad.

What crimes were focused on in the Casey stories? There were plenty of encounters with gangsters and more than a killing or two. In the twenty-one stories there were at least 18 murders, three kidnappings, one payroll robbery, a jewel robbery, counterfeiting, blackmail, illegal gambling, espionage and sabotage. The stories written in the 1940s. reflected an awareness of the Second World War.

Black Mask was where the stories began and formed the basis of the Casey legend. Since *Black Mask* had the reputation of publishing hard-boiled detective fiction, Casey was classified that way. Among the characteristics associated with hard-boiled fiction were a sleazy milieu, repeated violence, a cynicism about wealth and authority and a sense that nothing in society really worked. Coxe however saw Casey as tough, but never hard-boiled. Casey was no world-weary loner trying to make sense out of disorder. Any periods of depression didn't last long. He might wonder once in awhile whether the end was worth the means, but basically he was a pragmatist whose main goal in life was to take the perfect picture that told the whole story.

Cameraman of the Pulps
Black Mask in 1934 and 1942
Avon's 1946 Collection

The Casey Short Stories and Novelettes

"Return Engagement." *Black Mask* XVII (March 1934): 73-84.

Tom Wade, fresh from the small town comes to the city and wants more than anything to be a successful cameraman for the *Globe*. In an encounter with gangsters he not only loses his camera and fails to get the pictures city editor Blaine wants, but loses his job. With the help of Jack Casey, the *Globe's* veteran cameraman, Wade infiltrates the mob's quarters and gets pictures no one else can. Not only does Blaine re-hire him, he gives Wade a raise. Illustrated by Arthur Rodman Bowker. [Filmed by Grand National as *Here's Flash Casey*, 1937; also known as *Meet Flash Casey*.]

"Special Assignment." *Black Mask* XVII (April 1934): 72-83.

When a fire breaks out at the Hub Oil Company in Belleville, Casey is the only *Globe* cameraman available to cover the story. Wade, on another assignment, has been shot and is asking for Casey from his hospital bed. Casey gets one terrific shot before turning his camera over to rewrite man Kimball and heading for the hospital. Wade, in quest of pictures of an accident took a picture of the killer of detective Sam Burke. Of course, the killer and Casey are both after the plates from Wade's camera. Illustrated by Arthur Rodman Bowker.

"Two-Man Job." *Black Mask* XVII (May 1934): 43-61.

Curiosity about a parked sedan leads Casey to photograph the owner and his friends. The car is a gangland armored vehicle and the owner demonstrates a physical objection to being the object of such scrutiny. Further investigation on the part of Casey links the driver and his companions to a series of payroll robberies and the murder of a guard. With Wade's help (after all, it's a two-man job) Casey gets additional photos of the men that help put them in jail. Illustrated by Arthur Rodman Bowker.

"Push-Over." *Black Mask* XVII (June 1934): 83-101.

A kidnapped victim is returned safely to his family; the lawyer go-between is murdered; the police try to fit the blame on the city's public enemy number three. Casey's plan to get the pictures and the story for the *Globe* hits two obstacles: the lawyer's bodyguard, a private detective, and a clever woman working for the rival *Express*. Cracked plates have two meanings here, dental and photographical. They call Casey a "push-over" where women are concerned, but not when he gets crossed. Illustrated by Arthur Rodman Bowker.

"Hot Delivery." *Black Mask* **XVII (July 1934): 79-93.**

Casey and Wade are covering the failed attempt by four men to break Buck Hannan out of jail. The gunmen capture the two cameramen and use their camera gear and police cards to go back and spring the boss. It takes some fancy work on the part of Casey to foil the plot, capture the gunmen and get enough exclusive pictures to satisfy the editor of the *Globe*. Illustrated by Arthur Rodman Bowker.

"Mixed Drinks." *Black Mask* **XVII (August 1934): 88-106.**

It is Casey's day off when Mae Rigo, widow of Nick Rigo, the racketeer, is found dead. Editor Blaine is looking for a cameraman to cover the story and thinks Wade may have what he needs. The trouble is, Wade can't be found. Even though he doesn't know how to drink, he's downed more than his share of mixed drinks at Steve's Restaurant. Casey and racketeer Joe Arnstein's associates are all after the picture Wade took that will establish who shot Mae and Stumpy Greenberg. It looks grim for Casey, but Lieutenant Logan of the Central Bureau arrives in time. Illustrated by Arthur Rodman Bowker.

"Pinch-Hitters." *Black Mask* **XVII (September 1934): 61-77.**

When Casey sees Jim Degnan, a witness to a recent gangland kidnapping, he thinks he's drunk. What he doesn't know is that he's been shot and is dying. Casey is teamed with Mallon, a recent addition to the *Globe's* reportorial staff, on this one, but his new partner is not around when the bullets start flying. Fortunately for Casey, Wade pinch hits for Mallon and calls in Lieutenant Logan before it's too late. Illustrated by Arthur Rodman Bowker.

"Murder Picture." *Black Mask* **XVII (January 1935): 73-97.**

A photo of a race track gambling raid taken by Wade also includes the kid brother of the new managing editor of the *Globe* in an embarrassing situation. Before the tangled web is sorted out Casey has to come to Wade's rescue and shows he knows how to use a .38 automatic. Blaine, Wade and Casey are all fired by the *Globe* and go out to look for jobs on the *Express*. Illustrated by Arthur Rodman Bowker.

"Casey—Detective." *Black Mask* **XVII (February 1935): 68-88.**

It's winter in the city and Casey's camera is back in the office of the *Express* when Doris Eaton is murdered., her body lying on a copy of the *Blade*. Casey calls his paper and Eddy, the office boy, delivers his equipment to him.

No one but Casey notices the edition of the paper under the dead woman and that bit of detective work breaks the alibi of the killer. Illustrated by Arthur Rodman Bowker. [Reprinted *Flash Casey—Detective* (Avon, 1946)]

"Earned Reward." *Black Mask* **XVIII (March 1935): 101-121.**

Casey is covering a fire when he literally stumbles on the body of Shorty Prendell, a photographer for the *News*. Prendell has been shot in the chest. It all involves a missing judge and a photo that Casey, for once, didn't take. Casey and Logan, entitled to the reward for finding the judge give it to Prendell's widow instead. Illustrated by Arthur Rodman Bowker. [Reprinted as "Reward for Survivors" in *The Saint Detective Magazine* (August 1958) and in Peter Haining's C*rime Movies II* (Severn Books, 1997) and *The Mammoth Book of Movie Detectives and Screen Crimes* (Carroll & Graf, 1998)]

"Women are Trouble." *Black Mask* **XVIII (April 1935): 10-44.**

Casey isn't exactly pleased when Blaine assigns the new reporter, Helen Draper, to cover the Jenny killing with him. Women are trouble, he believes. Her attitude that a reporter's job is thrilling doesn't make things any better. In spite of having to rescue her from gunmen he comes to have a grudging respect for her ability to learn on the job. Illustrated by Arthur Rodman Bowker. [Reprinted in *Flash Casey—Detective* (Avon, 1946); filmed by MGM in 1936.]

"Thirty Tickets to Win." *Black Mask* **XVIII (June 1935): 48-74.**

A day at the tracks in Rockville Park instead of working and Casey has only his small personal camera with him when he sees the body of Lew Gordon on the floor of the telephone booth. Tickets on the winner of the race, *Silk Maid*, have been stolen from the dead man and cashed for $27,000. If it weren't for the money that made someone shoot Gordon, why was Fuzzy Hunt killed as well? A showdown at a gambler's apartment includes Casey, Wade and former cop Delemater. Illustrated by Arthur Rodman Bowker.

"Buried Evidence." *Black Mask* **XVIII (July 1935): 72-90.**

Casey's on vacation so Blaine turns to Wade to cover a jewel robbery and shooting on Maybury Street, Wade stumbles over a dead policeman, finds a scrawled clue to the killer and follows the trail to a jewel robber with the cop's bullet in his shoulder, truly buried evidence. Wade gets his pictures and the story with the aid of a cab driver ... and all the way keeps asking himself what would Casey have done. Illustrated by Arthur Rodman Bowker.

"Mr. Casey Flashguns Murder." *Black Mask* **XVIII (October 1935): 32-61.**

Fred Parker, aspiring news photographer, comes to Casey for advice. Some find it amusing that he calls Casey "Mr. Casey." When Parker disappears after taking a potentially hot picture, it's Casey to the rescue. Parker's young wife is relieved when Casey finds Parker, the young photographer gets a job he badly needs with the *Globe* and Casey expects a new respect from his colleagues – that's Mr. Casey, if you please. Illustrated by Arthur Rodman Bowker.

"Portrait of Murder." *Black Mask* **XVIII (February 1936): 58-82.**

Casey is at the waterfront covering a fire when the sedan speeds by. At first he thinks it's joy riders, but after being hit on the head he knows better. When he comes to he learns about the death of Ben Harvey, waiter at the *Blue Grill* and the star witness at the Sanford trial four years earlier. The "portrait" of the title is a framed one of Harvey which hides a typewritten affidavit with proof that Sanford was innocent in that old case. Illustrated by Arthur Rodman Bowker.

"Murder Mixup." *Black Mask* **XIX (May 1936): 8-30.**

Herman Elwood, maker of counterfeiting plates, is dead, but the Treasury agents don't have either the plates or the man behind the printing of the money. The police are questioning a girl when Casey comes on the scene. He speaks up for her because he knows her. She is Rose Nielson, one of the few people who calls him Jack. The trail to the counterfeit money leads to another murder and Casey begins to question the value of his job as a photographer. Illustrated by Arthur Rodman Bowker. [Reprinted in Joseph Shaw's *The Hard-Boiled Omnibus* (Simon & Schuster, 1946)]

"Fall Guy." *Black Mask* **XIX (June 1936): 62-82.**

Norma Patten, née Lamont, former vaudeville and burlesque singer, asks Casey to get the negatives of some old semi-nude advertising poses of her and gives him a sheaf of fifty-dollar bills with which to buy them from the man who holds them. When Casey calls on the photographer who took the pictures he finds him dead. The shyster go-between is his next stop, but Sal Ambrose is shot and killed right in front of him. Casey's investigations reveal who is behind the blackmail scheme and also suggest why he is the "fall guy" in this situation. Illustrated by Arthur Rodman Bowker.

"Too Many Women." *Black Mask* XIX (September 1936): 34-58.

Edith French is another woman eager to become a reporter who is assigned to Casey by Blaine. When Dan Marcy, fresh from prison for running a lottery, is shot and killed, Edith follows the trail of the story even though it puts her in harm's way. Casey's work on the case brings him in touch with Stella Nissen, an old friend, who also knew Marcy. It's at that point he begins to wonder if there aren't too many women involved in the Marcy murder case. Illustrated by Arthur Rodman Bowker. [Reprinted in *Flash Casey—Detective* (1946) and T*he Saint Mystery Magazine* (July 1962)]

"Casey and the Blonde Wren." *Black Mask* XXIII (August 1940): 52-66.

The blonde wren of the title is Nancy Allison of the British Women's Royal Navy Service, on assignment with Sir Eric Kirkman of Naval Intelligence. The murder of Sir Eric and the stolen plans of the harbor defenses are only two ingredients in the affair as Casey once more takes pictures without everyone's approval. Illustrated by Peter Kuhlhoff.

"Once Around the Clock." *Black Mask* XXIV (May 1941): 48-70.

Casey helps Lew Bronson home from *Pinelli's Grill* when it is obvious he is in no shape to drive himself. Bronson was once a piano player who accompanied Alma Sinclair, the singer, and it is rumored that he went to prison to cover up for her. When Alma is found shot to death, it appears Bronson is the killer, especially when Casey finds a .32 in Bronson's coat pocket. The events take place in a 24-hour period from one midnight to the next. Both ends of the drama find Casey at *Pinelli's*. Interestingly, the text is divided into five chapters with titles, not a common structure. Illustrated by Peter Kuhlhoff. [Reprinted in *Flash Casey—Detective; Black Mask,* July 1951 and in Herbert Ruhm's *The Hard Boiled Detective* (Vintage Books, 1977)]

"Murder in the Red." *Black Mask* XXV (June 1942): 10-40.

Casey is collecting photographs in Bayport for a defense supplement for the *Express* and uncovers an extensive ring of saboteurs as well as a murder. The newly-developed infra-red film and flashbulbs give him an advantage in night-time photography. He solves the mystery and brings an estranged couple together. Again, the text is divided into six titled chapters. Illustrated by Peter Kuhlhoff.

5
Casey Short Story

Return Engagement
by
George Harmon Coxe*

Tom Wade set up his eight-year-old camera and focused it on a closed door at one end of the drab hall, cold in a blanket of damp, stale air. He shivered as he adjusted the shutter, paused in his shivering to wipe the sweat from his forehead

His hand shook when he sprinkled gray powder into the tray of his flash-gun. But what the hell! If he lacked the nerve to take a chance when opportunity knocked, he'd better quit the *Globe* and go back to the sticks. He sucked in a deep breath, whipped his muscles into submission and knocked on the door.

A gruff voice from inside the room called out: "Yeah?" challengingly.

Wade lifted the flash-gun. Lucky he remembered the name of Greek Joe's lawyer. He said: "It's Steinweg."

A lock clicked, the door-knob turned. Wade's finger tightened on the trigger of the flash-gun and he held his breath.

The door swung open and in that fraction of a second before the spark ignited the powder he saw a tall, broad man with a scarred face; behind him, visible over the angle of his shoulder, stood Greek Joe.

A blinding glare blotted out the picture with startling abruptness. A cloud of acrid white smoke hit the ceiling. Wade grabbed for the tripod legs, swung the camera over his shoulder and spun towards the stairway.

Greek Joe's curse rang in Wade's ears, and before he could take a step a vise-like hand caught his shoulder. He was jerked backward off his feet, yanked

---

* When "Return Engagement" appeared in *Black Mask* for March 1934, it was signed "George H. Coxe." On the table of contents page it was signed "George H. Coxe, Jr."

into the room with heels dragging over the doorsill. A fist caught him at the side of the neck, knocked him sprawling; the camera and tripod slapped down on top of him and tangled his legs as he tried to roll clear.

The big man reached out and grabbed him by the lapels, jerked him to his feet. Greek Joe had an automatic in his hand. Then the big fellow hit him again.

Wade's head smacked a table leg as he slid along on the back of his neck, He could not focus his eyes for a moment but he heard Greek Joe's string of curses break into intelligible speech.

"I damn' near plugged him. That flash scared hell out of me."

The big man said: "Can you imagine it? A mugg like that?"

Wade got to his feet, looked bewilderedly at Greek Joe. He was a short, round-bodied man, but he looked hard, rather than fat. His nose was thick and heavy, jutting brows made little shoe-buttons of his black eyes. He started towards Wade around one side of the table; the big man came the other way.

Wade backed up until the mantelpiece hit his shoulder-blades. What a spot he'd picked for himself! He wondered how far they'd go with him.

Greek Joe said: "Nobody followed us, huh? You're slippin', Gus. Now we gotta find us another joint."

Gus took another step forward, said: "It's a break he came instead of tippin' our mit to somebody else."

Wade felt the sweat come out on his forehead again. His brain throbbed and his mouth and throat were dry. He said: "Lay off. All I wanted was a picture."

Gus laughed. "Can you imagine that?" He swung his right.

Wade ducked, but he ducked right into Greek Joe, who cocked his wrist and slapped the flat of the automatic against the side of his head.

Wade could not remember how many times he was hit after that. The first clean-cut impression he had was when he slid into the hall on his face and Greek Joe said:

"Open your mouth about this, and we'll get tough with you."

Wade got unsteadily to his feet, fought the throbbing dizziness in his head. He looked at the closed door, realized that his camera was missing. Then he remembered the little camera he had tried to talk the skipper into buying. If he'd only had that in his pocket—

The germ of an idea took root in his brain, sprouted there. That optical shop was only a block and a half away. He could get there and back before he could reach the *Globe* offices. If he could get here before Greek Joe pulled out—

He burst into the little store two minutes later, ignored the two customers near the door and cornered the proprietor, a dapper little man who looked in open-eyed amazement at this disheveled apparition with the torn shirt and the bloodied, battered face.

"That camera," wheezed Wade. "You know, that imported one I was looking at."

The proprietor finally took it out of the showcase. Wade seized it eagerly, asked for film, exploded his story like a garbled radio program.

— "and charge it to the *Globe*. It'll be okey. But if I don't get it now I don't want it."

"But it's a hundred and forty dollars and—"

"Who cares?" Wade raced down the store and the proprietor was apparently too dumfounded to do more than make a half-hearted protest. "Call the *Globe* if you want"—Wade opened the door—"check with Blaine."

Wade slid his fingers lovingly over the sleek little instrument as he brushed through the pedestrians on the sidewalk and gained the comparative open space of the pavement.

This was what he should have had before if Blaine had only listened to reason. Why this camera would take anything, and it was so small you could slip it into your vest pocket. He passed a loafing taxi and the driver's razzing comment echoed in his ears as he swung around the corner.

He cut between a truck and a roadster, gained the middle of the street and ran the gauntlet of the traffic lines. Then he saw Greek Joe.

Halfway down the block he was just getting into a taxi; Gus was evidently giving orders to the driver. A stifling bitterness rose in Wade's throat, made it hard for him to breathe. He tried to increase his speed. Shouted once, although he knew it would do no good.

He was fifty yards behind the cab when it pulled out from the curb, a hundred yards away when it reached the corner and turned into the avenue. There was no other taxi in sight. He grabbed hold of a street-light pedestal and hung there, gasping, until a cop came up and said:

"What're you tryin' to prove?"

Wade said: "Nerts," and then had to show his police card and spend five minutes squaring himself.

Wade stood in the doorway of the huge city room and wished the next ten minutes was over with. He looked like a small boy coming home to tell his father the obvious fact that he had been in a fight.

Wisps of straight, reddish-brown hair stuck from under a battered felt hat; his round, ordinarily good-natured face was somber and battered. One blue eye had swollen shut, there was a cut on his cheekbone and his lip was split and bloodied. One hand held the twisted frame of the camera; the other gripped the bellows and lens. The tripod, little more than kindling, he had not bothered to bring.

He could see Blaine, the city editor, at his desk at the far end of the room, partly screened by a copy boy and the A. P. man, and the story he had rehearsed on his way to the office whipped through his mind as he started that long walk to the Desk.

Two days before, Greek Joe had killed Sid Vidal, a lieutenant of King Ricco. It was a peculiar kill for gangdom, obviously extemporaneous. The two had met in a night-club. Greek Joe had gone to Vidal's table and made some remark—just what, could not be learned. Vidal pulled a gun. Greek Joe grabbed it. The end came when Vidal fell with a bullet from his own gun in his heart.

Greek Joe had made no attempt to escape. He gave himself up, and because of the story of witnesses, was charged with manslaughter, released on $25,000 bail. The opinion was that he would beat the rap on justifiable homicide.

King Ricco was looking for Greek Joe. The King was one power in the city who had not been hurt by the repeal of prohibition. His work was almost identical with that of former years. The only difference was that he had his own distillery now and made whiskey legally. But he cut it illegally and he lined up his outlets as before, by coercion and strong-arm methods.

Greek Joe had disappeared. He had successfully dodged photographers coming out of the courthouse; there were no recent pictures available. Wade had seen him that afternoon quite by accident, had followed to get a picture instead of going to the assigned cornerstone laying. A suave, insolent voice cut into his consciousness.

"Maybe they had a riot before they sealed the cornerstone."

Wade looked up, met Blaine's piercing gaze for a moment, then looked down at the desk. The city editor leaned back in his chair and his thin lips dipped at the corners.

Blaine, a virtual czar because of the frequent absence of the managing editor, had none of the fictional characteristics of a city editor. None of this shirtsleeve, eyeshade stuff for him. He was always immaculately dressed, always worked in a coat, always wore a stiff collar, always spoke in a politely sardonic manner—that is, except when he was excited. Tall, slender, prematurely gray, he had a lean, predatory face and steady gray eyes.

He said: "Well?"

Wade held up the pieces of the camera. "It was eight years old anyway."

"Exhibit A, huh?" Blaine's thin smile was a bad omen. "How many shots did you get?"

"None." Wade took a deep breath, plunged headlong into his story. "—and I knew we didn't have anything good of Greek Joe. It was a swell break and I followed him. He was hiding out on—"

"So you got a half dozen assorted poses and—"

"All I got was a shellackin'. He didn't take to the idea."

"And you didn't go down to the Woman's Federation Building for the cornerstone? You didn't get a shot of that communist that tried to break up the meeting?"

Wade shrugged dejectedly. "All I've been doin' is taking tree plantings, and silk hats and press agent shots. When I saw Greek Joe I figured I had a chance to get a real beat."

"You're tired of tree plantings, huh?" Blaine's smile broadened, but not from good humor. "Maybe we've been wasting your time."

He broke off to answer the telephone, at the same time scanning a bit of copy tossed over from the Slot.

Wade was miserable. Until he had come to the city six months before, he had never been out of the small, upstate town where he was born except for brief trips. When the town's one newspaper got growing pains and branched from a good weekly to a shaky daily, Wade had been a combination reporter and photographer. But that paper was a weekly once more. His job had dissolved and he did not want to work in his father's shoe store.

He had come to the city, exaggerated his experience, overshadowed his greenness by his enthusiasm and cockiness, and finally talked Blaine into taking him on as an odd-job photographer at twenty-five a week.

He was not afraid to ask questions, he had a likable personality, and he managed to get by because Casey, the *Globe's* ace photographer, had taken an interest in him and given him a few pointers.

Blaine was talking again.

"So the cornerstone business wasn't quite important enough for a man of your talents?"

"No. But wouldn't you rather have a shot of Greek Joe and—"

"I might have," Blaine politely admitted, "but you didn't get it. And of course you wouldn't think of calling up and telling us about it before you tried to crash the place."

Wade's tongue stuck in the roof of his mouth. He could not meet Blaine's cool manner; and he could think of nothing to say, because he now realized the logic of Blaine's words, knew he'd been a sap to try the job as he had.

"And you're tired, huh?" Blaine sat up. "Well, we'll fix that. Go home and rest up. Take a little vacation; on second thought, maybe you'd better take a permanent one."

"But—"

Blaine held up his hand in mock gesture of concern. "We don't want to overwork you. And I don't want you dying on my hands." The voice hardened to a thin cutting note. "One more job like today's and they'll ship you home in a box."

"But—"

"You're fired!" Blaine whipped out the words, and began to read copy.

Wade was aware now that his face throbbed painfully. He felt tired, bitter, disconsolate. And he knew there was no use in arguing. He put what was left of the camera on the desk. As he started to turn away, Blaine looked up and said:

"And about that camera you bought today. The fellow called up, said you'd charged it to us. I told him we didn't want it—but you'd already gone out with it."

Wade defended his idea. "But I still had a chance to get some shots. I've been tryin' to get you to buy one of those—"

"And I told you a dozen times, we didn't want one. We want a camera in this business, not a sample."

"But they enlarge a thousand per cent and—"

"We don't want it," shouted Blaine, his thin face diffusing with anger. He got control of himself after a moment, spoke politely again. "You've got two weeks' pay coming. The *Globe's* big hearted that way. We'll apply it on the camera you bought. You'll owe us the difference."

Blaine shrugged. "Not that I ever expect to get it, but you owe it to us just the same."

Wade forgot his weariness in his anger. "All right, I owe it to you. And you'll get it, you hatchet-faced tailor's dummy. And when I pay off I'll come in and cram it down your dirty damn' throat!"

Jack Casey stopped Wade on the way out. He was a big, thick-chested fellow with curly brown hair and a profane manner. He was a prima-donna among the city's cameramen, but he could afford to be. He was the best, and everyone knew why. He had personality, he'd fight at the drop of the hat, and he had more guts than any other two photographers in the city. He could have gone over to any sheet in the city on a moment's notice—at more money. But he stayed with the *Globe* because he said, laughingly, that it had such a kind, fatherly city editor.

He said: "What's the matter, kid? Run into a door?"

Wade started to curse, finally broke into a rueful grin and told his story.

Casey's eyes widened as the tale unfolded. When Wade finished he said: "Listen, I got a *croix de guerre* with two palms the Frogs gave me. I'll bring 'em down tonight."

Wade looked surprised. He saw the twinkle in Casey's eyes, but he still didn't know why it was there. He said: "What—why—"

"A flash-gun in Greek Joe's face?" Casey grinned. "Oh, boy, oh, boy. You musta been nuts."

There was admiration in the big photographer's eyes for a moment, then his thick face grew thoughtful.

"Tied the can to you, eh? Tough. The skipper ain't a bad guy—but he's an egg about his assignments. You oughtta gone to that cornerstone business. But what the hell! Buck up."

Casey slapped Wade's back. "One of these other rags might take you on."

"I want to work for the *Globe*," growled Wade. "I want to come back here and make Blaine—"

"I know how you feel. Keep busy with that little box of yours. I never used one but I hear they're the business. Maybe you can run on to something that the skipper can use. Drop in and see us—and if you need a few bucks to tide you over—" Casey reached in his pocket.

Wade said: "Thanks. But I can get by for a while." He felt better already. It made a difference, having a guy like Casey with you.

During the next few days Wade pounded the pavements continually, firm in his determination not to go home. He'd had a taste of a city newspaper, had found it to his liking and he intended to hew to the line.

Even before he ever worked for a newspaper, he had been interested in photography. He had a dark room curtained off in his furnished lodging. He could do his own developing, printing and enlarging.

He finally got a break with the little camera. He got two night shots of a four-alarm fire that enlarged beautifully and appeared more spectacular than any taken by the newspaper photographers. He got twenty dollars for them from the branch of a photographic service which supplied newspapers all over the country.

That made him feel better and he began dropping into the *Globe* offices. He did not go when Blaine was there, but he sometimes came in on the lobster-shift around two in the morning.

On a Thursday morning, ten days after he had been fired, he found Casey there. It was about two-fifteen and Fesler, a lobster-shift city editor, Johnson, the night rewrite, Potter, a leg man, were munching sandwiches and talking about Greek Joe.

Casey was vociferously tight. When he saw Wade he yanked him down into an adjoining chair, offered half of his Swiss cheese on rye and said: "How's it, kid?"

"Oke." Wade grinned and sunk his teeth into the sandwich.

Potter, a stringy fellow with glasses and sandy hair so thin he looked bald from a distance, glanced at Wade, said:

"You certainly smoked him out. He hasn't been seen since."

"King Ricco," said Johnson, swallowing the last of his bread and fishing for a cigarette, "is burned up. He's had to take a bit of razz for not evening up for Vidal."

Fesler said: "He'd be better off if he—"He broke off as a phone rang, grabbed the pencil from behind his ear and pulled some copy paper towards him.

He said: "The desk—yeah. What? Yeah-yeah." He wrote two lines, said: "347 Hilton Street," and hung up. His eyes were like glowing coals, his neck thrust forward.

"Greek Joe," he snapped. "The King got him five minutes ago—347 Hilton —a prowl car heard the shooting—they got the King and two of his guns cornered in the house—"

Casey was on his feet, stone sober, before Fesler finished. "Oh boy, oh boy," he croaked, and leaped towards his cubbyhole of a workroom. Johnson snapped into life.

Wade stood up, excited, but undecided what to do first. He felt of the flat little camera in his pocket, inspected it to make sure it was loaded.

Fesler said: "Go with Casey, Potter. I'll get hold of Briggs and Mahone. Now for —— sake call back often. If it's big enough I'll rout out Blaine."

Casey came back loaded down with his camera and plate folders. He said: "Where's Terry?" Terry was the number two photographer. "On assignment?"

Fesler grunted: "Yeah, I'll try and get Murphy," and began talking to himself. "One and three with a flash and a bulletin lead—wonder what we got for cuts—"

He turned as telephones began to shrill, threw a telephone book at the dozing night office boy, said: "Answer 'em! See if anybody's in the art department!"

Casey grabbed Wade and dragged him towards the elevators.

The ride in Casey's roadster was short; but to Wade, it was a tonic in his blood. His bitterness towards Blaine, his own inexperience melted in the thought that he was with Casey, that Casey had brought him along, that there was going to be some action.

They got within two blocks of 347 Hilton Street with the car, ran the rest of the way to where a police line stopped them fifty feet short of the front door.

Three Forty-seven was on the corner, the last in a long row of three-storied brownstone fronts. The pavement behind the line was a mob scene. Family groups who had hurried to safety when the shooting began, huddled in vociferous knots. There were two fire trucks, three ambulances, a mess of blue-uniformed figures with here and there the white suits of internes standing out like ghosts in the night.

Casey and Potter stuck their police cards in their hatbands. Wade remembered his and followed suit. Casey, like the head man of a flying wedge, bucked his way up to the line that stretched across the street.

Wade could see the layout now. Ricco was evidently barricaded in a rear apartment. The side street—Maple—was absolutely deserted, but up on the roofs of the four-storied buildings which lined it he could see vague figures against the bleak, overcast sky.

As he looked up, a tongue of orange flame streaked over the top of the roof's retaining wall and a staccato burst of machine-gun fire clattered through the night air, reverberated through the brick-walled canyon and was lost in its own echo.

A savage answering burst which he could not see came from some point on the near side of the street. He realized Casey was talking with a barrel-chested police sergeant.

"The three guys in the prowl car cornered him. He got one of 'em."

"Where's Greek Joe?" rapped Casey.

"Still in there—so is the cop. The King smoked Joe out in this apartment. The guys in the prowl car chased him out but he got in an empty apartment at the back. Joe musta had an arsenal up there—they got two machine-guns, a couple shotguns.

"We got a squad up there on the roof" — the sergeant pointed across Maple Street just as another hail of leaden death streaked into the rear of number 347—"another bunch on the other side of the alley in back. Can't get up the stairs on account of King being at the back and commanding the stairs and hall; already lost another man when they tried to rush him. But we got a wrecking crew on the roof—going to dig through, drop some tear gas and—"

"Well, I gotta get some pictures." Casey started to push past the sergeant.

"Hold on there." The cop grabbed Casey. "Nobody goes past this line."

Casey began to swear. "What the hell? I can ease along this near wall to the front door and—"

The sergeant swung his blackjack on a thick forefinger, tapped it against the photographer's chest, thrust out an already jutting jaw. "Nobody, Casey! Nobody!"

Casey swore and for a moment Wade thought he was going to take a sock at the policeman, but he finally turned and pushed his way back through the crowd. Potter went in search of a telephone.

Wade, carrying the bulky plate case, tagged behind the big photographer without knowing just where he was going. Casey, still muttering angrily to himself, trotted a block down Hilton Street, two blocks down Spring Street; he turned right again, then cut down through an alley until he was in back of the four-storied apartments that housed the police machine-gun force on Maple Street.

They climbed a fire-escape, crossed two sets of roofs until they faced the side of the besieged 347. Casey said: "Keep down behind this wall," and began to move slowly towards the battery of police gunners about forty feet away.

Finally satisfied with his position, he said: "Okey. Get out the flash-gun. When I give you the word, hold it up and pull the trigger."

While Casey adjusted his camera, Wade sprinkled gray powder into the tray of the flash-gun. As he waited he remembered his own little camera and hurriedly got it out. He focused it, held it in his right hand, sighted experimentally at a shuttered window which at that moment spewed flame into the night.

Then Casey said: "Now!"

Wade stood up, pulled the trigger—opening the shutter of his camera at the same time. The flash-gun went "phuf" and a white glare blanketed the rooftops.

Casey cursed and yanked Wade forcibly down behind the retaining wall. "—— ——!" he wheezed. "I said hold it up—not stand up. You want to stop——"

He never finished the sentence. A cop crawled over and began to bawl him out in terse profane phrases.

Casey waited a moment as he changed plates said: "Listen, Lieutenant. We got a job to do, see? Just like you. We ain't crampin' your style, are we? You ain't tryin' to kid the King that you ain't here, are you?

"Keep your shirt on. One more shot'n we'll beat it—one of you and the boys. Sure—you cut loose with that typewriter, drive 'em away from the window and I'll take a shot of you in action that'll be on the front page tomorrow."

On the way down to the street Casey said: "They all fall for it. Now maybe we can get a couple shots from that roof back of the alley."

Ten minutes later they had these pictures of the rear of the death house, and Casey was chuckling because the officer in charge was going to keep all other photographers off the roof.

He said: "How we doin', kid?" and grinned. His felt hat was a battered crown now, his face was dirty and sweat stood out on his lip and forehead.

Wade moved around in a high-pressure trance. His heart was thumping like a triphammer and a triumphant feeling surged madly within him. This was something like it. And what a guy that Casey was! He heard him say, "If we could only get in that joint—" Then the big photographer was burrowing his way towards the police lines again.

Wade hesitated. So far he had not done much but lug the plates and handle the flash-gun. Of course he had some pictures—but if he could only figure out some way—

His brain snapped at a wild idea as his eyes caught sight of a milk wagon on the fringe of the crowd. A driver and helper were standing on the seat, peering over the heads of those in front of them.

Wade sprinted towards the wagon, expanding his idea as he moved. He slid to a stop on the pavement, stepped up on the wheel hub and yelled at the driver.

"You gonna be here a while?"

The fellow eyed Wade in disgust, cursed bitterly, said: "And how! We got milk to deliver in this block."

Wade gulped: "Will you let me have those white suits—coats and pants for ten minutes? Will you rent 'em for five bucks? I won't hurt 'em and—"

"You can have the horse for five bucks," growled the driver.

Wade let out an uncontrolled yelp of delight, climbed in the van-like body of the wagon, whipped off his topcoat. The driver slipped off the white coat and pants that covered his regular trousers and vest, put on the topcoat.

Wade, a white phantom, sprinted for the police line, barged through the crowd, finally found his man arguing with a cop. He pulled Casey by the coat-tail. The big man turned around with a snarl on his lips, checked the retort as his eyes widened in amazement.

"What the hell!"

Wade pulled him back down the street, explained his idea. "Get it? There's another one of these suits. They'll think we're internes. We can swipe a stretcher. You oughtta be able to talk us through the lines with that and—"

"Oh, boy! Oh, boy!" Casey's grin widened. He wet his lips. "And Blaine fired you!"

Five minutes later Casey, in white pants and a coat so tight he was just able to button it, sneaked a stretcher and a blanket out of a deserted ambulance.

He said: "The only way we can get the camera and plates inside is to carry them on this." He spread the blanket carelessly over the boxlike containers, grabbed up the forward handles. Wade took the rear end and they started through the crowd.

As they neared the police line Casey said: "I've gotta pick out some copper I don't know. And when I pull on this stretcher, get ready to run."

He followed along parallel with the line until he neared the same side of the street with number 347, then walked boldly up to a tall, gaunt policeman.

The fellow turned as Casey tried to edge past, said: "You can't go through here."

"The hell we can't," rapped Casey. "We just come from the Deputy Super. Ain't you heard? One of those cops in there is still alive. They say he's got a chance if we can get him to the hospital. We volunteered to the Super."

The cop hesitated, scowled.

Casey said: "Make up your mind! Does the cop get a chance for his life or do we spill this to the reporters?"

The cop turned sidewise, said: "I gotta make sure," and stepped towards a sergeant a few paces away.

Casey ducked under the line, shot forward. Wade followed, clinging to the stretcher handles. He stumbled as he went under the line, but Casey's steady pull on the stretcher jerked him erect and he broke into an awkward run.

He heard angry shouts behind him as they gained the stone steps of 347. But he did not turn his head. He kept his eyes on the back of Casey's thick neck, followed him up the steps and into the cool darkness of a stuffy vestibule.

The big photographer stopped, chuckled. "Well, we got to first base anyway." Then, apropos of nothing, he asked: "Say, how much did Blaine pay you?"

"Twenty-five a week."

"Oh, boy, oh, boy!" Casey put down his end of the stretcher and wiped the sweat from his face with his coatsleeve. Then he said: "Well, let's go up."

They moved slowly up a dimly lighted, narrow staircase to the second floor. In the background Wade could hear the muted bark of a machine-gun. Somewhere above him in the house, came a sharp, stuttering answer.

They went down the hall, started up the flight to the third floor. Near the top, Wade made out a group of four or five huddled figures silhouetted against the half-light of the hall above.

Casey pulled a quick retreat to the shelter of the second floor hall. "Hell! Captain Quinn's up there." He cursed softly, said: "It's up to you, kid. We gotta get through somehow. I'll keep my head turned the other way. Go up and talk turkey."

For an instant Wade's heart sank and he had a violent attack of jitters at the thought of his lone responsibility. But he whipped his nerves into submission, took a deep breath and climbed the stairs.

To the captain he presented an aggressive, assured ambulance man. He said the superintendent had called for volunteers—did they know for sure if the two cops were dead—this was their business—there was no risk. Even a killer like the King would not shoot an interne.

He concentrated on keeping all doubt from his voice. In the dim darkness the sweat poured from his face, but his tongue was glib and he realized he was winning out. Greek Joe and one cop were still in Joe's apartment; the other cop was in the hall. Nobody knew if they were dead or not. The King and his men commanded the hall and stairs from the door of the rear apartment. But the captain's resolve was weakening under Wade's dogged verbal assault. He saw this, pressed his advantage, turned and called to Casey:

"Okey, Mike." He went downstairs and took the front end of the stretcher.

The police drew aside, let them pass with a final word of caution. Casey kept his head down. They gained the upper hall, saw the inert form of a policeman against one wall, then ducked through the half-open door of Greek Joe's apartment.

The living-room was a shambles. A door was riddled with bullets; a cop lay sprawled in death in the little foyer; Greek Joe, a slug-torn, lifeless figure, lay across the living-room threshold.

Casey dropped the stretcher, wiped the sweat from his face with his coat-sleeve, snatched up the camera. They took pictures of Greek Joe, of the cop, of the splintered door. Wade worked in perfect co-operation with Casey, but his nerves jumped each time he heard the spasmodic bursts of machine-gun fire from the rear apartment. It sounded ominous, loud; much louder than when he had been on the roof with the police.

Casey, finally satisfied, stopped in the doorway to the hall. "Listen, kid," he whispered. "We'll take one shot of that guy in the hall, then run for it."

As they stepped out from the shelter of the doorway a momentary death-like silence swept through the hall. Wade's spine was like jelly and his fingers shook as he handled the flash-gun; but he took confidence from Casey's manner, carried through on his job. He stopped to throw the blanket over their photographic gear. Then Casey's voice rang in his ear, thrust a chill into his heart.

"Don't shoot! We're only carryin' these stiffs out."

Wade looked towards the door at the end of the hall. It was open about three inches; the stiff black barrel of a sub-machine-gun, looking as big and formidable as a one-pounder, slid out and drew down on them. Wade automatically lifted his hands, became a statue in chalk.

A low voice said: "Come here! Bring that stretcher, and come here!"

Wade heard Casey's whispered: "Oh, boy, oh, boy!" Then he was picking up the stretcher, moving on legs that were like cooked spaghetti into the face of the machine-gun.

The door opened, closed behind them. They stood in one end of a long living-room. There was no light on but there were glowing embers in the fireplace and light from the street filtered through the shattered shutters, so that Wade saw each feature of the room perfectly.

The glass had completely vanished from all three windows, lay in shimmering splinters on the floor; the walls and mantelpiece were etched with black holes; fragments of the shutters were everywhere. A man sat propped up against a table, his head on his chest. King Ricco, a slender black-haired figure with a wild look in his burning eyes, covered them with a sub-machine-gun. Another man, thick-set and swart, held an automatic in each hand.

Ricco said: "You guys must be tired of living. But you got guts, I'll say that."

"We came up," wheezed Casey, "to get—"

"To hell with them," rapped Ricco "We got a customer. Louis, here"— he jerked the gun towards the man on the floor—"ain't no good to us. Get him to a hospital."

He bent down beside the man, felt for his pulse, straightened up suddenly and spat out a curse.

"Hell! He's gone."

Ricco fell silent for a moment, started to curse again. He said: "But maybe—" He stopped, reached down and whipped the blanket from the stretcher.

The sight of the camera stiffened him. A sudden hail of death from a police machine-gun beat a sullen tattoo against the shutter of one window, whipping a spray of splinters into the room. Everyone ducked instinctively, waited, cautiously straightened up.

Ricco's thin face twisted in a leering smile. "Newspaper guys, huh? And me gettin' soft—was gonna give you a break." He began to take plates from the leather case, smash them against the corner of the table and toss them into the fireplace.

He seemed to take a vicious delight in this and he spoke bitterly as he worked.

"All right. You stuck your nose in here. I can use you. We'll get a truce and do a little bargaining. We ain't got nothing to lose and we might trade your hides for a chance to run for it. If we don't—"

He snatched up the box-like camera and threw it savagely against the wall.

Wade never knew exactly what happened next. The entire action was so unexpected, so lightning-like in its execution. He heard Casey bellow in rage, saw the camera crash against the wall.

As it sailed through the air, the long shoulder strap whipped out like an angry snake. Casey spun to one side. His big hand caught this strap and in one brief, continuous motion he swung the camera around his head like a cowboy throwing a lariat.

Wade heard the shout of alarm from the other man. He went into instant action, did not wait to see the camera strike. He heard it smash against Ricco's face as he left his feet and dived towards the other fellow who was swinging the automatic on Casey.

A gun roared in his ears, singed his neck; burned powder filled his nostrils. Then his shoulder struck a fleshy stomach and he crashed to the floor on top of a fighting, squirming madman. Some latent sadistic tendency sprang to life within him. He lost track of time and place. He was still astride the fallen gunman, pounding his fists into that swart face when Casey pulled him off.

The big photographer was raving about his smashed camera and plates. He continued to rave until another burst from the police gunners shook the room. That seemed to settle his anger. He took off his white coat, slid along to the window with his back to the wall, pushed open what remained of the shutter and waved his coat. The gunfire ceased.

While they waited for help, Ricco and his henchman recovered consciousness. Casey covered them with an automatic and Wade, remembering for the first time since he had come into the room, his own camera, took it out and found the flash-gun.

Casey watched in open-mouthed amazement. He said: "Did you—can you—" He broke off in a joyous whoop. "We'll get one shot nobody else'll get anyway. 'Cameraman rounds up gunmen.'" He laughed. "Can you imagine a photographer gettin' his picture took?"

Wade grinned and drew back for the picture. Casey posed. Wade got two shots before the police crashed in. He took one more of the police and the battered gunmen; then he and Casey ran for it.

Blaine, for once, was not sartorially perfect. His clothing showed the effects of a hurried dressing. His coat did not set quite right on his shoulders; his tie was askew and his vest had been buttoned up in the wrong buttonholes.

He sat at his desk as Casey told the story, but he could not keep still. His fingers drummed the desk top, he kept wetting his lips.

"Didn't you get any shots at all?" he asked bitterly.

"Sure." Casey grinned. "The kid got three that—"

"Well, don't stand there grinning, you big ape! Get busy!"

Casey's grin grew wary. "How about Wade? Is he fired or not? They're his pictures."

Blaine's face flushed. "What the hell is it to you?"

Casey lost his temper and pounded the desk. "If it hadn't been for his milk wagon idea we wouldn't have a thing. He's got three pictures that'll panic 'em. He's—"

Wade, his nerves still shaking, incredulous at Casey's defense of his cause, finally caught the spirit of the thing and began to argue for himself. "Three hell!" he barked. "I got at least a dozen—"

"You got what?" Casey jerked him around.

"I got everything you took. I handled the flash-gun, but I took a shot with my camera every time you did."

Casey grinned sardonically at Blaine "How do you like it?"

Wade, his fears forgotten, had command of the situation now and he knew it. He thought he ought to start rubbing it into Blaine, but he couldn't seem to work himself up to it. Blaine was okey. What the hell! All that mattered was that he work for the *Globe* again.

He said: "Am I fired, or not?"

"No, dammit, no! But hell! Don't stand there gawking. Do something!"

Casey started to pull Wade towards the dark room. Wade looked back over his shoulder as a happy thought struck him. "How about a raise?"

"Ten dollars a week," snapped Blaine. "Retroactive the day I made a mistake and let you go."

Casey opened the dark room door, said: "Blaine ain't a bad guy. He just takes a little handlin'."

Wade said: "What'd he mean, retroactive?"

Casey shut the door and his voice boomed from the darkness. "Don't ask me. Maybe it was a compliment, or somethin'."

6
Casey at the Movies

It is probably safe to say that all dramas and films about newspapers, reporters and photographers owe a debt to Ben Hecht and Charles MacArthur's 1928 play *The Front Page* as well as to the 1931 film version which featured Pat O'Brien and Adolphe Menjou.[1] Certainly, the cynicism of the editor and his volatile relationship with his number one reporter, the one who wants to get the story no matter what the cost, may be found in a number of films until *All the President's Men*, 1976, when the investigative reporter became the hero of the genre. Among the early films which reflect the influence of Hecht and MacArthur are three based on the works of George Harmon Coxe: *Women are Trouble*, 1936, *Murder with Pictures*, 1936, and *Here's Flash Casey*, 1937. Of these, the first and third are about our hero, Flashgun Casey, while the second is about Coxe's other cameraman, Kent Murdock.

How Many *Casey* Movies Were There?

There appears to be some confusion about the number of *Casey* films. Were there two or three? Even *Casey's* creator did not seem to be certain. In a background piece for the September 1941 *Black Mask* in which he introduced the serial "Killers Are Camera Shy" (published later as *Silent are the Dead*), Coxe asserted that *Casey* "appeared three times in movies — two of them pretty bad." In an article for *The Armchair Detective*, "Look for it in the *Morning Express*...," May 1973, this writer indicated that Coxe sold three *Casey* stories to the movies, one to M-G-M and two to Grand National. Only two films were actually made, though, *Women are Trouble*, based on the April 1935 *Black Mask* story of the same name and *Here's Flash Casey* based on "Return Engagement," *Black Mask*, March 1934 and "Murder Picture," *Black Mask*, January

---

1. The film was remade in 1940 as *His Girl Friday* with Cary Grant and Rosalind Russell and under the original title in 1974 with Jack Lemmon and Walter Matthau.

1935. The use of three stories in two films may account for the confusion, but the fact that the second *Casey* film went by two titles (*Here's Flash Casey* and *Meet Flash Casey*) may also have contributed to the uncertainty. A third factor might have been the Kent Murdock film, *Murder with Pictures,* mentioned above. So much attention from Hollywood in so short a time may have been something of which even a mystery writer could not keep track.

Women are Trouble

Women are Trouble was released in July 1936. The most detailed description of the film is found in the *American Film Institute Catalog of Motion Pictures Produced in the United States* (University of California Press, 1993). In lieu of an actual screening of the film, the following synopsis is based on that resource. An account of the cast and credits for the film will be found at the end of this chapter.

The Tim Gleason gang is responsible for a series of robberies and murders and Matt Casey, a reporter for *The Star*, has information he believes will help bring the gang to justice, so does the head of the liquor control board, a man named Eldridge. Casey and *Star* editor, Bill Blaine, are interrupted in their discussion of the situation by Ruth Nolan, a girl from a small town who wants a job as a reporter. Blaine turns her down, but she decides to prove her worth by getting an exclusive interview with Eldridge. Of course, she is just in time to witness his murder when his car is forced off the road. Her scoop on the murder makes Blaine hire her, but Casey still refuses to work with her. After all, he believes, women are trouble. Blaine sends the two of them to interview Murty, the man who drove the truck that killed Eldridge, but Casey won't let her accompany him to the actual interview. Instead, he tells her to stay in the car while he goes in to talk to Murty.

Ruth passes the time in the car practicing with a camera that she has found and takes a picture of someone leaving the building. When Casey comes back he tells her that Murty has just been shot. Ruth is pretty certain she has the picture of the killer in her camera. She doesn't tell Casey about this, but the killer knows she took his picture and explains to the rest of the gang that she is dangerous and they steal her camera. Blaine is furious until Ruth reveals that she had already removed the roll of film from the camera and put it in her purse, so *The Star* has a front page portrait of the gunman after all.

Ruth and Casey now try to interview the wife of Eldridge's killer, Mrs. Murty, but she doesn't want to talk to anyone. While Casey still has reservations about Ruth's methods of getting a story, he is beginning to find her attractive and even becomes jealous when Blaine escorts her to the Press Club masked ball. In retaliation, Casey escorts Blaine's ex-wife, Frances. Since everyone is masked, Blaine doesn't recognize his own ex-wife and makes a play for her. Two uninvited guests turn out to be a couple of gangsters determined to get Ruth out of the way. They kidnap her along with Blaine and the latter is about to be shot when Casey comes to the rescue. Unfortunately, Gleason, the ringleader of the gang, shows up and captures the three newspeople. Just as things look their worst, Inspector Matson arrives to save the day. The case closed, Casey admits that women aren't as much trouble as he had thought and Blaine remarries Frances to save on the alimony payments.

Stuart Erwin (left), Florence Rice and Paul Kelly
Women are Trouble

Reviews of the film were not very enthusiastic and even the ones in *The Motion Picture Herald,* June 6 and 20, 1936, and *Variety,* September 2, 1936, considered it no more than good entertainment. Apparently, the film received a certain amount of publicity at the time it was released because of a number of "firsts." It was the first story Coxe sold to the movies, it was the first screenplay written by Michael Fessier, it was the first film directed by Errol Taggart and the first film produced by Lucien Hubbard. As Coxe said in 1971, "it got a lot of publicity way beyond what it amounted to. It was a B picture."

Anyone familiar with the original story would have noticed the changes made for the movie. Let's begin with the characters: Jack Casey became Matt Casey and lost his role as photographer. Helen Draper, the small-town girl who wanted to be a reporter, became Ruth Nolan, a small-town girl who wanted to work for a big newspaper and learned to use a camera. Assistant District Attorney Eldredge became liquor control board head Eldridge, with his name spelled differently. Lieutenant Logan became Inspector Matson; city editor Blaine (with no first name given) became editor Bill Blaine and was given an ex-wife in the bargain. There were characters in the original story (including a number of reporters) who never appeared on the screen. Finally, there was no Press Club masked ball in the original story. Of course, many of the changes reflected the need to make things work on the screen.

What about the cast? Stuart Erwin, a good character actor, usually played the average citizen or the hero's slow-witted friend, but was hardly the person to portray Flashgun Casey, the big, rumpled cameraman with something of a temper.[2] Two years earlier, in 1934, he had played Ham Fisher's comic strip prize fighter in *Palooka* as a gentle giant with an accent like Will Rogers. Florence Rice (whose father was sportswriter Grantland Rice) usually portrayed sweet tempered women. As Julie Randall in the Marx Brothers film *At the Circus* (1939), she added some of the strong will needed of the would-be photographer Ruth Nolan.

Murder with Pictures

Before the next *Casey* film was presented to the public, Paramount released a film based on George Harmon Coxe's first novel, *Murder with Pictures*. The film starred Lew Ayres as Kent Murdock, the sophisticated photographer, and Gail Patrick as Meg Archer, the woman he had to prove innocent of murder. In the novel, this character was named Joyce Archer and Murdock eventually married her. In the film, Murdock's estranged wife, Hester, was turned into his fiancée Hester Boone (played by Joyce Compton). A photographic plate which revealed the murderer was the vital clue and *The New York Times*, November 21, 1936, found the most authentic part of the film to be the way Lew Ayres disposed of used flash bulbs by dropping them on the floor.

Here's Flash Casey

The second *Casey* film, *Here's Flash Casey*, was released in October 1937, slightly more than a year after *Women are Trouble*. The production company this time was Grand National Pictures and contemporary reviews indicate it was intended to be the first in a series. It starred Eric Linden as Flash Casey and

---

2. However, Judy Cornes in *Stuart Erwin, The Invisible Actor* (Scarecrow, 2001) considered Erwin's portrayal as "a world-weary reporter" in *Women Are Trouble* to be "memorable." His earlier role as the opportunistic newspaperman Johnny Sykes in *Viva Villa* (1934) was in contrast to the sympathetic and vulnerable Matt Casey who married the girl in the final reel of *Women Are Trouble*.

Boots Mallory as Kay Lanning. Officially, it was based on "Return Engagement" which had been published in *Black Mask* in March 1934; anyone with a knowledge of the entire *Casey* series to that time might have recognized elements from another story, "Murder Picture." Again, the following synopsis is based on the one in the *American Film Institute Catalog of Motion Pictures*, but unlike the first film, this writer was able to screen the movie.

The film opens by showing Flash Casey at college (Belmont) and establishes that his enthusiasm for photography began at an early age. By winning a photography contest, he makes enough money to stay in school until graduation. After college he goes to the big city and applies for a position as cameraman at *Globe Press*. Editor Blaine doesn't want to hire him until he takes a picture of the publisher's son, Rodney Addison, kissing Mitzi LaRue, a French dancer. Blaine only hires Flash (as he is called throughout the film) so he can get the negative and destroy it; pictures of young Addison's affairs are strictly forbidden at *Globe Press*. Flash is soon introduced to an older cameraman named Wade and becomes his assistant, but he makes a literal impression on Kay Lanning, the society editor, when he runs into her in the hallway. It is obvious Flash is more than a little smitten by Miss Lanning. Kay enlists Flash to help save *Snap News*, the pictorial magazine also published by the elder Addison. Flash gets a photo of a society wedding by hiding behind a floral delivery piece and turns the picture over to Pop Lawrence of *Snap News* instead of to his boss, Blaine. When Blaine learns of this disloyalty, he fires Flash, who is quickly hired by Lawrence. The regular photographer for *Snap News*, Gus Payton, has quit to start his own camera store, backed by a gangster named "King" Ricker.

Flash escorts Kay to a charity fund raiser and secretly takes pictures even though cameras are not allowed. He uses a candid camera he has borrowed from Gus Payton and gets a number of interesting shots, including one of the senior Addison with Miss LaRue. Flash has Payton develop the film and is unaware that Payton retouches some of them to show Addison and Miss LaRue in a compromising position. "King" Ricker takes the print to Addison and tries to blackmail him while Payton hides the negatives in Flash's desk.

Addison throws Ricker out and he and Kay head for the district attorney's office to file a complaint. When Ricker's men try to kidnap the two on the street outside, Flash interferes at which the gangsters shoot Addison from a nearby car and succeed in abducting Kay. Flash gets a photo of the crime and sets out in pursuit of the fleeing gangsters. When he is pulled over by the police, Flash calls Lieutenant Logan from a phone booth, then gets up and leaves the camera behind in his haste. The camera is soon picked up by a passing tourist who brings it to *Globe Press* as Flash's name, the name of the newspaper and the name of the Payton Camera Store are conveniently displayed on a label on the side of the camera. Flash manages to secure the camera before Blaine can get the photos because he wants to give the photos to *Snap News*.

Flash then teams up with Wade and the two steal an ambulance and disguise themselves as paramedics and gain entrance to the house to which Kay has been taken by carrying in a stretcher. They are recognized by Payton and a fight breaks out. Flash and Wade knock out Ricker and allow Kay to escape. The police arrive and Wade gets a photo of Flash and Kay in a final clinch.

Eric Linden (1935)

The reviews were not overwhelmingly favorable. *The Motion Picture Herald*, October 9, 1937, considered the film a pleasant diversion filled with blackmailers, gangsters, a murder, a kidnaping and a number of comic interludes. *The New York Daily News,* November 12, 1937, revealed the film was planned as the first of a series of four, but wasn't good enough to make anyone want to wait for even the first sequel. *The New York Journal American,* November 15, 1937, suggested there might be some possibilities to the film: the series potential was there and the actors were satisfactory in their roles, but it was juvenile fare.

Of course, Eric Linden was too young to be totally convincing as Casey as George Harmon Coxe wrote him and there were many scenes in the film which were the invention of screenwriter John Krafft and not the mystery writer. The entire college sequence was not in the original story, but in some ways it was not altogether inappropriate for many of Coxe's fictional heroes had college backgrounds. The story credit on the screen only mentioned "Return Engagement" and anyone who had read the story would recognize the use of a stretcher to gain entry to the gangster's house. The greatest difference was that the roles of Casey and Wade in "Return Engagement" were reversed for the film. In the original story, Wade was the newcomer who wanted a job as a cameraman, while Casey was the veteran. Of course, the newspaper in the story was just the *Globe,* but became *Globe Press* in the film and King Ricco in the original story became "King" Ricker. Anyone familiar with "Murder Picture" would recognize the concept of the photo of the publisher's son in a compromising position. In the original story, that situation led Casey, Wade, and even Blaine, to be fired from the *Globe* to go over to the competing *Express.*

Neither M-G-M nor Grand National was able to interpret the *Casey* stories and the characters satisfactorily for the silver screen. By making them comedic, they missed the drama. Stuart Erwin's gentle Matt Casey and Eric Linden's enthusiastic schoolboy did not represent the real Casey, the big man with a quick temper and fists to march. The experiment lasted only two years. After 1937 no one seems to have tried to bring Coxe's world to life on the large screen again, and that is to be regretted.

Filmography

Women Are Trouble
M-G-M. July 1936. 60 minutes.

Producers: Lucien Hubbard and Michael Fessier; Director: Errol Taggart; Assistant Director: Dolph Zimmer; Screenplay: Michael Fessier; Story: George Harmon Coxe;[3] Contributor to treatment: Richard Blake; Photography: Oliver T. Marsh; Art Director: Fredric Hope; Art Director Associates: Eddie Imazu and Edwin B. Willis; Film Editor: Conrad Nervig; Musical score: Edward Ward; Recording Director: Douglas Shearer; Sound: James K. Burbridge.

Cast: Stuart Erwin (Matt Casey); Paul Kelly (Bill Blaine); Florence Rice (Ruth Nolan); Margaret Irving (Frances); Cy Kendall (Inspector Matson); John Harrington (Tim Gleason); Harold Huber ("Pusher"); Kitty McHugh (Mrs. Murty); Raymond Hatton (Murty); George Chandler, Frank Jenks (Reporters); Robert Livingstone (Hotel Clerk); Wally Maher (Butch); Florence Lake (Clara); Frank Bruno (Gangster); Phil Tead (Granger); William Pawley (Mechanic); Ethel Wales (Hatchet-faced woman); Robert E, Homans (Lieutenant Mayer); Harry Burns (Escarel); Inez Palange (Italian mother); Frank Lackteen (extra).

---

3. The film was based on "Women are Trouble" in *Black Mask,* April 1935, but both the contemporary reviewers as well as the compiler of the entry for *The AFI Catalog* were unaware of this and credited Coxe with writing an original story for the film.

Here's Flash Casey
Grand National. October 1937. 58 minutes.

Presented by Edward L. Alperson; Producers: Max and Arthur Alexander; Associate Producer: Alfred Stern; Director: Lynn Shores; Assistant Director: Henry Spitz; Original screenplay: John W. Krafft; Photography: Marcel Pickard; Art Direction: Paul Palmentola and Fred Prebble; Film Editor: Charles Henkel, Jr.; Sound Supervisor: Terry Kellum; Production Manager: Harold Lewis; Technical Supervisor: A. E. Kaye.

Source: Based on the short story "Return Engagement" by George Harmon Coxe in *Black Mask,* March 1934. [Not credited: use of an idea from "Murder Picture" in *Black Mask*, January 1935.]

Cast: Eric Linden (Flash Casey); Boots Mallory (Kay Lanning); Cully Richards (Tom Wade); Holmes Herbert (Major Addison); John Creham (Blaine); Howard Lang (Pop Lawrence); Victor Adams ("King" Ricker); Harry Harvey (Gus Payton); Suzanne Kaaren (Mitzi LaRue); Matty Kemp (Rodney Addison); Dorothy Vaughn (Mrs. O'Hara); Maynard Holmes (Joe Gordon); Lester Dorr (Miller, reporter); Spec O'Donnell (Billy, copy boy); Virginia Dabney (Payton's moll, uncredited).

7
Casey on the Radio

Introduction

Like contemporary television, programming during the Golden Age of Radio followed trends that network executives thought would attract large numbers of listeners: as tastes changed, so did the programs.

One genre that remained popular throughout much of pre-talk and disc jockey radio focused on the adventures of people who worked for big city and small town newspapers. The number of such programs is legion and include: *The Daily Planet* reporters Clark Kent and Lois Lane of *Superman* fame, Britt Reid whose *Daily Sentinel* would report on the exploits of the *Green Hornet* and Steve Wilson, who as managing editor of *The Illustrated Press*, played initially by Edward G. Robinson, along with his sidekick (yes, most radio heroes enjoyed the adulation of female "pals") Lorelei Kilburn, played by Claire Trevor, mopped up crime in *Big Town*.

Using a different approach to the same general newspaper theme, *The Big Story* brought to listeners by Pall Mall cigarettes ("Outstanding and they are mild") saluted real life crusading reporters whose "big story" was dramatized and who were awarded on air cash prizes.

Other programs featuring the world of newspaper reporters included *Night Beat* with reporter Randy Stone of *The Chicago Star*, *Bright Star*, a syndicated show featuring Irene Dunne as editor of the *Hillside Evening Star* and Fred MacMurray as the paper's star reporter, *Rogers of the Gazette* with Will Rogers, Jr. in the title role, *Shorty Bell* with Mickey Rooney as a wannabe reporter who worked in newspaper circulation, *The Fourth Estate* narrated by well known journalist Mark Hellinger and *Night Editor* starring Hal Burdick.

Reporters were also well represented on daytime soap operas, including *Front Page Farrell* who worked for *The Brooklyn Eagle* and *Wendy Warren* which featured a female journalist who reported the news on the airwaves rather than in print.

Some lesser known radio dramas that featured newspaper people in leading roles included: *Deadline Mystery, Lucky Larson, Sandra Martin: Lady of the Press, Douglas of The World, Stand By For Crime, Special Assignment, Passport for Adams, European Confidential, Headline Hunters, San Francisco Final* and *The Lion's Den*.

If readers think that the authors may have missed an important program, have no fear. They saved their favorite newspaper adventure series for last.

How *Flashgun Casey, Crime Photographer* Came to Radio

Casey's transition from the pulps to radio was part trend, part the personal literary tastes of CBS executives and part serendipity.

During World War II, as part of its commitment to help the war effort by producing a series of programs extolling the efforts of our armed forces as well as the armed forces of our allies, a CBS vice president who was a fan of George Harmon Coxe's mystery stories invited the author to write some scripts for the network. One of the programs Coxe worked on was *The Commandos* which dramatized the heroic feats of Great Britain's commandos. The program was created by Phillips H. Lord of *Gang Busters* fame and produced and directed by Robert Lewis Shayon, later known for his work on *You Are There*. It was out of this working relationship that the radio *Casey* was born.

In a 1971 taped interview with co-author J. Randolph Cox, Coxe recounted how *Casey* arrived at CBS.[1]

> I happen to have had a couple of *Black Mask* fans at CBS, one of whom was a vice president and I did a little script work for him, mostly rewriting. When the vice president suggested that we try to get a *Casey* series going I agreed with the concept and said I would write an initial script that would set the formula but that I wouldn't write the scripts for the series.
>
> So I worked on the first script with Bob Shayon who was a young producer. When we went to the first audition, the script came out alright but I thought it needed something. Then, when we were sitting around having a beer and a sandwich, I said I knew a piano player that I thought was terrific and I wanted to help him if I could. He was playing in a place called the Ruban Bleu in New York with a trio and was accompanying Maxine Sullivan. "What the script needs," I said, "was a bar, and if we were going to have a bar, I was going to stick a piano in it."

---

1. The interview took place on August 10, 1971 in Old Lyme, CT. The above paragraphs are a paraphrase of the interview.

At that point, writer Ashley Buck came onto the scene and he invented the name Ethelbert for the role of the bartender. Buck also came up with the name the Blue Note Café for the bar which was the first time the name had ever been used. Now you can find Blue Notes in many parts of the county but that was the first Blue Note.

Coxe went on to recall some of the financial aspects of his relationship with the radio program.

So what I got out of it was a royalty which was fine with me because it allowed me to keep up my own work. And I had to make the deal with CBS myself because my agent was in Hot Springs. I made the deal with the vice president and a couple of CBS attorneys and the deal ended up being pretty good for me because CBS didn't put anything in the contract about television rights which wasn't very foresighted of them because later on when they wanted to put *Casey* on television I actually got a better deal and more money. I also told my agent that as long as I didn't write the scripts for the program I wasn't taking any bread out of his mouth so that he never got a nickel out of the deal. But I told him that if I started to write scripts for the program, then he would be entitled to his ten percent. He never quarreled about the deal and I kept all of the money. So that's the way it started and why it was very helpful financially to me.

Overview of *Casey's* Radio Career

The very first appearance of *Casey* on radio occurred on Wednesday evening, July 7, 1943, at 11:30pm. *Casey* replaced *Good Listening*, a program about which we know very little today and which was aired opposite NBC's *Author's Playhouse* and Mutual's *Dance Orchestra*. Initially, the program aired without a sponsor and was carried on a sustaining basis.

The premise upon which each weekly broadcast was based was quite simple: Casey was identified as a young, energetic photographer who was employed by the *Morning Express*, a major metropolitan newspaper, to provide photographs in support of mostly crime related stories. In sharp contrast to the tough and gritty Casey of the pulps, the new radio Casey was a softer, more gentle character who was partnered with an attractive female reporter, Ann Williams. Casey's natural curiosity, often based on the photos he had taken, caused him to follow certain clues leading to the solution of whatever mystery adventure the script writer had prepared for him.

Radio historian Jack French in his excellent book, *Private Eyelashes* (Bear Manor Media, 2004), described the relationship between Casey and Ann as professional with romance "strictly on the back burner." He also noted that depending on the script, Ann's role in solving the weekly mysteries ranged from negligible to total immersion, including one episode when Casey (played by Staats Cotsworth) was "out of town" and Ann solved the mystery entirely on her own.

While the author could find scant evidence of either Casey or Ann expressing romantic feelings toward one another, slight hints do appear from time to time to the effect that their relationship may have been something more than just professional. In the October 20, 1945 episode, "Cupid is a Killer," Casey pretends to make love to a woman who is the object of affection of a jealous killer in order to catch the killer red handed in an attempted murder. Casey implores Lt. Logan to let Ann know that the whole thing is a set-up, presumably so that she will not misunderstand. Logan, as a practical joke (and to get even with Casey for implying that he might be a dumb cop) fails to warn Ann that Casey's love making is only an act and her reaction to what she witnesses is nothing less than the anger that a jealous woman would express seeing the person she is fond of in the arms of another woman. If that isn't the behavior of two people who are "fond" of one another, then the author doesn't know human nature.

Casey's crotchety boss in the radio series was city editor Burke (Blaine in the pulps) who appeared in several episodes either giving Casey an assignment or challenging his judgment.

The law was represented by Logan, a second carry-over from the pulps and one who showed grudging respect for Casey's ability to spot clues often overlooked by others and who was either cooperative or cynical depending on the circumstances.

Initially a lieutenant in both the pulps and in the early radio broadcasts, Logan was "promoted" to Captain on April 10, 1945. In the episode "Death of A Rattlesnake" that only survives in script form, it is clear that Logan's promotion was not an accidental event but one bestowed upon him by the person responsible for writing most of the scripts, Alonzo Deen Cole.

ANN: Why do you think Bannon killed Smiley Lieuten__?
Uh— I forgot it's CAPTAIN Logan now.
LOGAN: (*Chuckles*) And I'm not forgetting Miss Williams that you and Casey had a lot to do with making me a captain.
ANN: I had nothing to do with it.
LOGAN: Casey did . . . Plenty.
CASEY: You're nuts.
LOGAN: OK pal. But thanks. To answer your question Miss Williams—

And finally, much of each week's adventure was discussed or narrated in the Blue Note Café presided over by the always amusing bartender, Ethelbert, and where the sound of a jazz pianist was heard in the background. The bar served as a focal point where Casey, accompanied by Ann, went to let off steam and review the facts of his most recent adventure.

A review of the initial broadcast appeared in one of New York City's tabloid newspapers a week later on July 14, 1943[2] and suggested that,

> ...the Casey show is a fast-moving presentation, guaranteed to keep the night owls awake for the stanza's full 30 minutes. The character Casey...has been endowed with cynicism, sleuthing ability, sentiment and hardboiledness expected of the radio and film version fourth estater. He (Casey) sasses the city editor, pitches woo and solves the mystery in forthright fashion.

After giving the program only mild approval, the reviewer went on to comment about the piano performance of Juan Fernandez[3], calling him a "...philosophical piano-playing nitery performer somewhat akin to Dooley Wilson (as in the movie *Casablanca*) minus the vocalizing." The reviewer added that the program offered a "highbrow" touch, noting that the bartender Ethelbert had read Wendell Wilkie's *One World*.

The writer concluded his not overly enthusiastic review observing that the program offered,

> ...conventional tried-and-true-entertainment, the acting was either overdone or generally satisfactory, depending on the actor, and the direction and producing was par for the course.

Readers who listen to recordings of the initial program, broadcast more than 60 years ago, will no doubt be struck, as the earlier reviewer was, with Ethelbert's intellectual proclivities. Clearly otherwise portrayed as a "dees, deem, dose" type of character, in the course of 30 minutes listeners hear that in addition to Wendell Wilkie, Ethelbert also reads *The New Republic, The Atlantic Monthly* and the *American Mercury* and that he can quote both Lord Dunsany and Thomas Paine. One may well wonder why a man with such high brow reading habits would be tending bar (meaning no insult to today's skilled bartenders).

---

2. The review can be found in the clippings file at both the New York Public Library for the Performing Arts and in the Coxe papers at the Beinecke Rare Book and Manuscript Library at Yale University. At both locations, the name of the newspaper is missing.

3. Some sources show the name of the program's early piano player as "Juan **H**erandez."

As the author was unable to find additional scripts portraying Ethelbert as a literary name dropper, it is likely that subsequent script writers found that characteristic less essential to the plot.

After its somewhat less than resounding reception, *Casey* continued on CBS as a sustaining program for three years and as a sponsored program for the next four years, going off the air on November 16, 1950 when the Philip Morris sponsorship contract expired and CBS was not able to line up a replacement sponsor. Although network staff pointed out to potential sponsors that at a weekly cost of $2,700 per program, *Casey* attracted more listeners per dollar than the *Lux Radio Theater, Fibber McGee and Molly, Amos 'n' Andy, Jack Benny, Charlie McCarthy, Red Skelton, Bob Hope* and *Bing Crosby*, by 1950 more and more companies were turning to television to sell their products.

Indeed, as discussed in greater detail in the chapter on television, four months after *Casey* was taken off the radio, the program reappeared on CBS television as a sponsored program. However, 18 months after the demise of the television *Casey*, and after being off the radio for three years, *Casey* returned to radio on January 13, 1954 with the same cast members and writers. For the next year and a half, the program continued to entertain its loyal fans, broadcasting its final episode on April 22, 1955.

Like its first three years, the program's final season was broadcast on a sustaining basis, taking over the 9:00–9:30pm time slot that had previously been filled by *On Stage*, a dramatic anthology featuring the husband and wife team of Elliott and Cathy Lewis. When the couple returned from their three week vacation on February 3, 1954, their program was rescheduled to the 9:30–10:00pm slot following *Casey*.

During its entire run on CBS, a total of 431 *Casey* programs were broadcast and all but 19 of the programs are identified by title in the Radio Log that appears in the next chapter. At least 23 of the 431 programs used scripts that had been done earlier and as many as 81 programs have survived and are in circulation among fans of Old Time Radio (OTR). These programs are identified in the Log.

Cast and Crew

Casey: The very first actor to portray Casey was Matt Crowley (1904–1983) of *Mark Trail* and *Jungle Jim* fame. While Crowley appeared in only the first three episodes, fortunately the premier broadcast of the series, "The Case of the Switched Plates," is one of *Casey* programs that has survived.

Crowley was followed for a short time by Jim Backus (1913–1989) of *Mr. Magoo* fame who took over the Casey lead on July 28, 1944 and continued in the role until sometime between August 26th and September 16th of 1943. No episodes in which Backus plays Casey are known to be in circulation.

Matt Crowley
Casey #1
July 1943

Jim Backus
Casey #2
August–September 1943

The third actor to portray Casey, and the actor that fans generally associate with the role, was the talented stage actor Staats Cotsworth (1908–1979).

Cotsworth continued in the Casey role until the program went off the air in 1955, repeating the pattern he had set earlier when he succeeded Richard Widmark and Carlton Young in the role of David (*Front Page*) Farrell where he also remained in that role until the end of the program's run. He also played Wolfe Bennett in *Lone Journey*.

Staats Cotsworth
Casey #3
September 1943–November 1950
January 1954–April 1955

Ethelbert: John Gibson (1905–1986), an actor known for his most distinctive voice, played Ethelbert, the Blue Note bartender for the program's entire run. Gibson is also remembered for his portrayal of Archie Goodwin, the clever legman for Nero Wolfe.

Ann[4] Williams: Jone (not to be confused with "June") Allison portrayed Ann in the very first broadcast but was replaced shortly thereafter by Alice Reinheart, famous for playing Chichi on *Life Can Be Beautiful*. Reinheart, in turn, was replaced by Lesley Woods (who also played Mary Wesley, *Boston Blackie's* female interest) who continued in the role until April, 1947 when she was replaced by Betty Furness. The final and longest lasting Ann was Jan Miner of *Hilltop House* fame who took over the role in 1947. OTR fans also remember Miner as Madge, the manicurist on television.

Lesley Woods

Jan Miner

Captain Logan: The program's fourth regular character, Captain Logan, was played by Jackson Beck during the show's early years and later by Bernard Lenrow who also played Geoffrey Barnes, the crime fiction connoisseur who each week introduced *The Molle Mystery Theater*. It should be noted that besides Casey himself and the city editor, Logan was the only other regular radio character who also appeared in the *Black Mask* pulps (when his rank was that of a lieutenant on the Boston Police Force.)

Burke: The *Morning Express* city editor was played by different actors as often the dialogue was so limited that the person reading the part's lines was also doubling.

---

4. Various references show the name of the character as Ann, Anne and Annie although on the air Casey frequently referred to the character as "Annie."

Jan Miner (Ann), Staats Cotsworth (Casey) and Bernard Lenrow (Capt. Logan) in a staged PR photo.

Silent characters: In a delightful interview for Richard Lamparski's *Whatever Became Of* series that aired on WBAI in New York City, ca. 1960s, both Cotsworth and Gibson recalled the character of Walter who appeared on the program from time to time but who never spoke a word. Instead, Walter would receive instructions from Ethelbert to go after some item needed for the bar. Whether the Walter character was used as a running joke or a way to fill time, remains an unsolved mystery.

A second "ghost" character who is referred to from time to time is Grace who can be described either as a bar fly or simply a frequent customer. Ethelbert speaks to Grace but her voice is never heard.

Guest actors: During its long run, a veritable "who's who" of radio giants appeared on the program, including: Bill Adams, Ed Begley, Ralph Bell, Peter Capell, Ted de Corsia, Roger de Koven, Joe de Santis, Robert Dryden, Hope Emerson, John Griggs, Jack Hartley, Raymond Edward Johnson, Joseph Julian, Ralph Locke, Mandel Kramer, James Kreiger, Abby Lewis, Arnold Moss, Santos Ortega, Bryna Raeburn, Karl Swenson, Maurice Tarplin, Chuck Webster, Miriam Wolff and Art Carney[5] to name but a few.

---

5. In a 1975 interview taped at a SAVE convention (Society of American Vintage Radio Enthusiasts), the precursor to the Friends of Old Time Radio (FOTR), that was later broadcast on Dick Bertel's *Golden Age of Radio* program on WTIC, Hartford CT, Cotsworth recalled that when Carney returned to broadcasting after World War II his legs were severely wounded and the program's director, John Dietz, was eager to help him out with roles on the program, even if they had to create a walk on part for the actor.

Announcers: Tony Marvin was, if not the program's first announcer, one of its earliest and his distinctive voice can be heard in the surviving episodes from 1946 through March, 1948. Marvin was replaced by Bill Cullen who became the spokesperson for Toni Home Permanents during the 1948–1949 season, and Cullen, in turn, was followed by Ken Roberts who stayed with the program until it went off the air in November, 1950.[6] During its sponsored years, Marvin, Cullen and Roberts would be on hand at the Blue Note, hawking their glass, beauty and tobacco products as though they were part of the story line. When *Casey* returned for its final season as a sustaining program the announcer for that entire run was Bob Hite.

Writers: Early writers for the program included Ashley Buck who, in collaboration with Coxe, wrote the first episode, Charles Holden, Milton Kramer, Robert Sloane and Gail and Harry Ingram and others whose names, when known, are identified in the Radio Log in the next chapter.

The best known writer, however, and one who was unquestionably responsible for the vast majority of the *Casey* scripts was Alonzo Deen Cole (1897–1971). Cole is known to have written at least 384 of the *Casey* scripts. The known Cole scripts are identified in the Radio Log in the next chapter.

A native of Minnesota, Cole learned his trade on the vaudeville circuit and got his start in radio as early as 1931 as both a performer and writer on WOR when he and his wife appeared on a program called *Darling and Dearie*. Shortly thereafter he created one of the earliest anthology horror programs in broadcast history, *The Witch's Tale,* which ran for a total of 352 broadcasts, from 1931–1938, before going into transcribed syndication.

Never one to waste a plot idea, Cole was adept at recycling material he had written for other radio shows. In October 1943, for example, he submitted a script for *The Shadow*, "The Knocker of Tolliver Level," that involved a murder in a coal mine. Not surprisingly, the Blue Coal Company, the show's sponsor, turned the script down. But, three years later, and with a few revisions, the script was transformed into a *Casey* script, "The Demon Miner," which was aired on March 20, 1947.

Similarly, Cole's October 5, 1931 script, "The Boa God," written for his *Witch's Tale* series and repeated twice on that program, October 31, 1933 and March 18, 1937, was recycled once more on *Casey* on December 4, 1947 with

---

6. In a telephone interview in February, 2005, Roberts laughingly related that these days his granddaughter was the public spokesperson for Philip Morris but that her message, unlike his, was to make the public aware of the harm that cigarettes can inflict.

slight revisions as "The Serpent Goddess." Another *Witch's Tale* script adapted for the series was "The Image," broadcast on February 8, 1932 and recycled on *Casey* as "Halloween Story" on October 31, 1946. Indeed, a "fun" exercise for OTR aficionados may well involve identifying other early Cole scripts that were recycled for his *Casey* assignment.

Not only did Cole borrow from his own previous ideas, but in at least two instances he recycled pulp stories by Coxe. The first was "Earned Reward," broadcast January 7, 1946 (and repeated November 20, 1947) based on the pulp story of the same name that appeared in the March 1935 issue of *Black Mask*. The second recycled Coxe story, "The Buried Evidence," was broadcast on December 26, 1946 and was based on the story, also of the same name, that appeared in the July 1935 issue of *Black Mask*.

Cole, in turn, had some of his own *Casey* scripts recycled in the form of comic book stories as discussed in greater detail in the chapter "Casey in the Comics."

Alonzo Deen Cole and Staats Cotsworth

Not a man of slight ego, in October, 1968, after reading an entry about his role as a writer for *Casey* in a reference book about radio, Cole took the time to write a four page letter to one of the authors to "clarify things." In the letter, he "informed" the authors that "...the masterminds of the CBS staff contrived a clumsy framework around the central character of several pulp magazine stories and a detective novel written by George Harmon Coxe which wobbled through five weeks on the air before I took over as developer and head writer. After excising a lot of dead wood from the show's primary conception and adding more solid timber, my escalating contract with CBS was constantly renewed throughout the series long lifetime." Cole went on to take issue with the authors' reference to him as "one of the show's writers," reminding them that he was responsible for 384 out of more than 400 original scripts used on the program.

Whether Cole was borrowing from earlier scripts or coming up with new ideas, CBS recognized that the program's chief writer might require an occasional "breather" and let it be known that it would pay freelance writers the sum of $200 for accepted *Casey* scripts. The network's instructions to writers were to follow the same format and use the program's regular characters. Ethelbert, for example, was described as a "dees, deem, dose" bartender.[7]

Music: Although Archie Bleyer, later of *Arthur Godfrey* fame, is generally credited with having composed the music for many of the programs, Cy Feuer, another well known musician, received on air recognition in 1949 for having also written music for some of the programs.

The jazz pianist most frequently credited on air for his participation on the program was Herman Chittison (1908–1967).[8] The pianist's popularity with the listening audience was highlighted in a feature story about Chittison that appeared in the July 14, 1950 issue of *NY Compass*. In the article, the writer noted that when CBS offered to send photos of the *Casey* cast to listeners, the station received 17,000 requests for the cast photo but also 10,000 requests for photos of just Chittison.

Teddy Wilson, who had earlier performed with Benny Goodman, filled in for Chittison on occasion and on January 17, 1954 became the Blue Note's full time pianist. Juan Fernandez and Lew White, a noted organist of the day, also made musical appearances at the Blue Note.

Director and producer: Albert Ward was the director of the very first *Casey* radio program and continued in that role through the middle of the following year. Although Rocco Tito was also known to have directed one or two programs during the show's early years, John Dietz took over as director after Ward stepped down and continued with the program to the end of its run. Dietz,

---

7. From an unidentified and undated newspaper clipping in the Coxe collection at the Beinecke Library.

8. The Kentucky Historical Society dedicated a special highway marker marking Chittison's place of birth in Fleming County, KY in recognition of the musician's accomplishments as an African American jazz pianist.

Herman Chittison

Teddy Wilson

who came to CBS in 1934 and who worked in almost every department from maintenance to engineering before becoming a director, was also associated with many other popular CBS programs including *Famous Jury Trials, Life Can Be Beautiful, Columbia Workshop* and *Suspense*, to mention just a few.

Chester Ranier is identified as producer of the premier broadcast and it is likely that he went on to produce subsequent episodes. Robert J. Landry, who is well known for having written about the business side of radio, was also a producer for the program.

Sound effects: Among the sound effects artists who were associated with *Casey* during its long run were Jerry McCarty, James Rogan, and Art Strand.

Although well known sound effects professional Robert Mott did not work on *Casey*, in his excellent book, *Radio Sound Effects* (McFarland, 1993), Mott relates the following incident that happened to one of his colleagues who did work on the program: During the broadcast, an actor carelessly stepped out his cigarette near the sound effects area which led the sound effects man to accidentally get the cigarette caught on the bottom of one of his shoes. Minutes later, while creating the sound of a chase scene on a wooden plank, the sound man's clean shoe produced one sound while the second shoe with the cigarette produced a more padded sound leaving listeners wondering how a one legged Casey could move so quickly.

Sponsorship

For its first three years on the air, from July 7, 1943–July 22, 1946, Casey was broadcast without a sponsor. On August 8, 1946, the Anchor Hocking Glass

Company picked up the program and continued to underwrite it until March 25, 1948.

The only *Casey* broadcasts in which there is a hint of a studio audience are those that were sponsored by Anchor Hocking and where there was a burst of applause at the conclusion of Tony Marvin's opening introduction.[9]

Anchor Hocking was replaced by Toni Home Permanents which sponsored the program from April 1, 1948–July 28, 1949, and on August 4, 1949 Philip Morris picked up the program and remained the sponsor until November 16, 1950 when it went off the air for a three year hiatus.

When the program returned to the air on January 13, 1954, once again it was on a sustaining basis.

In the Spring, 1947, the four regular *Casey* cast members, along with Tony Marvin, participated in a closed circuit "promo" written for officials and sales people of the Anchor Hocking Glass Company who were attending a convention at the company's Lancaster, Ohio headquarters.[10] The presentation starts with the pretext of a crisis at the Blue Note and Ethelbert explaining the presence of a CBS engineer who has set up the special microphone for the occasion.

> Staats Cotsworth (Casey) begins the presentation by informing the Anchor Hocking audience that some 35 million listeners, or one fourth of the population, tune into their *Casey* program. He then goes on to make the point that two years after the end of the war, consumers no longer need to buy any available product because now there is ample competition, thus stressing the need for effective advertising.
>
> Jan Miner (Ann) is next to speak, first explaining that she took over the role just a few weeks earlier, replacing Lesley Woods who had recently been married and was on her honeymoon. Then, after re-addressing the size of their audience, she stresses the program's two major responsibilities: that of providing clean, decent and worthy entertainment and of increasing the sales of the sponsor's product.
>
> John Gibson (Ethelbert) follows in his amusing, sometimes bumbling style, initially not knowing what to say but letting the Anchor Hocking officials know that he only serves "bottled" beverages. He also stresses

---

9. It is generally assumed that the applause came from a live audience as the use of "canned" audience sound effects was a rarity in the mid 1940s. Also, one can hear the faint if subdued sounds of reaction from an audience during other segments of the program. It should also be noted that Anchor Hocking used a live audience on another CBS program, *Hobby Lobby*, that aired from August 1945–August 1946, the year before *Casey* was broadcast.

10. A tape of the promo is in circulation.

the teamwork among cast members, particularly citing Herman Chittison, who, since joining the program, has a Saturday night program of his own, makes recordings and plays at night clubs, all the while continuing to play at the Blue Note.

The audience is then treated to a few bars of Chittison's piano before hearing from Bernard Lenrow (Captain Logan) who adds his encouraging words to the promo. Lenrow is followed by Tony Marvin who calls on Cotsworth to take a photo of the group. We are told by Marvin that like the character he plays, Cotsworth has becomes quite a photographer himself.[11]

Against All Odds, *Casey* Perseveres

When one considers the number of obstacles that could easily have led to the demise of a less popular program, it is amazing that *Casey* survived on radio for as many years as it did.

Title change: The first obstacle was the frequent change in the program's title. When the program debuted on July 7, 1943, it was known as *"Flash-Gun Casey," Press Photographer*. Then, on April 8, 1944 it became *Casey, Press Photographer*. By July 4, 1945, the title was shortened to simply *Crime Photographer*. It wasn't until March 29, 1947 that the title fans most associate with the program, *Casey, Crime Photographer*, came into existence and remained the official title until November 16, 1950 when the program went off the air. But even that title did not last. When *Casey* returned to the airwaves in 1954, the program title reverted back to *Crime Photographer*.

Time change: For avid fans who wished to follow Casey's adventures on a weekly basis, the changes in the program's title were a minor glitch when compared to the far more frustrating issue of the program's constantly changing schedule: even the most dedicated fan would be discouraged by never being sure on what day and at what time the program would be aired.

As the following table highlights, during *Casey's* entire run, it endured a total of 14 schedule changes, including being aired on six different days of the week. Only Sunday, not viewed as a great day for crime dramas unfolding in a

---

11. In his 1975 interview with Dick Bertel, Cotsworth recalled his interest in photography and how he and director John Dietz had once collaborated on a *Casey* script that featured the use of a Polaroid camera. The Polaroid Company was so pleased with the broadcast that it offered Cotsworth and Dietz their choice of either a free camera or 15 shares of stock. To his everlasting regret, Cotsworth admits selecting the free camera.

bar (which should be closed on the Lord's Day), was spared. The program also went through nine different time changes.

Crime Photographer Schedule Changes		
Time Period	Day	Time
Jul 7, 1943–Aug 4, 1943	Wed	11:30–12pm
Aug 12, 1943–Oct 21, 1943	Thu	11:30–12pm
Oct 30, 1943–Jul 8, 1944	Sat	11:30–12:00pm
Jul 15, 1944–Sep 9, 1940	Sat	5:00–5:30pm
Sep 12, 1944–Jun 26, 1945	Tue	11:30–12:00pm
Jul 4, 1945–Sep 5, 1945	Wed	9:00–9:30pm
Sep 12, 1945–Sep 26, 1945	Wed	10:30–11:00pm
Oct 20, 1945–Nov 24, 1945	Sat	1:30–2:00pm
Dec 3, 1945–Mar 4, 1946	Mon	10:30–11:00pm
Mar 12, 1946–May 28, 1946	Tue	10:00–10:30pm
Jun 3, 1946–Jul 22, 1946	Mon	8:30–9:00pm
Aug 8, 1946–Nov 16, 1950	Thu	9:30–10:00pm
Jan 13, 1954–Sep 29, 1954	Wed	9:00–9:30pm
Oct 10, 1954–Apr 22, 1955	Fri	8:00–8:30pm

One doesn't require the deductive skills of a Sherlock Holmes to conclude that once the program finally garnered a sponsor in 1946, there was not a single schedule change for the rest of the program's run until it went off the air in 1950. Whereas sponsors demanded a consistent schedule, sustaining programs, especially those like *Casey* that were carried by the network for three full years without sponsorship, could be moved frequently to meet the demands of those programs that enjoyed commercial support.

Logo or opening change: During radio's Golden Age, a program's opening became its logo or its symbol of identification. To this day, old timers react with instant recognition when hearing phrases like: "The weed of crime bares bitter fruit," "Lux Presents Hollywood," "Henry, Henry Aldrich," or "Yoo hoo, Mrs. Bloom," or hear marching feet followed by the sound of machine guns and the single word, "Gangbusters," or an orchestra playing the theme from the *William Tell Overture*. These and countless other program openings reminded folks that their favorite programs were about to be aired.

Casey, however, was an exception to this practice and, as illustrated below, utilized a variety of openings throughout its run.[12]

July 1943

Flashgun Casey, Press Photographer. (Musical interlude.) Out of a big city's roaring life, out of a great newspaper's pounding heart come the exciting adventures of a man with a camera, Flashgun Casey, Press Photographer. (Musical interlude.) Columbia presents a new adventure character, Flashgun Casey, Press Photographer, tough, daring, typical of the men who often risk their lives so that you may see the news as well as read it. Their salaries are not large and they seldom get much credit but their lives are packed with danger and thrills. Tonight and every Wednesday night at this time Columbia invites you to follow the story of Flashgun Casey and the people who pass in swift moving parade before the shutter of his camera. Tonight's story: "The Case Of The Switched Plates."

February 1944

Face the camera please. Hold it. Thanks. Look for it in the *Morning Express*. (Musical interlude.) *Casey, Press Photographer.* (Musical interlude.) Columbia brings you another adventure of Casey, Press Photographer. Tonight and every Saturday at this time Columbia invites you to follow Casey on his exciting assignment and to meet the strangely assorted people who pass in swift moving parade before the shutters of his camera. Tonight: "The Clue In The Clouds."

May 1947

The Anchor Hocking Glass Corporation brings you *Crime Photographer*. (Musical interlude plus piano tinkling.)

Casey:	Ethelbert, what on earth's going on over there?
Ethe:	Oh that's Grace. I can't get her away from that piano.
Casey:	Tell her to let Herman play.
Ethe:	Oh Grace. That's enough. Thanks.
Casey:	Besides this is the famous noise abatement week.
Marvn:	Well it may be famous Casey, but it's not as famous as

---

12. The absence of a consistent, easily recognizable opening most likely explains why *Casey* was not one of the 180 popular radio openings that were immortalized on the two volume set of long playing records, *Themes Like Old Times,* released in the 1960's.

my favorite line. Anchor Hocking is the most famous name in glass. (Musical interlude and applause.) Good evening ladies and gentlemen. This is Tony Marvin. Every week at this time the Anchor Hocking Glass Corporation of Lancaster, Ohio and its more than ten thousand employees bring you another adventure of Casey, Crime Photogragher, ace cameraman who covers the crime news of a great city. Written by Alonzo Deen Cole our adven ture for tonight: "King Of The Apes."

May 1949

Girl singing: The wave that gives that natural look is T O N I, T O N I. Toni, Toni Home Permanents, the wave that gives that natural look brings you *Crime Photographer*. Good evening everyone. This is Bill Cullen greeting you for Toni Home Permanents and inviting you to listen to another adventure of Casey, Crime Photographer, ace camera man who covers the crime news for the great city. Written by Alonzo Deen Cole our adventure for tonight: "Cupid Is A Killer."

August 1949

(Musical interlude.)
Roberts: Philip Morris presents, Crime Photographer.
Johnny: (Over the music of the *Grand Canyon Suite*:) "Call for Philip Morris." "Call for Philip Morris."
Roberts: It's a wonderful, wonderful feeling to wake up fresh with no cigarette hangover. Yes, you'll be glad tomorrow you smoked Philip Morris today.
Johnny: "Call for Philip Morris," (Followed by musical interlude.)
Roberts: Good evening, this is Ken Roberts greeting you for Philip Morris and inviting you to listen to another adventure of Casey, Crime Photographer, ace camera man who covers the crime news of a great city. Written by Alonzo Deen Cole, our adventure for tonight: "Death Of A Stranger."

January 1954

First on the scene, Crime Photographer. (Snap sound.)
Casey: Got it. Look for it in the *Morning Express.* (Musical interlude.)
Hite: CBS Radio brings back *Crime Photographer*, another adventure of Casey, ace camera man of the *Morning Express* who

covers the crime news of a great city. With the original cast, author and director, Crime Photographer played by Staats Cotsworth and written by Alonzo Deen Cole tonight presents: "Road Angel."

With at least five different and distinct openings, coupled with five different name changes and 14 different schedule changes, *Casey* clearly possessed more than simply "the luck of the Irish" to have remained on the air for as many years as it did.

Assessing *Casey's* Popularity

Casey's relative success over the years can be gauged by examining some of the many reviews and promotional pieces about the program that appeared in various publications during its initial years as well as by examining its ratings *vis a vis* other programs. It is also interesting to note how *Casey* has stood the test of time and is viewed today by contemporary OTR writers.

On April 7, 1945, *New York World Telegram* columnist Harriet Van Horn, later known for her appearance as one of the panelists on the popular television program, *Leave It To The Girls*, interviewed Staats Cotsworth about his Casey role and learned that Casey was the envy of real life newspaper photographers across the land who wrote him long letters offering advice, asking questions and sometimes voicing their dissent. One piece of advice was to stop using that old fashioned type camera that required a change of plates for every shot. Roll film, they suggested, was more practical, but not, Casey (Cotsworth) told Van Horn, for radio purposes where sound was important and the business of changing plates along with the "click" added to the drama.

Another reason for the professional envy, Cotsworth added, was that Casey was rarely assigned to cover county spelling bee championships or charity bazaars and he did not have to debase his art by having to scurry about after his subjects asking them their names "left to right." And finally, photographer fans envied anyone who could drink as much as Casey and still focus a camera.

According to one unidentified and undated review of the program that appeared at least one year after the Van Horn column,[13]

Crime Photographer is occasionally gabby in plot exposition in contrast with some of the trick whodunits on air today but the author, Alonzo

---

13. Regrettably, the source and date for this review, as well as the two following reviews, were not identified. However, as all three reviews note that the program was sponsored by Anchor Hocking, the reviews probably appeared sometime between August 8, 1946 and March 25, 1948.

Deen Cole, plants his elements carefully and this pays off in a story that is easier to believe and follow. Another valuable variation from current norm is the underplaying, fuller-bodied characterizations, both unusual in a bang-bang stanza.

Commenting on an earlier plot that involved an innocent man being released from prison after serving ten years for killing his wife, who it turned out, was still alive and wealthy, the reviewer added,

> That was a provocative premise and got conflict values established which offset the routine expectation of a real homicide.

Another unidentified reviewer considered the program "no better or worse than the next thriller" and hypothesized that,

> ...it's our suspicion that this show draws unfairly on untapped reserves in thrill starved working newspaper photographers who wish their lives *were* as eventful as Casey's.

The reviewer then added,

> Announcer Tony Marvin's eloquent assurances on his sponsor's behalf that beer taste better in bottles than in cans carries conviction. So would the show if Casey would only permit Captain Logan of the Homicide Squad to solve one teeny weeny crime.

And in the summer of 1946, still another reviewer had both positive and somewhat critical things to say about the program:

> After three years as a sustainer *Crime Photographer* went commercial for the first time last week...The program had been kicking around all segments of the network being heard early afternoons and late and in various spots in between. In the summer of 1945 it looked like it was sold when in a good hiatus spot it snagged a sensational 14 rating. Its more recent sustaining ratings have been 6–7 average.

> Under the competition of mid-season commercial programming in the heart of the evening *Crime Photographer* will need some pepping up, particularly in the acting division. Performances on the initial sponsored broadcast were for the most part sluggish and quite below the par of those achieved as a sustainer. The overall effect was that, after three years of amateur sleuthing, the *Crime Photographer* had gotten in a rut, and he and his gal Friday might just as well have been assigned to a Sunday School picnic for all the suspense and drama that they managed to convey. Fault, certainly was not with the scripter, Alonzo Deen Cole,

who, as usual, turned out a tight little story but each highlight fell flat because of the lack of conviction of the principles. To give it a distinctiveness apart from the host of other amateur sleuthing sessions, "Photog" should emphasize some specific traits in the leads and develop their personalities more fully. Lacking this added color the burden is placed wholly on scripter Cole, who gets — and certainly merits — star billing.[14]

Since two additional sponsors picked up the *Casey* series at the conclusion of Anchor Hocking's commitment, it is safe to assume that any weaknesses discerned by the previous reviewer had been properly addressed by early 1948.

In addition to reviews of the program, the program and its cast members were featured in several fan magazines of the day. The Summer, 1949 issue of *Radio Album*, for example, carried a pictorial story about *Casey* based on the episode "Blackout" that was broadcast on December 16, 1948. As was frequently the practice in those days, the radio cast posed for photographs dramatizing the series to be used by fan magazines for the purpose of creating greater interest in the program. The four page photo spread, headlined "Finger of Suspicion," featured 16 numbered photos that graphically depicted the plot from beginning to end.

Further evidence of *Casey's* popularity was his frequent appearance as a guest detective on a rival network's program, Mutual's *Quick As A Flash*, 1944–1951. That program, initially hosted by Ken Roberts, a former *Casey* announcer, devoted the first half of each broadcast to a quiz format pitting six contestants from the audience against one another in a race to determine how rapidly they could solve a series of puzzles put to them.

The second half of the broadcast featured a guest radio detective who would present a mystery for the panel to solve. Staats Cotsworth, in the guise of Casey, appeared on the program at least 20 times.[15] Other celebrity detectives who appeared over the years included *The Shadow, Mr. Keene, Mr. & Mrs. North, Nick Carter, Mr. District Attorney, Bulldog Drummond* and *Charlie Chan* to name just a few.

Looking back in time, contemporary OTR historians are of mixed opinions regarding the quality and merit of the *Casey* series. Jim Cox, the author of

---

14. In the 1975 WTIC Cotsworth interview cited earlier, taped almost 20 years after *Casey* left the air, the actor suggested that Cole, who enjoyed a sterling reputation as a radio writer, needed the intervention of cast members and director to create a succesful script. This writer, however, remains in tune with the contemporary critics cited above who praised Cole's scripts and felt that the performers may have needed more "pep."

15. OTR researcher Karl Schadow has identified the following dates on which Cotsworth appeared as Casey: 1946: 10/6; 1947: 1/12, 4/20, 9/14, 12/7; 1948: 3/7, 9/12, 12/12; 1949: 5/29, 10/1; 1950: 3/13–3/17 and 4/23 to 4/27.

many fine books about Old Time Radio, including *Radio Crime Fighters* (McFarland, 2002), referred to the program as "a kind of laid-back mystery drama without the startling revelations and intense action inherent in many other series." According to Cox, Casey "could turn into an amateur detective by merely studying a photo he had shot at a crime scene." On the other hand, John Dunning in his *On The Air: Encyclopedia of Old Time Radio* (Oxford, 1998), dismissed the series as having "had more history than substance." Dunning called *Casey* "a B-grade radio detective show, on a par perhaps with *The Falcon*, better than *Mr. Keene*, but lacking the polish and style of *Sam Spade*."

A somewhat different opinion was offered by OTR blogger Ivan Shreve (no relation to Moe Shreve, the *Shadow's* favorite cab driver), host of the *Thrilling Days of Yesteryear* Internet site. While professing admiration for Dunning, Shreve took issue with what he viewed as Dunning's unfair comparison of *Casey* to *Sam Spade*. Spade, in Shreve's view, represented "the gold standard of private eye dramas and to classify *Casey* as better than *Mr. Keen, Tracer Of Lost Persons* is damning with faint praise." Shreve went on to say that "What set *Casey, Crime Photographer* apart from its radio crime drama competition was its laid back atmosphere, chiefly personified in its backdrop of Casey and Annie's favorite watering hole."

Ratings

During the first three years that *Casey* was broadcast on a sustaining basis and often heard after 10:00pm, the program did not show up in the ratings as the rating companies such as C.E. Hooper Co., A.C. Nielsen Co. and Crossley, Inc. avoided making phone calls after 10pm in order to avoid irate listener reactions. To get around this problem and still get a sense of the program's following, CBS arranged that in one episode Casey would take a photo of Ethelbert, Captain Logan and Ann and then mention on the air that he had a few extra prints that listeners could obtain by writing to the station. Hoping to get a few thousand requests for the photo, CBS was more than pleased when it received more than 15,000 letters, a few of which even contained money which CBS dutifully turned over to the March of Dimes.[16]

Once the program was picked up by a sponsor and broadcast at 9:30pm, a more respectable time slot, all that changed. On July 20, 1949 *Variety* reported that Hooper listed *Casey* as being among the top 15 radio programs being aired for that summer and Hooper reported that *Casey* was more highly rated by the

---

16. By the time a reporter picked up this story in 1950 in an interview with Herman Chittison, the number of requests had grown to 17,000.

listening public than *Mr. District Attorney, Mr. & Mrs. North, The Big Story, Mr. Keen, The Fat Man* and *This Is Your FBI*, all rival mystery programs.

According to a second rating service, Air Features, a PR firm with a CBS affiliation, during the October to April 1949–1950 broadcast season, of the seven top mystery dramas being broadcast, *Casey* draw more listeners than four out of its six rivals.

Comparative Ratings October to April 1949–1950	
Casey	14.5
Mr. Keene	16.1
FBI In Peace & War	15.0
Suspense	14.3
Mr. And Mrs. North	13.9
Big Story	13.1
Gang Busters	12.1

From August 1946 to October 1950, *Casey* enjoyed an average rating of 14.2 which was 42% higher than the average rating of all evening sponsored programs for that period.

Despite its favorable ratings, though, by 1950, unable to interest a new sponsor in picking up the program, CBS took *Casey* off the air.

Looking back, perhaps *Casey's* single most lasting impact on American culture was creating the name, the Blue Note Café. For, as George Harmon Coxe put it in his 1971 interview, "There were no Blue Note Café's before *Casey* hit the CBS airways. But today while *Casey* may only be a radio memory, ads for Blue Notes appear frequently in New York newspapers and, no doubt, in newspapers in other cities, large and small, across the nation."

Plot Summaries

What follows is a sampling of some of the story lines used during the 1943–1955 run of *Casey*. With the exception of the first listing, all the scripts were written by Alonzo Deen Cole.

7/14/43: "Murder Off The Record." (2nd broadcast.) A broken record, snatches of song, a girl who hates her father and a man who hates democracy provide the clues leading to the killer's identity.

8/19/43: "No Answer." (1st known Cole script.) Death mysteriously comes to three persons who pick up a telephone receiver. Casey answers the fourth call and solves the crime.

4/8/44: "The Man Who Couldn't Be Killed." Afraid of being murdered because of threatening notes, a man holes up in an impregnable fortress but can't escape his fate. Revenge says it all.

8/29/45: "Chamber Of Horrors." A private collection of lethal instruments, a valuable dagger, a bald wife, a suspicious secretary, a photo designed to catch a thief catches a double murderer.

7/1/46: "Bloodless Murder." Suspicious series of heart attacks among family members, blacksheep half brother and murders revenged in an appropriate way.

3/6/47: "The Mysterious Lodger." Convicted murderess stabbed in similar fashion to that of her own crime victims. Revenge by brother of first victim a motive but Casey knows better.

9/2/48: "Little Feathered Friends." Attendant feeding ostriches at a zoo is forced into woods by two men with guns while a third gangster prevents Casey from following the action.

2/17/49: "The Chinese Room." A locked room mystery in which a suspect becomes the next victim. A small statue and a Confucius saying lead to the solution to the puzzle.

6/22/50: "Freak House." The murders of a diamond broker and a circus fat lady lead Casey into the intrigue of circus life and the unraveling of another mystery.

9/1/54: "The Man In Brown." Excessive bragging by armed robber and killer interests Casey who proceeds to work with mysterious blond to solve the mystery.

2/18/55: "One Grave For Three." Jewel thief under suspicion in a diamond robbery and murder leads Casey in his investigation.

Undated early cast photograph. Left to right: Jackson Beck (Lt. Logan), Alice Reinheart (Ann Williams), Staats Cotsworth (Casey) and John Gibson (Ethelbert).

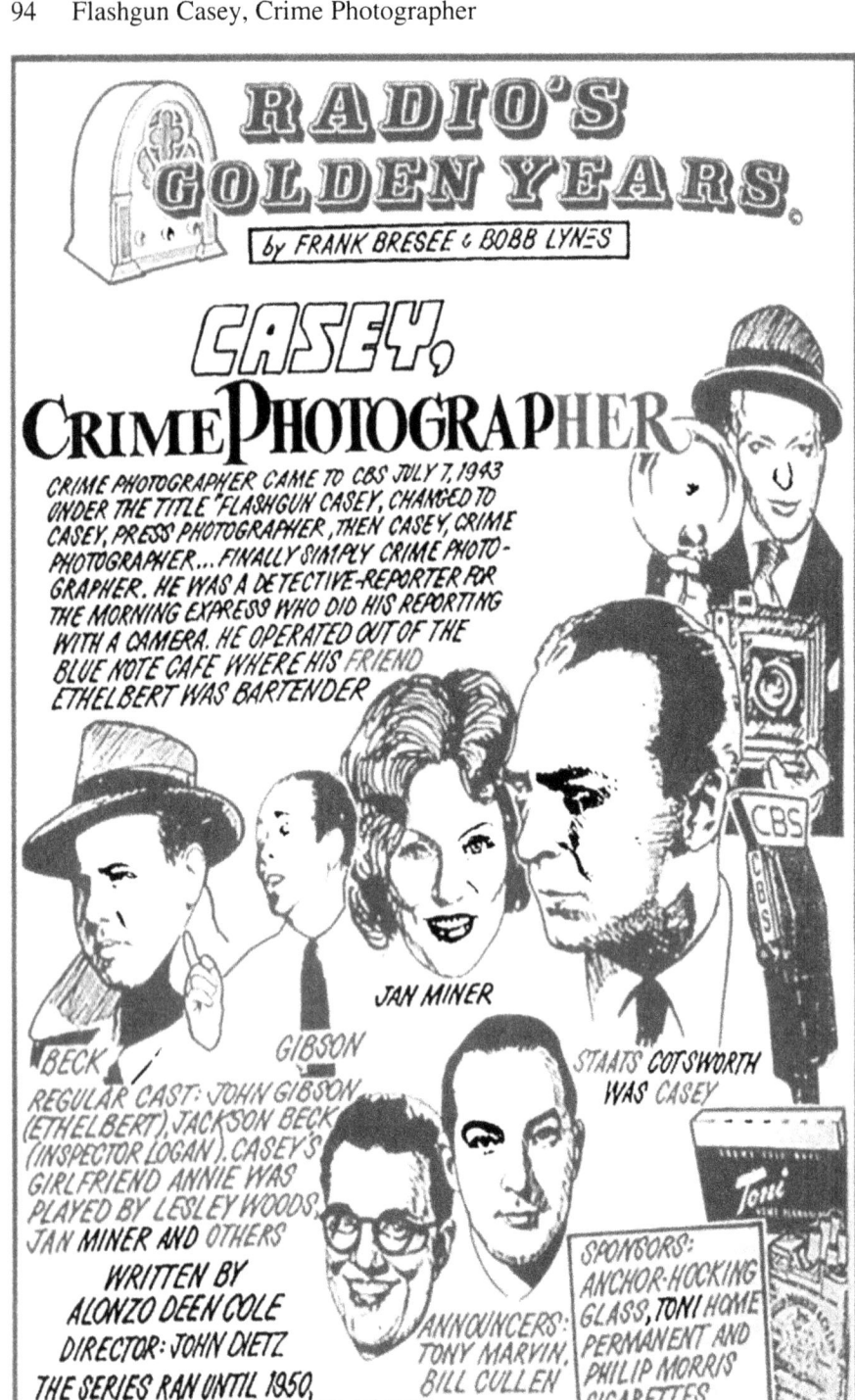

8
Radio Log

How This Log Was Compiled

The radio log was compiled using information from a number of different sources: earlier incomplete logs prepared by Old Time Radio collectors, files from the CBS Archives, the original scripts of Alonzo Deen Cole, the assistance of collector researchers and back issues of several newspapers, including *The New York Times, The New York Herald Tribune, The Chicago Tribune, The Washington Post,* the *New York Daily News,* the *New York Post* and the *New York Daily Mirror.*

Titles are shown for all but 19 programs broadcast in 1954. While the newspapers radio listings document that these programs were broadcast, regrettably, the listing information did not include the programs' titles.*

It is the author's hope that the publication of this log, minus the elusive 19 titles, will inspire other researchers to uncover any still untapped resources in an effort to successfully complete the log.

General Notes About the Log

1. All broadcasts were on CBS. Changing program titles are in bold.
2. C = program known to be in circulation. Where a script was repeated, both broadcasts are marked "C" although the listing with the * is the actual broadcast in circulation.
3. ADC = script known to be by Alonzo Deen Cole, many of which are in the personal collection of one of the co-authors of this book.
4. When known, the names of the authors of other scripts appear after the program title.

---

*At least one other well respected OTR researcher has noted that CBS data for 1954 was less than complete. If there is an explanation that transcends more than the *Casey* program, that explanation remains a mystery.

FLASH-GUN CASEY, PRESS PHOTOGRAPHER

Wednesday – 11:30pm

C	07/07/43	# 1 The Case Of The Switched Plates (Ashley Buck with George Harmon Coxe)
	07/14/43	# 2 Murder Off The Record
	07/21/43	# 3 The Lost Melody
	07/28/43	# 4 Love Is A Whisper
	08/04/43	# 5 The Case Of The Painted Walls

Thursday – 11:30pm

- 08/12/43   # 6 Murder Comes In Threes
- 08/19/43   # 7 No Answer (ADC)
- 08/26/43   # 8 Five Thousand Dollar Reward (ADC)
- 09/02/43   # 9 The Case Of The Whispering Gun
- 09/09/43   # 10 Hoodoo For Hire (ADC)
- 09/16/43   # 11 Pattern For Murder (ADC)
- 09/23/43   # 12 Case of the Pretty Bandit (ADC)
- 09/30/43   # 13 Kidnapping of the Rare Book Dealer (ADC)
- 10/07/43   # 14 Murder For Breakfast (ADC)
- 10/14/43   # 15 The Case Of The Indignant Lady (ADC)
- 10/21/43   # 16 Picture In The Park (ADC)

Saturday – 11:30pm

- 10/30/43   # 17 A Butterfly Dies (ADC)
- 11/06/43   # 18 Death In The Dentist's Chair
- 11/13/43   # 19 Ghosts Work For Money (ADC)
- 11/20/43   # 20 The Killer's Kid (ADC)
- 11/27/43   # 21 The Man With The Crippled Arm
- 12/04/43   # 22 The Last Will And Testament (ADC)
- 12/11/43   # 23 Mystery Girl (ADC)
- 12/18/43   # 24 Set To Kill
- 12/25/43   # 25 Christmas Is A Family Day (ADC)
- 01/01/44   # 26 Casey Begins A New Year (ADC)
- 01/08/44   # 27 Casey Goes Into Society (ADC)
- 01/15/44   # 28 Casey Compounds A Felony (ADC)
- 01/22/44   # 29 Casey Remains To Dance (ADC)
- 01/29/44   Pre-empted
- 02/05/44   # 30 Casey And The House With The Hedge (ADC)
- 02/12/44   # 31 Casey And The Man Called John Doe

	02/19/44	# 32 The Mystery Of The Ten Dollar Bills
C	02/26/44	# 33 The Clue In The Clouds (Charles Holden)
	03/04/44	# 34 Casey And The Strong Woman
	03/11/44	# 35 Man Overboard (ADC)
C	03/18/44	# 36 Casey And The Self-Made Hero (ADC)
	03/25/44	# 37 Star Witness (ADC)
	04/01/44	# 38 The Case Of The Glowing Ghost (ADC)

CASEY, PRESS PHOTOGRAPHER

	04/08/44	# 39 The Man Who Couldn't Be Killed (ADC)
	04/15/44	# 40 It's A Dog's Life (ADC)
	04/22/44	# 41 The Strange Invitation
	04/29/44	# 42 Air Tight Alibi (Robert Sloane)
	05/06/44	# 43 A Matter Of Reputation (ADC)
	05/13/44	# 44 Killer On Parole (ADC)
	05/20/44	# 45 The Murder In The Rain
	05/27/44	# 46 The Little Man Who Wasn't There (Robert Sloane)
	06/03/44	# 47 Skeleton On Horseback (Charles Holden)
	06/10/44	# 48 Photo Finish (Robert Sloane)
	06/17/44	# 49 Lamb To The Slaughter (ADC)
	06/24/44	# 50 The Cinderella Girl (ADC)
	07/01/44	# 51 Old Nobody (ADC)
C	07/08/44	# 52 The Case Of The Self-Made Hero (First Repeat) (ADC)

Saturday – 5:00pm

07/15/44	# 53 A Picture Of Murder (ADC)
07/22/44	# 54 Danger For Blondes (ADC)
07/29/44	# 55 One Of The Family (ADC)
08/05/44	# 56 The Last Beat (ADC)
08/12/44	# 57 Little Black Dog (ADC)
08/19/44	# 58 Man Hunt (ADC)
08/26/44	# 59 Victory Garden Murder (ADC)
09/02/44	# 60 Gun Boy (ADC)
09/09/44	# 61 The Birthday Present (ADC)

Tuesday – 11:30pm

09/12/44	# 62 The Case Of The Laughing Dog (Robert Sloane)
09/19/44	# 63 An Old Girlfriend (ADC)
09/26/44	# 64 Anonymous Letter (ADC)

10/03/44	# 65 Treatment For The Doctor (ADC)
10/10/44	# 66 Beaten By A Nose (ADC)
10/17/44	# 67 Bad Luck For Sale (ADC)
10/24/44	# 68 Hanged By The Neck (ADC)
10/31/44	# 69 The Diary Of Death (Charles Holden)
11/07/44	Pre-empted
11/14/44	# 70 Picture And The Frame (ADC)
11/21/44	Pre-empted
11/28/44	# 71 The Substitutes (ADC)
12/05/44	# 72 Trial Balloon (ADC)
12/12/44	# 73 A Girl Named Kate (ADC)
12/19/44	# 74 Group Photograph (ADC)
12/26/44	# 75 The Unknown Caller (ADC)
01/02/45	# 76 Engagement Ring (ADC)
01/09/45	# 77 Key To Room 424 (ADC)
01/16/45	# 78 The Professional Widow (ADC)
01/23/45	# 79 Beware Of The Dog (ADC)
01/30/45	Pre-empted
02/06/45	# 80 Don't Call The Cops (ADC)
02/13/45	# 81 Suicide Note (ADC)
02/20/45	# 82 Diamonds And Tombstones (ADC)
02/27/45	Pre-empted
03/06/45	# 83 Complete Acquittal (ADC)
03/13/45	# 84 The Picture In The Park (Repeat) (ADC)
03/20/45	# 85 Incredible Evidence (ADC)
03/27/45	# 86 The White Monster (ADC)
04/03/45	# 87 The Impossible Crime (ADC)
04/10/45	# 88 Account Settled (ADC)
04/17/45	# 89 Outline In Clay (ADC)
04/24/45	# 90 Gambler's Luck (ADC)
05/01/45	# 91 The Killer's Kid (Repeat) (ADC)
05/08/45	Pre-empted
05/15/45	# 92 Free Confession (ADC)
05/22/45	# 93 The Unexpected Guest (ADC)
05/29/45	# 94 A Degree Of Arson (ADC)
06/05/45	# 95 The Invisible Man (Robert Sloane)
06/12/45	# 96 The Strange Case Of Mr. Strange (ADC)
06/19/45	# 97 Vacation In Maine (ADC)
06/26/45	# 98 Man Overboard (Repeat) (ADC

CRIME PHOTOGRAPHER

Wednesday – 9:00pm
	07/04/45	# 99 The Cat's Paw (ADC)
	07/11/45	#100 The Double Cross (ADC)
	07/18/45	#101 Uncle John (ADC)
	07/25/45	#102 The Retired Camera (B. Edgar Marvin)
	08/01/45	#103 Danger For Blondes (Repeat) (ADC)
	08/08/45	#104 The Bird Expert (ADC)
	08/15/45	#105 Hot Ice (ADC)
	08/22/45	#106 A Tiger On The Loose (ADC)
	08/29/45	#107 The Chamber Of Horrors (ADC)
	09/05/45	#108 Gun Boy (Repeat) (ADC)

Wednesday – 10:30pm
	09/12/45	#109 A Walk In The Rain (ADC)
	09/19/45	#110 Death Insurance (Field)
	09/26/45	#111 One Of The Family (Repeat) (ADC)

Saturday – 1:30pm
C	10/20/45	#112 Cupid Is A Killer (ADC)
	10/27/45	Pre-empted
	11/03/45	#113 The Case Of The Battered Playboy (Kane)
	11/10/45	#114 The Last Of The Faradays (Max Ehrlich)
	11/17/45	#115 The Little Man Who Wasn't There (Repeat) (Robert Sloane)
	11/24/45	#116 Strictly Confidential (ADC)

Monday – 10:30pm
	12/03/45	#117 No Evidence (ADC)
	12/10/45	#118 The Considerate Burglar (ADC)
	12/17/45	#119 Death Of A Rattlesnake (ADC)
	12/24/45	#120 Two New $100 Bills (ADC)
	12/31/45	#121 A Date With Hester (Max Ehrlich)
C	01/07/46	#122 Earned Reward (ADC)
	01/14/46	#123 The Finger Of Death (ADC)
	01/21/46	#124 The Fighting Fool (ADC)
	01/28/46	#125 Iron Mike (ADC)
	02/04/46	#126 The Prince Of Darkness (Ashley Buck & Tom Taggert)
	02/11/46	#127 Killers Can Be Beautiful (ADC)

	02/18/46	Pre-empted
C	02/25/46	#128 Graveyard Gertie (ADC)
	03/04/46	#129 Motive For Murder (ADC)

Tuesday – 10:00pm

	03/12/46	#130 Beaten By A Nose (Repeat) (ADC)
	03/19/46	#131 Family Argument (ADC)
	03/26/46	#132 Buccaneer's Cove (ADC)
	04/02/46	#133 The Body Was Buried Deep (ADC)
	04/09/46	Pre-empted
	04/16/46	Pre-empted
	04/23/46	#134 The Joker (ADC)
	04/30/46	#135 The Butterfly (ADC)
	05/07/46	#136 The Man That Nobody Liked (ADC)
	05/14/46	Pre-empted
	05/21/46	Pre-empted
	05/28/46	Pre-empted

Monday – 8:30pm

C	06/03/46	#137 The Reunion (ADC)
	06/10/46	#138 Mr. Big (ADC)
	06/17/46	#139 Social Afternoon (ADC)
	06/24/46	#140 The Poker Game (ADC)
	07/01/46	#141 Bloodless Murder (ADC)
	07/08/46	#142 The Man Called John Doe (Repeat) (ADC)
C	07/15/46	#143 A Tooth For Tooth (Charles Holden)
	07/22/46	#144 A Girl Named Kate (Repeat) (ADC)

Thursday – 9:30pm

	08/08/46	#145 Three Sapphires (ADC)
	08/15/46	#146 Unlucky Day (ADC)
	08/22/46	#147 The Fat Lady Dies (ADC)
C	08/29/46	#148 The Red Raincoat (ADC)
C	09/05/46	#149 The Handkerchief (ADC)
	09/12/46	#150 Johnnie's Got A Gun (ADC)
C	09/19/46	#151 The Duke Of Skid Row (ADC)
	09/26/46	#152 The Bronze Peacock (ADC)
	10/03/46	#153 Happy Birthday to You (ADC)
	10/10/46	#154 The Carved Bed (ADC)

	10/17/46	#155 The Tip Off (ADC)
	10/24/46	#156 The Prison Break (ADC)
	10/31/46	#157 The Halloween Story (ADC)
	11/07/46	#158 Missing Persons (ADC)
	11/14/46	#159 The Cuckoo
	11/21/46	#160 The Searchlight And The Tomb
	11/28/46	#161 The Thanksgiving Dinner
	12/05/46	#162 Room 1110
	12/12/46	#163 Dangerous Characters
C	12/19/46	#164 Christmas Shopping (ADC)
	12/26/46	#165 The Buried Evidence
	01/02/47	#166 The Last Of The Faraday's (Repeat) (Max Ehrlich)
	01/09/47	#167 Dead Pigeon (Harry Ingram)
C	01/16/47	#168 The Surprising Corpse (ADC)
	01/23/47	#169 The Purloined Payroll
	01/30/47	#170 Held For Ransom
C	02/06/47	#171 The Gray Kitten (ADC)
	02/13/47	#172 Please Be My Valentine
C	02/20/47	#173 The Twenty Minute Alibi
	02/27/47	#174 The Red Headed Kid (B. Edgar Marvin) same plot as 7/ 25/45
C	03/06/47	#175 The Mysterious Lodger (ADC)
	03/13/47	#176 The Undercover Man

CASEY, CRIME PHOTOGRAPHER

C	03/20/47	#177 The Demon Miner (ADC)
	03/27/47	#178 Blood Pact
	04/03/47	#179 The Girl On The Dock
	04/10/47	#180 The Ugly Duckling
C	04/17/47	#181 The Box Of Death (ADC)
C	04/24/47	#182 The Gentle Strangler (ADC)
C	05/01/47	#183 King Of The Apes (ADC)
C	05/08/47	#184 The Laughing Killer (ADC)
	05/15/47	#185 Mad Dog
C	05/22/47	#186 Pickup (ADC)
	05/29/47	#187 Out Of The Past (ADC)
	06/05/47	#188 The Haunted House (Repeat of 4/01/44 broadcast with a different title.) (ADC)
	06/12/47	#189 In The Sweet Name Of Charity (ADC)

	06/19/47	#190 Find The Papers
	06/26/47	#191 A Package For Annie (Max Ehrlich)
C	07/03/47	#192 Acquitted (ADC)
C	07/10/47	#193 The Lady Killer (ADC)
C*	07/17/47	#194 Casey And The Self-Made Hero (Second Repeat) (ADC)
C	07/24/47	#195 Photo Of The Dead (ADC)
C	07/31/47	#196 Bright New Star (ADC)
C	08/07/47	#197 Death In Lover's Lane (ADC)
C	08/14/47	#198 The Chivalrous Gunman (ADC)
C	08/21/47	#199 The Busman's Holiday (ADC)
C	08/28/47	#200 Hide-Out (ADC)
C	09/04/47	#201 The Loaded Dice (ADC)
C*	09/11/47	#202 Graveyard Gertie (Repeat) (ADC)
C	09/18/47	#203 The Tobacco Pouch (ADC)
C	09/25/47	#204 The Treasure Cave (ADC)
C	10/02/47	#205 The Miscarriage Of Justice (ADC)
C	10/09/47	#206 The Wedding Breakfast (ADC)
C	10/16/47	#207 The Camera Bug (ADC)
C	10/23/47	#208 The Lady In Distress (ADC)
C	10/30/47	#209 Great Grandfather's Rent Receipt (ADC)
C	11/06/47	#210 The Case Of The Blonde Lipstick (Milton Kramer)
C	11/13/47	#211 Too Many Angels (Al Barker)
C*	11/20/47	#212 Earned Reward (Repeat) (ADC)
C	11/27/47	#213 After Turkey - The Bill (ADC)
C	12/04/47	#214 The Serpent Goddess (ADC)
C	12/11/47	#215 The New Will (ADC)
C	12/18/47	#216 The Life Of The Party (ADC)
C	12/25/47	#217 The Santa Claus Of Bums' Blvd. (ADC)
C	01/01/48	#218 Hot New Year's Party (ADC)
C	01/08/48	#219 Queen Of The Amazons (ADC)
C	01/15/48	#220 The Miracle (ADC)
C	01/22/48	#221 Ex-Convict (ADC)
C	01/29/48	#222 The Piggy Bank Robbery (ADC)
C	02/05/48	#223 Music To Die By (ADC)
C	02/12/48	#224 Key Witness (ADC)
C	02/19/48	#225 Witchcraft (ADC)
C	02/26/48	#226 The Fix (ADC)
C	03/04/48	#227 Tough Guy (ADC)
C	03/11/48	#228 Fog (ADC)

C	03/18/48	#229 Murder In Black And White (ADC)
C	03/25/48	#230 Blind Justice
	04/01/48	#231 Sleeping Dogs Awake (ADC)
	04/08/48	#232 A Present For Percy (ADC)
	04/15/48	#233 The Considerate Burglar (Repeat) (ADC)
	04/22/48	#234 You Die Today (ADC)
	04/29/48	#235 Half Guilty (ADC)
	05/06/48	#236 "X" Marks The Spot (ADC)
	05/13/48	#237 Dead Man's Fortune (ADC)
	05/20/48	#238 My Brother's Keeper (ADC)
C	05/27/48	#239 Gun Wanted (ADC)
	06/03/48	#240 Murderers, Ltd. (ADC)
	06/10/48	#241 Letters From Mexico (ADC)
	06/17/48	#242 Wife Number Eight (ADC)
	06/24/48	#243 No Tears For Terry
	07/01/48	#244 Missing Heiress (ADC)
	07/08/48	#245 Old Joe (ADC)
	07/15/48	#246 Farewell Performance (Harry Ingram)
	07/22/48	#247 In For Trouble (ADC)
	07/29/48	#248 Man Hater (ADC)
	08/05/48	#249 Pattern For Murder (Harry Ingram)
	08/12/48	#250 The Pirates (Repeat) (ADC)
	08/19/48	#251 On The Record (ADC)
	08/26/48	#252 Kangaroo Court (ADC)
	09/02/48	#253 My Little Feathered Friends (ADC)
	09/09/48	#254 Winning Streak (ADC)
	09/16/48	#255 2,000 Suspects (Harry Ingram)
	09/23/48	#256 Finger Man (ADC)
	09/30/48	#257 A Poison Pen (ADC)
	10/07/48	#258 Old Blankety Blank (ADC)
	10/14/48	Pre-empted
	10/21/48	#259 Only Saps Work For Wages (ADC)
	10/28/48	#260 Election Bet (ADC)
	11/04/48	#261 The Ghost Seekers (ADC)
	11/11/48	#262 The Mystery Man (ADC)
	11/18/48	#263 String Of Beads (ADC)
C	11/25/48	#264 Holiday (ADC)
	12/02/48	#265 The Wild Man (ADC)
	12/09/48	#266 The Genius (ADC)

	12/16/48	#267 Blackout (a.k.a. Finger Of Suspicion) (Harry Ingram)
	12/23/48	#268 Two Days Before Christmas (ADC)
	12/30/48	#269 Meet The Wife (ADC)
	01/06/49	#270 The Box Of Ashes (ADC)
	01/13/49	#271 Tiger On The Loose (Repeat) (ADC)
	01/20/49	#272 Action Photograph (ADC)
	01/27/49	#273 Pick Up Your Marbles (ADC)
	02/03/49	#274 Unwelcome Party (ADC)
	02/10/49	#275 The Grandson Of Mr. Smith (ADC)
	02/17/49	#276 The Chinese Room (ADC)
	02/24/49	#277 Blood Money (ADC)
	03/03/49	#278 You Are The Killer (ADC)
C	03/10/49	#279 The Scene Of The Crime (ADC)
	03/17/49	#280 An Attempt To Murder (Repeat) (ADC)
	03/24/49	#281 Terror (ADC)
	03/31/49	#282 I'll See You Hanged (ADC)
	04/07/49	#283 Murder In The Air (ADC)
	04/14/49	#284 Too Many Knives (ADC)
	04/21/49	#285 Rest Cure (Harry Ingram)
	04/28/49	#286 Death From The Dead (ADC)
C	05/05/49	#287 The Wolverine (ADC)
	05/12/49	#288 The Booby Trap (ADC)
C	05/19/49	#289 Cupid Is A Killer (Repeat) (ADC)
	05/26/49	#290 The Return From The Grave (ADC)
	06/02/49	#291 Brotherly Hate (ADC)
	06/09/49	#292 Deadline – Midnight (Harry Ingram)
	06/16/49	#293 Notice To The Public (ADC)
	06/23/49	#294 The Dragon Head (ADC)
	06/30/49	#295 The Lily (ADC)
	07/07/49	#296 Murder Farm (ADC)
	07/14/49	#297 Crazy Like A Fox (ADC)
	07/21/49	#298 Durable Dennis (ADC)
	07/28/49	#299 Murder-Go-Round (ADC)
C	08/04/49	#300 Sell-Out (ADC)
C	08/11/49	#301 The Death Of A Stranger (ADC)
	08/18/49	#302 Big Danger (ADC)
C	08/25/49	#303 The Snow Ball (ADC)
	09/01/49	#304 Scrub Woman (ADC)
	09/08/49	#305 Peace Mission (ADC)

	09/15/49	#306 The Maniac (ADC)
	09/22/49	#307 The Blackmailer (ADC)
	09/29/49	#308 Unstandard Model (ADC)
	10/06/49	#309 The Weasel (ADC)
	10/13/49	#310 Museum Of Murder (ADC)
C	10/20/49	#311 The Coffin (ADC)
	10/27/49	#312 The Vampire (ADC)
	11/03/49	#313 Fall Of The Cards (ADC)
C	11/10/49	#314 Thunderbolt (ADC)
C*	11/17/49	#315 The Upholsterer (ADC)
	11/24/49	#316 A Gift For Thanksgiving (ADC)
	12/01/49	#317 Murder At the Auction (ADC)
	12/08/49	#318 Witness For The Prosecution (ADC)
	12/15/49	#319 Appointment For Murder (ADC)
	12/22/49	#320 A Picture for Christmas (ADC)
	12/29/49	#321 The Chisler (ADC)
	01/05/50	#322 Justice (ADC)
	01/12/49	#323 The Love Story (Harry Ingram)
	01/19/50	#324 Wanted - A Gun (ADC)
	01/26/50	#325 Unsolved Murder (ADC)
	02/02/50	#226 Four Forefingers
	02/09/50	#327 The Bad Hunch (ADC)
	02/16/50	#328 The Girl Hitch-Hiker (ADC)
	02/23/50	#329 The Jinx
C	03/02/50	#330 The Bad Little Babe (ADC)
	03/09/50	#331 The Quarrel (ADC)
	03/16/50	#332 Platonic Friendship (ADC)
	03/23/50	#333 The Rest Cure Murder (ADC)
	03/30/50	#334 Death Calls A Number (ADC)
C	04/06/50	#335 The Fire (ADC)
C	04/13/50	#336 The Disappearance Of Mr. Dizzel (ADC)
	04/20/50	#337 Junior Bad Man (ADC)
	04/27/50	#338 Dead Pigeon (Repeat) (Harry Ingram)
C	05/04/50	#339 The Suicide (ADC)
	05/11/50	#340 The Diamonds Of Mrs. Divonne
	05/18/50	#341 The Buried Treasure (ADC)
	05/25/50	#342 Doll Face (ADC)
	06/01/50	#343 Death Threat (ADC)
	06/08/50	#344 Unknown Passenger (ADC)

C	06/15/50	#345 Unlucky Numbers (Gail & Harry Ingram)
	06/22/50	#346 Freak House (ADC)
	06/29/50	#347 The Master Mind (ADC)
	07/06/50	#348 Collision (ADC)
	07/13/50	#349 Murder At The Yacht Club (ADC)
	07/20/50	#350 The Lorelei Killer (ADC)
	07/27/50	#351 The Red Hots (ADC)
	08/03/50	#352 Written In Blood (ADC)
	08/10/50	#353 The Love Death (ADC)
	08/17/50	#354 Gun Crazy (ADC)
	08/24/50	#355 The Woman With Golden Hair (ADC)
	08/31/50	#356 The Fatal Visitor (ADC)
	09/07/50	#357 The Mascot (ADC)
	09/14/50	#358 Hit And Run (ADC)
	09/21/50	#359 Inside Job (ADC)
	09/28/50	#360 The Man Of Mystery (ADC)
	10/05/50	#361 Alibi (ADC)
	10/12/50	#362 The Eyes Of Death (ADC)
	10/19/50	#363 A Scheme For Liquidation (ADC)
	10/26/50	#364 On The Spot (ADC)
	11/02/50	#365 The Deadly Wolf (ADC)
	11/09/50	#366 Woman Of Mystery (ADC)
C	11/16/50	# 367 The Upholsterer (Repeat) (ADC)

CRIME PHOTOGRAPHER

Wednesday – 9:00pm

C	01/13/54	#368 The Road Angel (ADC)
C	01/20/54	#369 Source Of Information (ADC)
	01/27/54	#370 (Title Unknown)
	02/03/54	#371 (Title Unknown)
	02/10/54	#372 (Title Unknown)
	02/17/54	#373 (Title Unknown)
	02/24/54	#374 Portrait Of An Artist
	03/03/54	#375 (Title Unknown)
	03/10/54	#376 (Title Unknown)
	03/17/54	#377 (Title Unknown)
	03/24/54	#378 (Title Unknown)
	03/31/54	#379 Dateline (ADC)
	04/07/54	#380 (Title Unknown)

04/14/54   #381 Full Circle (ADC)
04/21/54   #382 Casey Visits A Circus (ADC)
04/28/54   Pre-empted
05/05/54   Pre-empted
05/12/54   #383 Yellow Streak
05/19/54   Pre-empted
05/26/54   #384 The Legacy (ADC)
06/02/54   #385 (Title Unknown)
06/09/54   #386 (Title Unknown)
06/16/54   #387 (Title Unknown)
06/23/54   #388 (Title Unknown)
06/30/54   #389 (Title Unknown)
07/07/54   #390 (Title Unknown)
07/14/54   #391 (Title Unknown)
07/21/54   #392 (Title Unknown)
07/28/54   #393 Target Unknown
08/04/54   #394 (Title Unknown)
08/11/54   #395 (Title Unknown)
08/18/54   #396 Pictures Can Lie
08/25/54   #397 The Moth
09/01/54   #398 The Man In Brown (ADC)
09/08/54   #399 For The Family Honor
09/15/54   #400 Death In The Rain (ADC)
09/22/54   #401 Street Carnival (ADC)
09/29/54   #402 The Strangling Ghost (ADC

Friday – 8:00pm
10/08/54   #403 The Protection Racket
10/15/54   #404 Life For Sale (ADC)
10/22/54   #405 The Football (ADC)
10/29/54   #406 Black Magic (ADC)
11/05/54   #407 Showdown
11/12/54   #408 Widgeon Is A Ducky Word!
11/19/54   #409 Poor Little Rich Kid (ADC)
11/26/54   #410 No Publicity
12/03/54   #411 Juanita
12/10/54   #412 What's In A Name?
12/17/54   #413 Ex-Con (ADC)
12/24/54   #414 A Red Wagon For Junior (ADC)

12/31/54	#415 A Dead Man's Message (ADC)
01/07/55	#416 Unbury The Dead (ADC)
01/14/55	#417 Peaches (ADC)
01/21/55	#418 Criminal For A Day (ADC)
01/28/55	#419 The Watchdog (ADC)
02/04/55	#420 The Late Unlamented (ADC)
02/11/55	#421 Valentine (ADC)
02/18/55	#422 One Grave For Three (ADC)
02/25/55	#423 Panic (ADC)
03/04/55	#424 Bogey-Man Story (ADC)
03/11/55	#425 The Homicide Ring (ADC)
03/18/55	#426 Check - And Double Check (ADC)
03/25/55	#427 The Death Watch (ADC)
04/01/55	#428 Death Visits Five (ADC)
04/08/55	#429 Top Secret (ADC)
04/15/55	#430 Battleground (ADC)
04/22/55	#431 Casey Visits A Circus (Repeat) (ADC)
	FINAL BROADCAST

9
Casey Radio Scripts

Determining which of the more than 400 different radio scripts that were broadcast between 1943–1955 should be included in a volume such as this is no easy task. Indeed, an entire collection of such scripts could easily form the basis of a volume — or two. To paraphrase one of the author's favorite posters: "So Many Books, So Little Time," selecting only two *Casey* radio scripts is akin to: "So Many Choices, So Little Space."

In deciding which scripts to use, one clear determining factor was to avoid programs known to be in circulation as doing so would add little for Casey fans who are already familiar with those plots.

A second criteria was to avoid scripts that reflected the often mundane nature of the average radio detective program of the period that typically dealt with larceny, arson, kidnapping, robbery and murder by gun, knife, poison, strangulation, etc.

In the first script, "Hanged By the Neck," Casey and Ann are returning from an assignment and not untypically run into a crime in which the police would end up pinning the crime on the wrong person if not for Casey's insight and intervention.

In selecting the second script, "The White Monster," the author confesses that he was influenced by his admiration of Cole's earlier career as the creator of *The Witch's Tale* and the writer's ability to let his imagination run amok and create stories like "Witchcraft," "The Case of the Glowing Ghost," "The Invisible Man" and "The Chamber of Horrors" that suggested horror but delivered a tamer product. "The White Monster" also treats the reader to a rare instance in which the police are ahead of Casey in solving the crime.

110   Flashgun Casey, Crime Photographer

Hanged by the Neck (#68)
Broadcast October 24, 1944

Written by Alonzo Deen Cole, Directed by John Dietz and Supervised by Robert J. Landry.

CAST: Casey, Ann, Ethelbert, Hayes, Pasquale, Mariana, Cop, 2nd Cop (bit), Trenchard, Frank, Doctor (bit), Voices.

CUE:	COLUMBIA BROADCASTING SYSTEM
	(. . . . . . . 30 seconds . . . .)
CASEY:	(*COLD*) Face the camera, please . . . hold it!
SOUND:	FLASH BULB & SHUTTER CLICK
CASEY:	Thanks. (*FADING*) You'll see it in the Morning Express.
ANCR:	The adventures of CASEY . . . PRESS PHOTOGRAPHER!
MUSIC:	UP . . . THEN UNDER & BACK
ANCR:	Columbia brings you another adventure of Casey, Press Photographer, written by Alonzo Deen Cole and played by Staats Cotsworth. We invite you to follow Casey on his exciting assignments and to meet the strange assorted people who pass in swift moving parade before the shutters of his camera. Tonight's adventure: — (*ORGAN EFFECT*) — "Hanged by the Neck!"
MUSIC:	OVERTURE TO DRAMA

* * *

ANCR:	Nearly midnight. A dark and narrow road. (*) A leisurely moving automobile AND — Casey and Ann Williams:
SOUND:	FADE IN AUTOMOBILE MOTOR AT * ABOVE & HOLD UNDER
ANN:	(*A YAWN . . . THEN*) Excuse me.
CASEY:	Sleepy, Ann?
ANN:	No . . . it's the suburban quiet and the suburban air that's making me — (*STIFLING A YAWN*) — yawn. How soon'll we be back in the city, Casey?
CASEY:	We're in the city now . . . crossed the line couple minutes ago.
ANN:	Really? There's nothing but farms along here . . . I thought —
CASEY:	(*CHUCKLES*) Didn't you know our town had a farming section? There's a lot of milk and eggs and garden truck produced between here and Old Turnpike — and Big Swamp.

ANN: I did know it ... just wasn't thinking. (*SLIGHT PAUSE*) Don't believe I've ever been over this road before —
CASEY: It's a short-cut to the Turnpike.
ANN: I'm twisted, Casey — Big Swamp's over that way?
CASEY: No ... it's about half a mile this way.
ANN: Oh.
CASEY: If we turned into that side road we'd run smack into it.
ANN: I'd just as soon not ... it sounds messy.
CASEY: It is. Far back as I can remember, the city's been promising to drain those marshes, but — it hasn't. Here's Old Turnpike.
ANN: Now we can shoot straight into town.
CASEY: Uh huh.
ANN: Going to stop at the office and leave the pictures you took tonight?
CASEY: What for? That assignment we just finished in the sticks is for a Sunday feature ... we'll turn our stuff in tomorrow.
ANN: That'll be time enough, I guess.
CASEY: And plenty. (*PAUSE*) Say, Annie! — feel like paying a little social call?
ANN: Social call? It's almost midnight!
CASEY: That won't matter in this case. You know Jim Hayes.
ANN: Police Lieutenant Hayes?
CASEY: Yeah. I just happened to think ** He was transferred to the Old Turnpike precinct station a couple months ago and, since we're in the neighborhood —
ANN: We ought to stop in and say hello ... he did some nice things for us when he was down town.
CASEY: Yeah ... Jim's a swell old egg. Let's see exactly what time — ten minutes to 12 ... he should still be on duty or just about to come on duty so we'll catch him either way. The station's just down the road ... we'll stop.
ANN: Okay. That was a pretty raw deal they gave Lieutenant Hayes — transferring him way out here, miles from his home, just because he made a little mistake.
CASEY: When a cop puts the pinch on a guy with political influence and the guy turns out to be innocent, it's a BIG mistake, Annie ... and that's the kind Jim made. Unfortunately, he's longer on honesty and impulse then he is on brains and diplomacy. (*) Here are the old green lights ... pile out.

SOUND:	CAR STOPPED & MOTOR CUT AT * ABOVE ... CAR DOORS OPENED AT ** BELOW & CLOSED AD LIB, THEN FOOTSTEPS CROSSING SIDEWALK & UP SHORT FLIGHT OF STONE STEPS ... HEAVY DOOR OPENED AT **** CLOSED AD LIB
ANN:	Okay. ** I've never understood why police stations have green light at their doors ... that's a "come on" signal.
CASEY:	(*CHUCKLES*) Why don't you write a letter-to-the-editor about it?
ANN:	(*CHUCKLES*) I think I will.
CASEY:	And I'll write one complaining that women are always on the wrong side of a guy when he has to open a door for em. Let me get around you and ** — Here. (***)
ANN:	Lieutenant Hayes is on the desk.
CASEY:	We're in luck. (*PROJECTS*) Hello, Jim!
HAYES:	(*FADING ON*) What are you two doin' way out here??
CASEY:	We were in Hewitt County on a routine job ... we were driving back this way and —
ANN:	As we saw a light in your window, we thought we'd drop in —
CASEY:	For a cup of tea.
HAYES:	Say — it's good to see ya!! This is the only excitin' thing that's happened since I been pastured out here with the cows and the goats! (*EAGERLY*) Come on up here, back of the desk ... there's a couple of extra chairs — sit down!
ANN:	Thanks, Lieutenant.
HAYES:	How're things down town, Casey?? — I don't know what's goin' on any more.
CASEY:	Everything's just about the same, Jim.
HAYES:	Nothin's ever just the same down town! — there's always somethin' new. Out here — Well, I'm seriously considerin' the matter of puttin' chicken coops back in the cell block and tryin' to raise broilers ... a cop exiled to this neck of th' woods has little else to do.
CASEY:	I've always heard this precinct was a great place to take a rest cure.
HAYES:	(*WITH A SIGH*) It's all of that. The farmers 'round Big Swamp do nothin' but get up in the mornin', work all day, then go to bed ... the people in the defense plants down the road do nothin' but tend to their own business ... and, outside of them two classes, there's no one out here except a couple very law-abidin' store keepers. Miss Williams, if it wasn't for an occasional traffic violation on the Turnpike, there'd be no need for cops out here at all. And I'm a cop who's used to workin' for his pay.

ANN:	Cheer up, Lieutenant . . . they won't keep you in these back woods long.
CASEY:	Of course not, Jim! — you'll be down town again pretty soon.
HAYES:	(*SADLY*) I'm not so sure of that . . . and neither are you two. When an old bull gets himself in wrong, as I did, he's likely to stay in wrong until he dies, retires or — puts over somethin' to prove he ain't the dumbbell everyone's decided he is. The smartest thing I can hope to put over in this forsaken place is — maybe to find a dog somebody reports is lost.
CASEY:	Cheer up, Jim . . . you'll get a break. Say — you go off duty pretty soon, don't you?
HAYES:	In — seven minutes . . . a sergeant relieves me at 12.
CASEY:	When he gets here, how about you, Miss Williams and I finding a comfortable joint where we can have a steak sandwich, maybe a drink or two, and a little restful gab?
HAYES:	I'd like to, Casey . . . but it takes me so long to get home from here—
ANN:	Lieutenant Hayes has a wife and family, Casey.
CASEY:	Yeah . . . that's so.
HAYES:	But I <u>will</u> take y'up on — well, a quick drink after the Sarge gets here, Casey. (*) I hear someone comin' up the steps now . . . it must be him —
SOUND:	QUICK FOOTSTEPS OUTSIDE AT * ABOVE . . . NOW DOOR THROWN OPEN
PAS:	(*A MIDDLE-AGED ITALIAN . . . EXCITEDLY, OFF & FADING ON*) Mister Polizaman! Mister Polizaman —!!
HAYES:	Huh??
MAR:	(*20; VERY <u>SLIGHT</u> ITALIAN ACCENT . . . EXCITEDLY, HALF OFF & FADING ON*) Something terrible has happen'!!
PAS:	You musta go quick to Mister Trenchard's farm —!!
MAR:	(*QUICK . . . OVERLAPPING*) There, you will find in his barn!
PAS:	(*QUICK . . . OVERLAPPING*) We see it with our owna eyes !
MAR:	And came right here to tell you —!
PAS:	Immediatamente!
MAR:	It was terrible —! (*BOTH CONTINUE AD LIB UNTIL **)
HAYES:	Wait a minute!. Wait a —!! (*TOPPING*) WAIT A MINUTE! (*) One at a time!! You, Mister — What's this all about??
PAS:	I —! (*EXHAUSTED FROM EXCITEMENT*) <u>You</u> tella him, Mariana . . . you speaka da gooda Englis.
MAR:	(*RATHER BREATHLESS NOW*) Officer, I am Mariana Simoni . . . thees is my father, Pasquale Simoni.

HAYES:	Okay. Why are you here?
MAR:	We think we have just see — a murder.
HAYES:	You think —??
CASEY:	A MURDER ??
ANN:	Casey—!
HAYES:	(*TENSE & RAPID*) Talk fast, young woman . . . and talk straight!
MAR:	You know where issa Asa Trenchard's farm?
HAYES:	No, but go on!
MAR:	Five–six minutes ago, my father and me, we drive past his place—
PAS:	Anda we see, Mister Polizaman —!
MAR:	Wait, Papa! As we drive past his place, Officer, we see through the doorway of his barn —
PAS:	We see a mans —!
MAR:	A man whose feet are not upon de floor . . . a man who twist and turn around . . . a man who is HANGING BY HIS NECK!
HAYES:	Hanging by his neck??
PAS:	From a ROPE!
MAR:	A man, we think is — MURDERED!
HAYES:	If you saw a guy hanging, he was probably a suicide!
MAR:	We do not think so.
HAYES:	We'll soon find out! (*PROJECTS*) You guys in the on-call room! — cut the pinochle game and come here!!
MEN:	AD LIB RESPONSE OFF . . . FADE ON UNDER:
HAYES:	Collins, you take charge of this desk until Sergeant Rosen relieves you! McIntyre and Adams, you come with me!
CASEY:	We're going, too, Jim!
HAYES:	Okay, Casey . . . there'll be room in the squad car for you and Miss Williams. Come on, you Simonis — we'll have a look at this "murdered" guy who's hanging by the neck!
MUSIC:	BRIDGE

* * *

SOUND:	SIREN OF POLICE CAR . . . THEN RAPID MOTOR & HOLD UNDER
HAYES:	You know where this Asa Trenchard's farm is, Adams?
COP:	Yes, Lieutenant . . . Trenchard has the acreage next to the Garcia place — back by Big Swamp.
HAYES:	Bear down on the gas and get us there.
COP:	We'll make it in three minutes.

HAYES:	Now, Miss Simoni, let's have your full story — First, where do you and your father live?
MAR:	On Pickens Road . . . by Big Swamp.
HAYES:	How come you were passing Trenchard's place at this time of night?
MAR:	Papa and me — We pass it every week day night in our automobile . . . at about 15 minutes to 12 o'clock.
PAS:	Si . . . Mariana anda me, we worka in defensa factory. Mr. Polizamans.
MAR:	We are on the midnight shift.
HAYES:	Okay. And when you drove by Trenchard's place tonight, you saw a guy hanging in the doorway of his barn.
MAR:	Not IN the doorway . . . THROUGH the doorway we see the hanging man.
CASEY:	This is a pretty dark night, Miss Simoni . . . there must have been a light in the barn if you were able to see —
HAYES:	(*CORDIAL AGREEMENT*) I was just gonna ask about that, Casey!
MAR:	There was a light inside the barn — from a lantern, Papa think.
CASEY:	And you believe the hanging man you saw was murdered.
HAYES:	WHY do you believe that?
MAR:	Papa —
PAS:	I tella dese polizamans, Mariana! It issa because theesa Mr. Trenchard issa badda-temper' mans . . . allaways, he issa having quarrel witha peoples. AND, when he hava quarrel, he allaways—
MAR:	He always say: — "Some day I see you hanged!"
HAYES:	He always says that to the person he's sore at, eh?
PAS:	Si.
MAR:	Yes. Only this morning, Papa hear him say that to Joe Gracia!
PAS:	He anda Joe Garcia have badda quarrel —
MAR:	It was in Hadley's store on de Turnpike . . . Papa and other men see and hear. And, before, I have hear Mr. Trenchard say that thing to other peoples.
HAYES:	So now you think he's really hanged somebody?
MAR:	We SEE somebody hanging in his barn.
CASEY:	(*DRYLY*) With a light in the barn so the hanging body can be seen from road.
HAYES:	I was just gonna remark on that, Casey.
PAS:	(*STUBBORNLY*) It wassa what we see.
HAYES:	Have you two ever had any quarrels with this guy, Trenchard?
PAS:	No, no!

MAR:	Papa and me — we have quarrel with nobody!!
HAYES:	Adams — you've been stationed in this precinct a long time— What do you know about Trenchard?
COP:	He's a big, raw-boned guy about 50 years old, Lieutenant . . . he was born on that little farm he runs. Lost his wife 'bout 5 years ago and has lived alone ever since. These people have his disposition right — he's a tough egg to get along with. I've heard him tell guys he'd see em hanged someday, but it always sounded to me like — just a corny expression.
ANN:	(*SOTTO VOCE*) My grandfather used to say things like that when he got made, Casey.
CASEY:	(*LOW*) So did my old man Annie.
COP:	There's the Trenchard place just ahead Lieutenant.
HAYES:	Slow down and cut your lights . . . then drive in to this barn.
COP:	Yes sir.
HAYES:	(*SOTTO VOCE*) It still sounds like a suicide to me, Casey.
CASEY:	To me, too, Jim. Sour old guy, living alone, gets bored with it all and gives himself a neck-tie party.
HAYES:	Yeah. Is that the barn, Miss Simoni, where you and your father—
MAR:	Yes.
HAYES:	There's no light in it now.
ANN:	(*LOW*) A suicide couldn't have turned out his lantern after he'd hanged himself, Casey.
CASEY:	No, but the lantern could wink out by itself. Ann.
ANN:	That's so.
HAYES:	Stop here, Adams . . . this is close enough.
SOUND:	STOP CAR . . . OPEN DOORS AT *
COP:	Yes, sir.
HAYES:	Now we'll see — (*) Come on, boys — with your flashlights. Was it through that doorway you saw the hanging man, Simoni?
PAS:	Yes.
MAR:	(*PUZZLED*) The door it is closed now.
HAYES:	(*DRYLY*) So I see. Open it, McIntyre.
2nd COP:	Yes, sir.
SOUND:	SLIDING BARN DOOR OPENED UNDER:
MAR:	The man — we see him hanging just behind the door —-
HAYES:	There's no one hanging there now!
MAR:	No-o.
PAS:	Mariana —??

COP:	(*HALF OFF*) Nothin' in this barn but a couple cows, Lieutenant.
SOUND:	MOVEMENT AND LOWING OF DISTURBED COWS ... ANTICIPATE
HAYES:	Miss Simoni, sure you and your father didn't dream this whole thing?
MAR:	No, no —!
PAS:	We SAW, Mr. Polizaman —!
CASEY:	(*SLIGHTLY OFF*) I don't think they were dreaming, Jim ... look at that beam up there.
HAYES:	Beam, Casey?
CASEY:	Yeah. There's a light colored streak on each side of it — at the top ... as though it had been recently chafed by — maybe a rope.
COP:	(*HALF OFF*) There's a lotta rope hangin' on this peg, Lieutenant — heavy rope. And one of the pieces has a runnin' noose on the end. See?
HAYES:	Yeah. (*SLIGHT PAUSE*) Adams, you and McIntyre go to the house and see if Trenchard's there ... if he is, bring him here quick and don't say WHY.
COP:	Yes, sir.
2nd COP:	(*FADING*) Okay, Lieutenant.
HAYES:	Hand me that milkin' stool, Casey ... by standin' on it, I can reach that beam.
CASEY:	Here, Jim.
HAYES:	(*PAUSE*) There's been a rope — or somethin' — pulled over this beam not very long ago ... the only place where it ain't dusty on top is between them chafe marks we noticed, Casey.
ANN:	If a man was hanged here, what's happened to his body?
HAYES:	That's what I wanta know!
CASEY:	It couldn't have been over 12 minutes from the time the Simonis say they saw the hanging man until we got here ... if his body was taken down and hidden, whoever did it worked fast.
HAYES:	Yeah. (*HALF OFF*) There ain't any body in this part of the barn ... (*FADING*) ... I'm climbin' up to the hay loft.
ANN:	(*LOW*) This is screwy, Casey.
CASEY:	Plenty screwy, Ann. Let's take a look around outside.
ANN:	Okay.
MAR:	We come with you, Mr. Casey ... I do not like to be in this barn.
PAS:	I do notta like it, too, Mariana.
CASEY:	You folks had better stay here until the Lieutenant tells you otherwise. Come on, Ann.

MAR/PAS:	*LOW, UNHAPPY AD LIBS . . . FADING*
CASEY:	(*AFTER PAUSE*) Hmm . . . ground's hard as concrete out here— there'll be no footprints to tell the cops anything.
ANN:	(*HALF OFF*) No. (*PAUSE*) What's this Casey?
CASEY:	What?
ANN:	(*FADING ON*) This funny looking rubber gadget . . . I just picked it up.
CASEY:	Let's see it.
ANN:	It has a little hook on one end . . . here.
CASEY:	Hmm . . . some gimmick that's used around a cow barn, I guess. Only — (*PUZZLED*) I've seen things like this before somewhere and I haven't spent much time around cow barns. (*MOCK SEVERITY*) You should never pick up things at the scene of a crime, Ann.
ANN:	We don't know yet that there's been any crime! And why are you sticking the thing in your pocket??
CASEY:	I'm a gadget collector. Besides —
HAYES:	(*OFF*) Casey — where are you?
CASEY:	Here, Jim!
ANN:	Did you find anything in the hay loft, Lieutenant?
HAYES:	(*FADING ON*) Nothin' but hay, Miss Williams. I poked all through it with a pitchfork . . . there's no body hid in it.
CASEY:	If anyone around here had a body to dispose of in a hurry, Jim, I think there'd be just one place they'd drop it.
HAYES:	Where's that?
CASEY:	In Big Swamp.
HAYES:	That's just what I was thinkin'! and this farm is right at the edge of Big Swamp . . . a corner of it ain't no more'n three-four minutes walk from this here barn.
ANN:	Lieutenant — the men you sent for Trenchard are coming back.
HAYES:	And the big guy between em must be Trenchard. Now we'll see—
COP:	(*OFF . . . FADING ON*) Here's the man you wanted, Lieutenant!
TREN:	(*50 . . . A SOUR, BELLICOSE FARMER. FADING ON*) Are you the big police mucky-muck who had these fellers get me outa bed??
HAYES:	I want to ask you a few questions, Trenchard.
TREN:	(*ANGRILY*) First, I', gonna ask YOU some! What's the big idea of comin' onto my farm in the middle of the night and bustin' up my sleep??
HAYES:	(*TENSE*) What time did you go to sleep?

TREN:	At half past eight, like I usually do! — I get up at 4 in the mornin'.
HAYES:	And you've been sleepin' ever since half past eight??
TREN:	Yes . . . until these fellers woke me up just now!
HAYES:	Then how did you get that <u>fresh mud</u> on your shoes???
TREN:	Mud?
HAYES:	Let's have a closer look! (*EXCITEDLY*) Casey, feel this mud . . . it's still wet — and it's <u>black muck from the swamp!</u>
CASEY:	It's that alright, Jim.
TREN:	(*PUZZLED*) I don't know —
HAYES:	Trenchard, if you hadn't been outside your house during the last four hours — in THOSE SHOES — that mud woulda dried out by now! Who was the man you hanged tonight?? — whose body have you hidden in Big Swamp???
TREN:	You must be crazy!! — I dunno what ye're talkin' about!
HAYES:	Oh, no??
TREN:	NO!! What's more, I dunno where this mud came from . . . I ain't been near the swamp all day and there warn't no mud on my shoes when I took em off tonight and left em on the back stoop!
HAYES:	You left your shoes on the back stoop?
TREN:	I always leave em there when I go inta the house . . . so's I won't mess up my clean floors!
HAYES:	(*HEAVY SARCASM*) Now you're gonna tell me the shoes walked down to the swamp all by themselves and got muddy.
TREN:	(*ROARS*) I ain't gonna tell you nothin' 'til you tell me what this crazy business is about!!
HAYES:	You know what it's about, Trenchard! Now stop lying and come clean!!
TREN:	(*FURIOUS*) Don't call me a liar! — I don't let no man alive — !!
HAYES:	That's right — hang onto him, boys!
TREN:	(*STRUGGLING*) Lemme go!! Oh — someday I'll see all of ye— HANGED BY THE NECK !!!
HAYES:	(*HAPPILY TRIUMPHANT*) Well — **! You and Miss Williams are witnesses to that Casey. Put the bracelets on Trenchard, boys . . . he and all of us are going to the swamp and have a look around.
MUSIC:	BRIDGE

* * *

HAYES: We're strikin' soft ground now, Casey ... look at those footprints.
CASEY: Not only footprints, Jim ... there's a tire track.
HAYES: Yeah — a single tire track ... like a wheelbarrow'd make.
ANN: I noticed a rubber-tired wheelbarrow standing under Trenchard's toolshed when we passed it, Lieutenant!
HAYES: I noticed it, too, Miss Williams. Hey, McIntyre —!
2nd COP: (*OFF*) Yes, sir?
HAYES: Bring Trenchard here!
TREN: (*SUPPRESSED FURY ... OFF, FADING ON*) He don't havta-BRING me! What d' ye want?
HAYES: Just keep walking as you're doin', Trenchard. Now you can stop.
TREN: I'll make you pay for all this —!
HAYES: Shut up! (*EXCITEDLY*) Look at the footprints this guy just made in the soft ground, Casey! — it's his shoes that left those others.
CASEY: Same shoes alright.
HAYES: And when we bring his wheelbarrow down here and check it —
TREN: (*RATHER PLAINTIVE NOW*) Will you fellers PLEASE tell me?
HAYES: Quit stallin'! You killed a man tonight, brought his body here in your wheelbarrow and threw it in the swamp — Who was that man??
TREN: You're crazy —!
HAYES: (*ANGRILY*) Okay ... go on playin' dumb! It won't be hard to find the body with your tracks leading directly to the spot where you duped it. Take him back to the house, McIntyre!
2nd COP: Come on, Trenchard.
TREN: (*FURIOUS AGAIN ... FADING*) I'll see you all hanged for this ... someday I'll see you hanged —!
HAYES: Adams —!
COP: Yes, sir?
HAYES: Call precinct headquarters and get a car out here to locate the body in this swamp.
COP: (*FADING*) Okay, Lieutenant.
HAYES: (*PROJECTS*) And come back here when you've made your call!
COP: (*OFF*) Yes, sir.
HAYES: (*CONTENTEDLY*) Well, Casey — soon as that body's brought up from the mud and identified, this case'll be all sewed up.
CASEY: Umm ... I wonder.
HAYES: You wonder what?

CASEY:	If there's a body under the mud I wonder if Trenchard was so stupid as to have done all the things he seems to have done.
HAYES:	You only have to take one look at that guy to know he's stupid! Besides, we got here so fast, he didn't have time to cover his tracks . . . we surprised him and all he could do was play dumb.
CASEY:	(*UNEASILY*) Maybe so, Jim . . . but I'd take things a little easy if I were you.
HAYES:	Easy nothin'!! This case may get me back down town again! When we find the guy who's been murdered – (and I'm sure we will find him!) – I'm gonna put the pressure on Trenchard fast and hard.
CASEY:	Somehow, I wish you wouldn't until —
FRANK:	(*35 . . . EASY. INGRATIATING MANNER. OFF, ANXIOUSLY*) Joe! Oh, Joe.
HAYES:	Huh?
FRANK:	Is that you over there, Joe?
HAYES:	(*PROJECTS*) There's no Joe here! Who are you?
FRANK:	(*FADING ON*) Who are YOU —? Oh — a cop! I didn't make out your uniform in the dark.
HAYES:	Yeah, I'm a cop.
FRANK:	I saw flashlights bobbing around over here . . . I was out looking for my brother and I thought maybe — (*WORRIED*) You're not here because — something's wrong, Officer?
HAYES:	Do you live on this next farm — where you were out lookin' for your brother?
FRANK:	Yes. My name's Frank Garcia.
HAYES:	(*TENSING*) Garcia —?
FRANK:	Yes. You probably know my brother, Joe . . . he's lived here for years, and all the year around — I'm just an occasional visitor during the fall and winter.
HAYES:	No. I don't know him. One of you Garcia fellers had a fight with Trenchard this mornin', didn't you?
FRANK:	I wouldn't call it a "fight" . . . Trenchard and my brother had some words down at Hadley's store — but words is all it amounted to. They're always cussing each other out.
HAYES:	Don't like one another, eh?
FRANK:	No. Trenchard's to blame for it — he's always got a chip on his shoulder . . . Joe is naturally a sweet guy.
HAYES:	Would you say Trenchard hated your brother?

FRANK:	I'd say he hasn't any love for him. Why —?
HAYES:	When did you see your brother last, Mr. Garcia?
FRANK:	He went out after we had dinner . . . it was my night to wash the dishes — we're both bachelors. He don't usually stay out late so, when it got around 11 o'clock, I began to worry a little . . . about half an hour ago, I started out to look for him and — (*SLIGHT PAUSE*) Why are you asking me all this, Officer?
HAYES:	I —
COP:	(*OFF*) I've talked to Headquarters, Lieutenant.
HAYES:	Oh — it's you, Adams.
COP:	(*FADING ON*) Yes sir. The crew's on its way here to look for that body.
FRANK:	"Look for a body"??
HAYES:	(*WITH ROUGH SYMPATHY*) Mr. Garcia, you stay here with us . . . and maybe you'd better get set for a shock.
FRANK:	A – a shock?
ANN:	(*DRYLY . . . SOTTO VOCE*) Lieutenant Hayes is hardly what you'd call a diplomat, Casey.
CASEY:	(*SAME TONE*) No Ann . . . old Jim is just a nice old, honest, thickhead.
MUSIC:	BRIDGE . . . HOLD INTO SCENE & UNDER

* * *

MAN:	(*OFF*) We've got it, Lieutenant — the body of a man!
HAYES:	(*EXCITEDLY*) bring it to the hard ground, boys, and lay it down!
FRANK:	(*OFF . . . FADING ON — ANGUISHED*) Is it Joe, Lieutenant?? Let me see —!
HAYES:	Hold everything, Mr. Garcia. Wash some of the mud off that poor stiff's face, boys, so we can —!
FRANK:	Hurry . . . hurry, I've got to know! (*PAUSE . . . CHOKED*) Oh — I can tell now. That's the body of Joe — my bother.
MUSIC:	UP FOR BRIDGE, THEN UNDER

* * *

HAYES:	What's your opinion, doctor?
DOC:	This man died around 11 o'clock, Lieutenant.
CASEY:	Around <u>eleven,</u> Doctor?
DOC:	That's right, Casey . . . maybe a little before.
HAYES:	That fits okay! Go on, Doc.
DOC:	There's a severe contusion of the scalp, as though he'd been struck

DOC: (cont'd.)	heavily on the head, but — pending autopsy — I'll say that death was brought about by strangulation . . . he was garotted — choked with a heavy cord or rope.
HAYES:	That's all I wanta know!
CASEY:	Take it easy, Jim.
HAYES:	Whatta y' mean, "take it easy", Casey?? — I'm arrestin' Trenchard for murder!
MUSIC:	UP . . . THEN UNDER
TREN:	You policemen are crazy!! — I haven't hanged anyone . . . I dunno what this is all about!
HAYES:	(*ROUGHLY*) Come on Trenchard . . . we're takin' you to jail!
MUSIC:	HIT & BRIDGE

* * *

SOUND;	BARROOM EFFECTS . . . PIANO BEHIND
ETH:	(*HURRIED & HARASSED*) Here's yer Martini, Mr. Pizer.
MAN:	Thanks, Ethelbert.
2nd MAN:	(*HALF OFF*) How about my scotch and soda, Ethelbert?
ETH:	Scotch and soda? — oh, yeah! Here, Mr. Johnson.
3rd MAN:	Gimme a beer, bartender.
ETH:	Uh — a beer. (*PAUSE*) Ya got it.
GIRL:	(*OFF*) Oh, Ethelbert —!
ETH:	I — (*PROJECTS DEFIANTLY*) Grace, I'll take YOUR order later! (*PLAINTIVELY*) Gee Casey — every time you and Miss Williams come in and start to tell me somethin' interestin', this bar suddenly gets busy. Now! — when we was interrupted, you was sayin' you don't believe this guy, Trenchard, did the hangin'.
CASEY:	I said I don't believe he did the MURDER, Ethelbert. After the Medical Examiner performed an autopsy this morning, he definitely decided that Joe Garcia wasn't hanged.
ETH:	Wasn't hanged??
ANN:	He was strangled with a rope after he was knocked out by a blow on the head, Ethelbert . . . but the M.E. says he wasn't strung up to a beam and left dangling —
CASEY:	Either before his death or afterwards.
ANN:	(*SIGHS*) Now the whole case is a mess of contradictions.
CASEY:	(*DRYLY*) Not to our friend, Lieutenant Hayes, Ann . . . old Jim's still positive he arrested the right guy.

ANN: I think he did . . . and so does Logan who's head of the Homicide Bureau! If Trenchard didn't actually hang Joe Garcia, every evidence proves that he put his body in the swamp.

CASEY: Does it?

ANN: (*IRRITABLY*) Oh, I realize that there are some things that can't be easily explained —!

CASEY: And PLENTY of things! First, if Trenchard was the killer, you've got to put him down as an utter moron, which I don't believe he is. He made no attempt to obliterate his footprints near the swamp — or the track of his wheelbarrow. He didn't even wash the swamp mud off his shoes!

ANN: (*UNCOMFORTABLY*) Lieutenant Hayes thinks our police car got there before Trenchard had time to cover up —

CASEY: (*IRRITABLY*) Old Jim's bullheadedness may keep him in a back woods precinct for the rest of his life if Trenchard hires a half-smart lawyer to defend him! — he's trying to make square pegs fit into round holes!! Trenchard had plenty of time, assuming he was the killer . . . the Medical examiner sticks to his original opinion that Joe Garcia died not later than 11 o'clock — a good 45 minutes before the Simonis say they saw a man hanging in that barn!

ETH: But if this Gracia WASN'T hanged, how could them Spumonis have seen him hangin'?

ANN: (*WITH A SIGH*) That's just ANOTHER little problem, Ethelbert.

CASEY: (*DRYLY*) Yeah.

ETH: I can figger that one! — they DIDN'T see what they said they saw.

CASEY: (*IMPATIENTLY*) That's the way Jim Hayes — and even Logan — tried to brush it off! But a check-up on the Simonis has established them as A-one citizens with a top-notch reputation for honesty, and they have no known motive to tell any lies in this case. What's more, they haven't made a single important change in their original story.

ETH: But CASEY — when they say someone hangin' who wasn't hung —!

CASEY: They've never said they saw JOE GARCIA hanging . . . it was just a man!

ETH: You think somebody else was hung and —

CASEY: I don't know what to think! (*PAUSE . . . HALF TO HIMSELF*) Something was hanging in Trenchard's barn . . . from a rope that left scars on that beam.

ETH: Hmm. Well — it's too deep for me!
CASEY: Give me another drink, Ethelbert.
ETH: How 'bout you, Miss Williams?
ANN: No . . . one's my limit.
ETH: (*FADING*) Oh sure . . . I ferget —
CASEY: (*THINKING ALOUD*) Trenchard was framed, Ann . . . I'm sure of it. Trenchard is a big, strong guy; Joe Garcia was a little fellow. Why should Trenchard have trundled his body to the swamp in a wheelbarrow when it'd have been much simpler to have carried it?
ANN: (*SHORTLY*) I want to have that hanging man explained before I tackle anything else.
CASEY: (*THINKING*) That hanging man was part of the frame . . . he's the key to the whole thing, but I can't figure —
ETH: (*FADING ON*) Here's yer drink, pal.
CASEY: (*ABSENTLY*) Thanks, Ethelbert.
ETH: Say — it musta been a perty sad thing when that Frank Garcia identified his brother's body right after it'd been pulled outa the swamp, Miss Williams.
ANN: It was.
ETH: How did the feller take it?
ANN: He seemed badly broken up. Show people are emotional, you know.
CASEY: (*VAGUELY*) Show people?
ANN: Frank Garcia is in the show business, Casey.
CASEY: Yeah? I didn't know —
ANN: I had a long talk with him after the body was found . . . while you were busy taking pictures and arguing with Lieutenant Hayes. He's very interesting . . . he spends all his summers with the circus.
CASEY: Circus? (*SLIGHT PAUSE, THEN SHARPLY*) Circus??
ANN: (*PUZZLED*) Yes.
CASEY: What's he do?
ANN: He's a ticket seller.
CASEY: (*DISGUSTEDLY*) Ticket seller?
ANN: I gathered that he used to be a performer, but he hurt his back some years ago and —
CASEY: (*SHARPLY AGAIN*) What kind of performer was he?
ANN: He didn't say.
CASEY: (*TENSE*) What circus was he with, Ann . . . did he tell you?
ANN: Yes . . . the big one . . . Farnum and —
CASEY: Their headquarters are in Jacksonville, Florida —

ANN:	I believe so. Where are you going??
CASEY:	(*FADING*) Excuse me . . . I'm going to make a long distance phone call.
ETH:	Miss Williams! — WHY has he suddenly decided to —
ANN:	Ethelbert — that's a $64 question.
MUSIC:	BRIDGE

* * *

SOUND:	MOTOR CAR UNDER
HAYES:	(*IRRITABLY*) There's Trenchard's farm just ahead, Casey — Will y'tell me NOW why you've driven us out here??
CASEY:	Be patient another minute, Jim . . . I've told you I want to show you something rather than talk about it.
ANN:	(*WEARILY*) You've already heard all I know, Lieutenant Hayes. Casey suddenly decided to make a long distance phone call to somewhere . . . next thing, I'm rushed into this car without any explanation; we pick you up and — here we are.
SOUND:	CAR STOPS. CAR DOOR OPENED AT * . . . BARN DOOR OPENED AT **
CASEY:	(*CHEERFULLY*) Yep — here we are, Ann! (*) Pile out you two.
HAYES:	We're goin' into the barn?
CASEY:	Uh huh.
HAYES:	(*IRRITABLY*) Okay! (*SLIGHT PAUSE*) I'll open the door. (**)
ANN:	(*AFTER BIZ*) Well — now, what're we going to see?
CASEY:	A demonstration of how the Simonis saw a man hanging in here last night.
HAYES:	They didn't see any man hangin'!
CASEY:	Oh yes, they did! And — the man they saw hanging was the murderer of Joe Garcia.
HAYES:	(*PATIENTLY*) Listen, Casey . . . if they saw a guy hangin', the guy would be dead himself.
CASEY:	Not if the guy was accustomed to hanging.
ANN:	Casey . . . WILL YOU — ?
CASEY:	(*CHUCKLES*) Okay, Ann. (*SLIGHT FADE*) I'll take a piece of rope off this peg . . . just a short piece — (*SLIGHT EFFORT*) — ** throw one end over that beam and — (*SLIGHT PAUSE*) — tie it. Now, we're all set for the hanging.

HAYES: (*SNEERS*) Ain't y' gonna tie a noose on the other end?
CASEY: No.
HAYES: Y'mean a guy just hung on to that loose end with his hands?
CASEY: He wouldn't have looked as thou he were hanging by the neck if he had, Jim . . . and the Simonis were positive about that. His head was thrown back, they said . . . and his hands dangled at his sides. Here's how it was done.
HAYES: What're you hookin' onto that rope?
ANN: Casey! — it's that gadget I found outside last night!
CASEY: Yes, Ann. All of us have seen this gimmick used dozens of times, but I didn't figure what it was until you said Frank Garcia had been with a <u>circus.</u>
ANN: Frank Garcia?
CASEY: Yeah. This rubber gadget with a hook on one end is the bit trapeze artists use when they hang by their teeth.
HAYES: I've seen them things —!
CASEY: Of course you have, Jim. My long distance call was to the head quarters of the circus Frank Garcia works for . . . they told me the kind of performer he used to be before he hurt his back — (so badly he'd have to carry the body of a small man in a wheelbarrow instead of on his shoulder!) . . . he was a trapeze artist.
ANN: You think Frank Garcia killed — his OWN BROTHER?
CASEY: It isn't a pretty thought, Ann . . . but remember Cain killed Abel.
HAYES: (*SHARPLY*) Let's have your whole idea, Casey.
CASEY: Jim — I think Frank Garcia was one of those chumos who planned the "perfect crime." Trenchard was a known enemy of Frank's brother, Joe . . . Trenchard's pet threat was that he'd see his enemies "hanged." Trenchard and Joe had a quarrel, before witnesses, yesterday morning. Last night, around 11 o'clock, Frank knocked his brother unconscious; then strangled him with a rope—
HAYES: (*TENSE*) Wait a second, Casey — I'm gettin' this now. Frank knew Trenchard left his work shoes on the back stoop . . . he put on them shoes, took Joe's body to the swamp in Trenchard's wheelbarrow and — replaced the shoes.
CASEY: That's it, Jim.
ANN: Then he wanted the police to get here while the fake tracks he'd made were fresh!

CASEY:	Yes, Ann. The Simonis always passed this place at around 11:45 . . . a light in the barn was sure to attract their attention. And, when they saw a man apparently hanging by his neck in here —
HAYES:	What a dum-bell I've been!!
CASEY:	YOU, Jim? What a dumbbell I was not to recognize this rubber gadget when Ann found it! And what a dumbbell Frank Garcia was to drop it when he left this barn!! — this thing, with his teethmarks on it, is going to send him to the chair!
ANN:	Don't try to hog the dumbbell honors, gentlemen! — I haven't been so bright, either.
HAYES:	But WHY did Frank Garcia kill his brother, Casey?
CASEY:	I don't know why, Jim —
FRANK:	(*OFF . . . SOFTLY*) Suppose you ask ME.
ANN:	What — ??
HAYES:	Garcia —!!
FRANK:	Put up your hands! (*QUICK & SHARP*) Don't reach for your gun, Copper!!
HAYES:	(*PAUSE . . . BITTERLY*) Okay.
CASEY:	(*DRYLY*) You seem to have been — hiding in that cow stall, fella.
FRANK:	Yeah. (*FADING ON*) I was looking for a little — "rubber gadget" I lost last night when you three unexpectedly appeared . . . I thought it best to keep out of sight. (*CHUCKLES*) I've been greatly interested in your conversation.
HAYES:	You know we've got you dead to rights, Garcia . . . be sensible and drop that gun!
FRANK:	You're funny, Lieutenant. You only have me "dead to rights" as long as you three are alive and have that — gadget . . . which won't be long.
HAYES:	(*BELLIGERENTLY*) You think —??
FRANK:	Don't Move!! (*EASY AGAIN*) I think all of you are going to take a trip to Big Swamp in a minute . . . to a part of the swamp where dead bodies aren't easily recovered. And, this time, I'll obliterate all tell-tale tracks.
CASEY:	(*PAUSE . . . QUIETLY*) You seem to hold the top hand, Garcia.
FRANK:	I think so, Mr. Casey. (*SHARPLY*) Let's get started . . . turn around and start walking!
HAYES:	Look here, Garcia —!!
CASEY:	Wait a minute, Jim! And you, too, Garcia!
FRANK:	Why ?

CASEY:	(*EASILY*) You suggested we ask you why you killed your brother... I'd like to know.
FRANK:	(*PAUSE, THEN A SNEERING CHUCKLE*) Dying man's last request, eh?
CASEY:	Something like that.
FRANK:	(*SLIGHT PAUSE*) Okay... I'd like to tell you. (*SUDDENLY BITTER & LOSING HIS VENEER OF CULTURE*) Joe was a skunk! Until I hurt my back couple years ago and had to take a lousy charity job of ticket-taker, I was in the big money! And I spent it! I was generous! — any of my old circus pals will tell you I never kept my pockets buttoned. Was Joe generous when I was outa the chips?? No! — he was a stingy hick who'd lived in the backwoods all his life and didn't appreciate a circus guy! He'd let me come and live with him here all winter when the big show was layin' off — But what'd he give me to have a good time on?? He'd only stake me to a lousy couple bucks a week! And him ownin' a swell payin' little farm and a lotta dough he'd stuck away in the bank! Well — finally, I figured... if my own half-brother won't give me a break, I'll TAKE it — !
ANN:	Half-brother?
FRANK:	Yeah... that skunk and me only had the same father. Well — Joe didn't have any family, outside of me, so I was his heir. I decided it was time he died, so I'd get what was comin' to me! Now you know all about it!
CASEY:	Thanks — (*EFFORT*) — Garcia!!
SOUND:	HEAVY BLOW & BODY FALL... FRANK GROANS
HAYES:	You knocked him cuckoo, Casey!!
CASEY:	The old trick, Jim: — when a guy has a gun on you, get him talking about himself and he forgets you and the gun!
ANN:	(*A DEEP SIGH*) I'm glad he forgot it! — I didn't want to take a walk to that swamp.
CASEY:	Think of the walk this sweet-smelling egg is going to take, Ann... to the hot-seat.
MUSIC:	BRIDGE

* * *

SOUND:	BARROOM EFFECTS... PIANO BEHIND
ETH:	So Lieutenant Hayes has been transferred downtown again, Casey?

CASEY:	Yes, Ethelbert . . . he's back in his old precinct, starting today.
ETH:	On account of how he solved the Gracia case, eh?
ANN:	(*DRYLY*) Yes. Ethelbert. According to official records, Lieutenant Hayes solved the Garcia case all by himself.
ETH:	Hmmmmm. (*PAUSE*) Casey — it's time that you and Miss Williams had a drink on the house.
MUSIC:	UP FOR FINISH.

• • •

ANCR:*	You've been listening to Casey, Press Photographer played by Staats Cotsworth, a new series of adventure programs based on the fictional character created by George Harmon Coxe. Casey, Press Photographer is directed by John Dietz and produced for Columbia by Robert J. Landry. Tonight's story was written by Alonzo Deen Cole.
MUSIC:	BRIDGE
ANCR:	Join us again next week at this same time for another swift moving story of Casey, Press Photographer. This is CBS, the Columbia Broadcasting System.
MUSIC:	UP FULL THEN OUT.

* THE END *

* Cole's original copy of this script did not contain a Closing segment. In order to present the script as a "complete" episode, the author has added on the Closing from the February 26, 1944 broadcast, the closest (by date) sustaining broadcast in circulation.

The White Monster (#86)
Broadcast March 27, 1945

Written by Alonzo Deen Cole, Directed by John Dietz and Supervised by Robert J. Landry.

CAST: Casey, Ann, Ethelbert, Sheriff, Herb (double). Jaffers. Hank.

CUE:	COLUMBIA BROADCASTING SYSTEM (. . . . . . . 30 seconds . . . .)
CASEY:	(*COLD*) Face the camera, please . . . hold it!
SOUND:	FLASH BULB & SHUTTER CLICK
CASEY:	Thanks. (*FADING*) You'll see it in the Morning Express.
ANCR:	The adventures of CASEY . . . PRESS PHOTOGRAPHER!
MUSIC:	UP . . . THEN UNDER & BACK
ANCR:	Columbia brings you another adventure of CASEY, PRESS PHOTOGRAPHER, written by Alonzo Deen Cole and played by Staats Cotsworth. We invite you to follow Casey on his exciting assignments and to meet the strangely assorted people who pass in swift-moving parade before the shutters of his camera. Tonight's adventure: — (ORGAN EFFECT) — The White Monster.
MUSIC:	OVERTURE TO DRAMA . . . UP & UNDER

* * *

ANCR:	11:30 in the morning. The Blue Note Café. Only a few customers are in the place and Ethelbert, the bartender, is languidly polishing glasses when the street door opens and —
SOUND:	ONLY A SLIGHT MURMUR FROM THE BARROOM HABITUES AT THIS HOUR & NO PIANO. A GLASS CRASHES AT *
CASEY:	(*OFF . . . BIG & CHEERY*) Hi, Ethelbert!
ETH:	(*STARTLED*) Oops! — (*) — Casey!! Look what y' made me do, yelling like that.
CASEY:	(*FADING ON*) 'Smatter — getting jittery in your old age? I never saw you drop a glass before.
ETH:	I — I think I got spring-fever . . . my mind ain't on my work and —
ANN:	You need a little sulphur and molasses.
ETH:	Mebee you're right. OH! — hello, Miss Williams!

ANN: (*CHUCKLES*) I came in with Casey . . . you just notice me?
ETH: Now y'see what I mean.
CASEY: (*LAUGHS*) Too bad we can't take you with us today . . . a little of the old back-to-nature treatment might cure what ails you.
ETH: You and Miss Williams goin' back to Nature, Casey?
ANN: In about two hours from now we're catching a train for Beaver Lake.
ETH: Beaver lake?
CASEY: Yeah . . . and we've just got time for a thin beer before we grab some lunch and go to the station.
ETH: Comin' right up. What's takin' y' way upstate to Beaver Lake?
ANN: Special assignment.
CASEY: And, for once, I'm glad to get one of those out-of-town jobs . . . this gives me a chance to visit an old friend.
ETH: Y' know someone at Beaver Lake?
CASEY: A guy who lives not far from there. I haven't seen him since I was a punk, but I've always gotten a couple letters a year from him . . . he was a great pal of my old man's. I may have bragged about knowing him to you, Ethelbert . . . Dr. Alvin Jaffers.
ETH: Jaffers? I don't recollect you mentionin' that name, Casey.
CASEY: Maybe I haven't. In my old man's time, Doc Jaffers was one of the world's great brain surgeons . . . a lot of his original methods are still considered tops in the medical colleges.
ETH: One of them skull carvers, eh?
CASEY: One of the BEST . . . he saved a lot of people from hopeless insanity before he retired.
ETH: A guy like that <u>reetired</u>?
CASEY: About 18 — 19 years ago.
ETH: Why . . . too old to work?
CASEY: No. He was a fairly young guy then. He lost his wife . . . it broke him all up and — he's the kind who don't come back after a kayo punch.
ANN: Casey says he was very devoted to his wife . . . after she died, he had to get away from everything and everyone he'd known — so he bought himself a place in the woods near Beaver Lake and never leaves there.
ETH: The poor guy. He keeps in touch with you count of bein' pals with yer old man, Casey?
CASEY: That's it mostly . . . but Doc and I were good friends, too, even

CASEY: (cont'd.)	though I was only a high school kid when he went away. I've always meant to pay him a visit, but — Well, the chance never came along until today.
ETH:	Now y'll drop in and surprise him?
CASEY:	Yeah.
ANN:	You may not have time, Casey . . . remember we have a little job of work to do in Beaver Lake.
CASEY:	I'll TAKE time, Ann. Anyway, our job up there won't take long.
ETH:	What is the job y're gonna do?
CASEY:	We're investigating a screwy report that may make a good Sunday feature story.
ANN:	Some people think they've seen a monster near Beaver Lake.
ETH:	A — MONSTER??
ANN:	It's described as a huge white ape.
ETH:	There ain't no monkeys in this part of the country! — and, 'specially, not big white ones except in zoos.
CASEY:	Even in zoos, the white variety are little fellas.
ANN:	Just the same, the Sheriff of Beaver County got a report early this morning that something of the size, shape and general appearance of a gorilla — and all white! — had tried to attack some people in an automobile.
ETH:	Was them people <u>sober?</u>
CASEY:	That's one of the things we're going upstate to find out . . . the paper hasn't been able to get any details from our correspondent up there.
ETH:	I bet it turns out to be one of them sea-serpent yarns.
CASEY:	Sure it will . . . but people like to read sea-serpent yarns.
ANN:	Let's get started, Casey . . . we've got to have lunch and pack a few things before we go to the train.
CASEY:	Okay, Ann. Here's for the beer, Ethelbert.
ETH:	Thanks. How long'll it take you to get to Beaver Lake?
CASEY:	It's quite a trip . . . we won't pull in there 'til nearly 7 o'clock. Which is good time for us, Ann. The Sheriff, whom we'll see first, will be through with his dinner by then . . . we'll get his story quick and get to the next persons concerned — by 8 or half past, we should have all the stuff we need and be on our way to Doc Jaffers.
ANN:	The train we're taking doesn't carry a diner. When do WE eat dinner?

CASEY: We can grab a sandwich somewhere and eat it on the fly.
ANN: Hump! (*SIGHS*) If I stick around with you, Casey, I foresee a very dyspeptic future.
MUSIC: BRIDGE

* * *

SHER: (*55 ... A SHREWD, GENIAL, RURAL TYPE*) Sit down, Miss Williams ... and Mr. Casey.
CASEY: Thanks, Sheriff.
ANN: (*A TOUCH OF LONGING*) I hope we haven't taken you away from your dinner.
SHER: Nope, I was jest finishin' when you phoned from the depot that y' wanted to see me ... (*CHUCKLES*) ... anyway, I wouldn't keep big city newspaper folks awaitin' while I had a second hunk of pie.
ANN: (*A MURMURED SIGH*) Pie.
SHER: You folks et yet?
CASEY: We're having dinner later ... after you give us the dope on that matter —
ANN: Humph.
SHER: I'll give you the dope in short order: — you've wasted yer time comin' here to Beaver Lake ... there ain't nothin' to that "white monster" story.
CASEY: You've proven it's altogether phoney?
SHER: No-o ... can't say I've PROVEN anything about it. But a yarn like that jest don't stand t'reason.
ANN: Will you tell us exactly what happened, Sheriff?
SHER: Okay. 'Bout one o'clock this mornin', I got an excited phone call from Mr. Ira Crawford —
CASEY: Ira Crawford?
SHER: You folks have prob'ly heard of Mr. Crawford ... he writes plays.
CASEY: Ira Crawford has written some darn successful plays.
SHER: He lives up here mosta the time ... has a fine big house 'tother side of the Lake. Well — he starts tellin' me about this "monster" —
CASEY: Crawford saw the thing?
SHER: No. HE didn't see it ... but some folks who'd just arrived at his house had and he said they'd been scared half t' death. He asked me to come out to his house right away and talk to them folks, which I did.

ANN: Who were these — folks?
SHER: They were three actresses, Miss Williams.
CASEY: Actresses?
SHER: Uh huh. They'd driven up from the city to spend a week-end with Mr. Crawford and his wife.
ANN: What are their names?
SHER: A Miss Effie Nolan; a Miss Katherine Tucker; and Miss Tucker's mother, who goes by the stage name of Bertha Ransome.
CASEY: Oh, oh! — Annie, I've heard that Nolan and Tucker are listed for parts in the new play Crawford's putting into rehearsal soon.
ANN: This is beginning to have the familiar odor of a publicity gag, Casey.
SHER: I'm just a hick law officer, folks . . . but that's the way it smelled to me.
CASEY: Publicity stunts sometimes make good copy. What did the three women tell you, Sheriff?
SHER: They said they took a wrong road drivin' to Crawford's house and got lost — they took the wrong turninn' just this side of Sintenville, which is 'bout ten miles from Crawford's; and it's easy to b'lieve that part of their story 'cause the roads in that section are mighty confusin'. Well — they drove around for mebee half an hour 'til they lost all sense of direction. Then Miss Nolan, who was drivin, thought she saw a signpost ahead and slowed down for a look. Their car was almost at a dead stop when this "white monster" jumped outa the woods 'bout 50 yards away and come a chargin' at the car —
CASEY: All three women saw it?
SHER: So they say.
ANN: Exactly how did they describe it?
SHER: They all agree it was about 5 feet tall when it stood up and was almost as wide . . . its arms were as long as its legs and it moved mostly on all fours.
CASEY: And it was white.
SHER: Naked white . . . a dirty gray white — and without any hair.
ANN: All apes have hair!
SHER: (*CHUCKLES*) This was a very SPECIAL kinda ape, Miss Williams . . . the way them women described it, it was like an ape and like a man — yet NOT like either.
CASEY: (*DRYLY*) Sounds a little complicated.

ANN: What happened after they saw — what they saw?
SHER: Miss Nolan stepped hard on the gas. They say the "monster" jumped outa the car's way and, as they passed it, it gibbered and screamed — like it was mad enough to bite nails in two.
CASEY: But they passed it okay and got safely away.
SHER: Uh huh. Then after drivin'— (for how long and over what roads they didn't remember) – they finally found themselves at Mr. Crawford's house, where they all had highsterics. They were still havin' em when I got out there . . . and I must admit that, 'till I found out they were actresses, them highsterics looked like the genuwine article.
ANN: They certainly told a crazy story, Casey.
CASEY: TOO crazy . . . and too pointless — a publicity build-up has got to have something fairly solid behind it. (*SLIGHT PAUSE*) They couldn't even tell you where they saw their "white monster" Sheriff?
SHER: No . . . it just happened somewhere between Crawford's place and Sintenville — which covers a lot of acreage. I don't pertend to know anything about your business, but I don't think you folks can make enough news outa this yarn to pay for your trip here.
CASEY: I'm afraid you're right.
ANN: Anyway, we'll have to follow it up. Where can we rent a car to take us to Ira Crawford's place, Sheriff?
SHER: Three squares south of here, corner of Main Street — Bill Hackett's Garage . . . Bill rents out cars and drivers.
CASEY: We'll need a driver to pilot us around here.
SHER: You won't learn anything more'n I've told you when y' get to Crawford's.
ANN: I've got to interview these three women and get their first hand stories.
CASEY: And I've got to take back pictures of em, even if the paper won't use em.
SHER: But you won't see them three ladies tonight . . . they took a train back to the city just an hour before your train pulled in here.
ANN: I thought you said they were to be week-end guests at Crawford's.
SHER: They made out the "monster" had scared em so they couldn't bear to stay in these parts another night.
CASEY: (*HAPPILY*) Since that's the case, we can go right out to Dr. Jaffers, Ann!

ANN:	I guess so.
SHER:	Dr. Alvin Jaffers?
CASEY:	Yes.
SHER:	Why you goin' to his place? — he don't know anything about this monkey business.
CASEY:	I'm going on a personal matter . . . the Doctor is an old friend.
SHER:	Is that so! Fine old gent, the Doctor . . . although we never see much of him here in town.
CASEY:	I understand he leads a kind of a hermit's life.
SHER:	He hardly ever leaves that place of his back in the woods . . . drives in for 'bout an hour each week to buy provisions and get mail; that's all. (*SLIGHT PAUSE*) He know you're comin' to see him?
CASEY:	No, I'm going to surprise him.
SHER:	Hmm. (*SLIGHT PAUSE*) You a VERY old friend?
CASEY:	Known him since I was this high.
SHER:	Guess it's alright then. Doc don't welcome ordinary comp'ny . . . I've known him goin' on the 20 years he's been here, and we're real friendly — but I've never been invited inside his house and neither has anybody else I know of.
CASEY:	That so?
SHER:	Yup.
ANN:	Casey, you'd better phone him before we start out there.
CASEY:	That'd half kill the surprise, Annie. And it's okay . . . Doc looks on me as a son. How far is it to his place, Sheriff?
SHER:	Quite a piece — almost to Sintenville. Get Bill Hackett to drive you himself . . . the roads are tricky out that way and Bill knows the way to Doc's place.
CASEY:	What if we can't get Bill?
SHER:	Then ask for Pat . . . he's okay. Better not take a chance on the only other driver, though; he ain't been in this section long and only knows the main routes . . . his name's Herb.
CASEY:	Bill and Pat are okay, but not Herb.
SHER:	That's right.
CASEY:	Thanks for everything, Sheriff — you've been very kind to us.
ANN:	Indeed you have.
SHER:	Sorry I couldn't help you get a worthwhile story.
CASEY:	(*CHUCKLES*) Of course, we didn't expect to find any real white monster here . . . we only hoped the yarn would have — angles.

SHER:	It has angles ... but they ain't square ones.
CASEY:	That's it. So long, Sheriff.
SOUND:	DOOR OPENED. CLOSED AT * ... SMALL TOWN STREET EFFECTS UNDER
ANN:	Goodbye.
SHER:	Goodbye and good luck. (*)
CASEY:	Let's get down to that garage, Ann.
ANN:	We're going to EAT before we start for your Doctor friend's ... it's nearly half past seven.
CASEY:	I'll buy sandwiches ... we'll east as we ride.
ANN:	NO ... we're sitting down to a decent dinner — at a table.
CASEY:	That'll take the best part of an hour! —we'll be driving out to Doc's in the dark instead of enjoying this pretty country.
ANN:	I prefer to enjoy a satisfied stomach.
CASEY:	(*SIGHS*) Okay.
SOUND;	DISTANT ROLL OF THUNDER
CASEY:	Hmm ... that sounds like rain coming.
ANN:	I'm STILL going to eat.
CASEY:	(*WEARILY*) Alright ... alright. (*PAUSE*) What did the Sheriff say?—if we can't get Bill to drive us, we take — who?
ANN:	Uh — Herb, but not Pat.
CASEY:	Is that right?
ANN:	(*PAUSE ... THINKING*) Yes ... I'm sure.
CASEY:	That's good ... I wasn't. We must remember ... if we can't get Bill take Herb. (*LOW THUNDER*) Listen to that ... it's going to rain alright.
MUSIC:	BRIDGE

* * *

SOUND:	MOTOR CAR & LIGHT RAIN ... HOLD UNDER. FADE RAIN OUT AT *
ANN:	We've been driving an awfully long time, Casey.
CASEY:	Yeah, it's way after 9 o'clock. The Sheriff said it was "quite a piece" to Doc's place and we've had to take it easy since this rain started but — (*SLIGHT PROJECTION*) Say, Herb —
HERB:	(*THE DRIVER ... SLIGHTLY OFF*) Yes, sir?
CASEY:	How much farther do we go?
HERB:	I — I ain't got no idea, Mister ... t' tell the honest truth, I been lost for a good half hour.

CA & AN:	<u>Lost???</u>
HERB:	Yeah . . . these roads are awful tricky and I'm new in this section anyways.
CASEY:	Oh, oh!
ANN:	Casey — it was PAT we should have taken when we couldn't get Bill!
CASEY:	NOW you remember that. (*WEARILY*) Stop at the first house we come to, Herb, and ask directions.
HERB:	I'm gonna do that, Mister — if we ever git outa these woods and see another house.
ANN:	That may not be for some time . . . houses seem to be few and far between around here.
CASEY:	Houses that can be seen through the trees when it's so dark as this . . . everyone turned their lights out at 9 o'clock and went to bed.
ANN:	Dr. Jaffers'll probably be in bed and asleep by the time we find his place . . . and you'll give him a double surprise by waking him up.
CASEY:	Doc hasn't acquired county habits . . . according to his letters he works half the night.
ANN:	At what? He's retired from active practice, hasn't he?
CASEY:	Yes . . . but he keeps up his research work, reads all the medical journals and writes a lot. At least that's what I gather.
ANN:	(*PAUSE*) How did his wife die, Casey? I don't believe you ever told me.
CASEY:	She died in childbirth . . . only about a year after they were married.
ANN:	(*SYMPATHETICALLY*) Oh.
CASEY:	The kid died, too — a month or two later, I think . . . I've forgotten what my folks told me about it and Doc never mentions it. You see, he got a double wallop.
ANN:	(*PAUSE*) Do you think it left him — altogether sane?
CASEY:	Sane??
ANN:	A man who gives up a fine career and leads a hermit-like existence in this wilderness for so many years —
CASEY:	(*A TOUCH OF DEFENSIVE ANGER*) Get the idea out of your head that you're going to meet a partial screwball or a weak sister, Ann . . . Doc's as solid a guy as you'll ever see.
ANN:	How do you know? — you haven't seen him for so long —
CASEY:	I read his letters, don't I? And you heard the Sheriff, who sees him often, call him a fine old gentleman!

ANN:	But why doesn't he ever invite anyone into his home?
CASEY:	Because he's smart! — after you invite some people into your house they start to call when they're not invited . . . Doc's protecting his privacy! (*)
ANN:	He's getting no chance to protect it from US tonight . . . I wish you'd phone him —
CASEY:	I tell you it'll be alright! — Doc'll always have the welcome mat out for ME and for anyone who's with me. All we have to worry about is WHEN do we find his place.
ANN:	(*WEARILY*) Okay.
CASEY:	(*PAUSE*) It's stopped raining.
ANN:	I'm glad of that.
CASEY:	Say, Driver!! — I see lights through those trees!
HERB:	There's a house back there! (*) I'll pull up right here and go ask where we are.
SOUND:	CAR BRAKES APPLIED AT * ABOVE . . . HALT CAR NOW WITH MOTOR RUNNING. CAR DOOR OPENED AT ** BELOW. SECOND CAR DOOR AT ***
CASEY:	Also ask how to get to where we're going. (**)
HERB:	I'll git straight directions. (*WITH A SLIGHT FADE*)
CASEY:	While he's getting em, Ann, I'm going to get out and stretch my legs. (***)
ANN:	I can stand a little of that . . . we've been sitting in this jalopy a long time.
CASEY:	Look out for the mud here . . . I stepped into a mess of it.
ANN:	I just did, too. That house is set pretty far back from the road . . . it'll take our Herb some time to get there and come back.
CASEY:	Yeah . . . he's not a fast mover.
SOUND:	OFF: AN ANGRY, HALF HUMAN-HALF ANIMAL, SERIES OF GIBBERING SNARLS THAT MOUNT IN FURY . . . THEY REACH PEAK AT *, THEN FADE OUT VERY QUICKLY. A FURIOUS SNARL OFF AT **. ANOTHER, CLOSER AT ***
ANN:	(*PAUSE FOR EFFECT*) What's that?
CASEY:	Darned if I know.
ANN:	Listen . . . it's behind those trees.
CASEY:	Some animal — or bird, I guess.
ANN:	(<u>BIG</u> . . . *TERRIFIED*) Casey — LOOK!!!
CASEY:	Good Lord!!
ANN:	(<u>BIG</u>) A huge WHITE APE !! (*)

CASEY:	It CAN'T be!!
ANN:	Those women did see something — THAT!!
CASEY:	It's run across the road — toward that house!!
HERB:	(OFF — ** A SCREAM OF TERROR)
ANN:	Our DRIVER —!!
CASEY:	Herb —!?! (**)
HERB:	(OFF) Help!! (A GASP) Hel—11
CASEY:	I'm coming, guy —!
ANN:	NO — you can't leave ME!!
CASEY:	Ann —!
ANN:	You haven't a gun . . . you can't stop that thing we saw — it's a GORILLA!!
CASEY:	It's coming back!!
ANN:	With our driver —!!
CASEY:	He's hanging limp in the thing's arms . . . only dead guys look like that !! (***)
ANN:	The Thing sees US!!!
CASEY:	It's dropped Herb! Get into that car!!!
ANN:	YES!!
SOUND:	CAR DOORS SLAMMED UNDER FOLLOWING. MOTOR ROARS IN START AT *
ANN:	(SCREAMS) Ahh — it's coming toward us!! START THE CAR? CASEY . . . START — — !! (*)
CASEY:	I've got it going!!
SOUND:	CAR ROARS AWAY, FADING WITH VOICE
ANN:	(FADING) Get away from the THING, Casey . . . get AWAY FROM THAT THING!!
SOUND:	A HALF HUMAN-HALF ANIMAL GIBBER OF RAGE
MUSIC:	BRIDGE

* * *

CASEY:	(QUIETLY . . . WEARILY) And that, Sheriff, is all there is to the story — except that, after driving for hours, it seemed we finally found a place where we could phone you . . . I told you the same thing over the phone as I'm telling you now. A guy at the joint I phoned from told us how to find our way into town and — here we are.
SHER:	(QUIET . . . KEEN) I wanted to hear yer story at closer range than I got it from you over the phone. (PAUSE) so there really IS a white-ape-thing.

ANN:	(*SHAKEN & NERVOUS*) It's just as those women described it to you last night, Sheriff . . . we SAW it; HEARD it — we knew it killed our driver.
CASEY:	I feel like a heel . . . I didn't do anything to help the guy; all I did was run away.
SHER:	I don't know what else you could have done, Mr. Casey . . . you were unarmed and you had Miss Williams to think of.
ANN:	What can that Thing be??
SHER:	(*HELPLESSLY*) I give up, Miss Williams. Matter of fact, if I hadn't gotten Dr. Jaffers on the phone right after you phoned me and if he hadn't said Mr. Casey here could be depended on 100%, I wouldn't believe you any more than I did them actresses.
CASEY:	So you talked to Doc.
SHER:	Yeah . . . he's on his way over here—I figgered we could use the advice of a feller like him. I also got phoned orders out to every constable and deppity in this section to search for that — "white monster" and the body of pere Herb. But you not knowin' WHERE y' saw what y' saw is going to complicate the search. Y' can't give me <u>any</u> description of that house y' stopped in front?
CASEY:	The only things Miss Williams and I really noticed about the place were a broken rail fence and a big granite boulder at the roadside.
ANN:	The house itself was so hidden by trees, we could only make out several lighted windows.
SHER:	(*SIGHS*) There's a lotta broken fences and boulders in this section — also trees that hide houses. (*PAUSE . . . TENSE*) Say! — was in front of that house the only place you got outa the car, except at where you phoned me??
CASEY:	Yes.
SHER:	Hold up them feet of your'n.
CASEY:	Feet?
SHER:	Yes. (*SLIGHT PAUSE*) Red clay mud . . . and Miss Williams has it on her shoes, too!
ANN:	What has mud to do —?
SHER:	Ma'am, there's only half a dozen places in this county where y'll find red clay like that, and where Casey phoned from ain't one of em . . . in one of them half dozen places is where you saw the ape-thing! Lemme get on that telephone —
SOUND:	PHONE RINGS. RECEIVER UNCRADLED AT *. RECRADLED AT **

SHER:	Um — seems it's callin' me. (*) 'Lo . . . Sheriff Frost speakin'. — — Oh. 'lo, Dan. — — Where?? — — Hmm . . . near Benton Corners, huh. — — No sign of whatever did it? — — Leave everything just as it is 'til I can get out there. — — so long, Dan. (**) They've found pere Herb's body.
CASEY:	They have??
SHER:	Yeah . . . near every bone in it broken.
ANN:	(*A SHUDDER*) I — I knew it'd be that way.
SHER:	They found it in a place where there ain't no red clay.
CASEY:	That Thing probably carried it some distance.
SHER:	I'm figuring that. (SIGHS) Guess we're not gettin' very far from where we started. My men saw no sign of the ape-thing.
SOUND:	KNOCK AT DOOR. IT IS OPENED AT * & CLOSED AT **
SHER:	Come in! (*)
MAN:	(*HALF-OFF*) Dr. Jaffers is here, Sheriff.
SHER:	Oh — (*PROJECTS*) Come right in , Doc!
JAF:	(*55; HIGHLY CULTURED, VERY GENTLE . . . STRAINED & NERVOUS. OFF:*) Thank you, Sheriff.
CASEY:	(*QUIET WARMTH*) Hello, Doctor.
JAF:	(*FADING ON*) It's good to see you, Casey
CASEY:	It's swell to see you. (**) Let me introduce Miss Ann Williams . . . Dr. Jaffers.
ANN:	How do you do.
JAF:	It's nice to know you, my dear. I — I was greatly shaken when Sheriff Frost telephoned me about the distressing experience you two young people have had.
CASEY:	We'll get over it, Doc. It was quite different, though, from the evening I'd planned to spend with you.
JAF:	You — you were trying to find my house when — this thing happened . . . and couldn't find it.
CASEY:	Yeah.
JAF:	Thank Heaven no harm came to you. (*LESSENED STRAIN . . . FONDLY*) It — it's been a great many years since I've seen you, my boy! You're a little taller and a lot heavier, but I knew you instantly.
SHER:	I know you two fellers have a lot of gettin'-together and reminescin' to do, but I've gotta job that comes first. Doc — a man with your brains and experience oughta be able to figure what this ape-thing really is.

JAF: (*STRAINED AGAIN*) From the description you gave me over the phone, Sheriff, I — I can't imagine. I — I can offer you no explanatory theory whatsoever.

SHER: (*DISAPPOINTED*) That's too bad ... I kinda counted on you.

JAF: Have — have they found the victim?

SHER: Yeah.

JAF: (*PAUSE*) Dead?

SHER: Crushed up like an eggshell.

JAF: (*AN ANGUISHED MURMUR*) I'm so sorry.

SHER: (*PAUSE ... TENSE & THINKING*) The thing CAN'T be a white, hairless gorilla ... there ain't no such thing! It's gotta be a MAN who looks and acts like a gorilla.

CASEY: I've seen lots of guys who looked and acted like gorillas, Sheriff, but none of em resembled the Thing we saw tonight It — well, it's something you might dream about after eating cold lobster, welsh rarebit, pickles and ice cream at one sitting ... you shouldn't see it when you're wide awake, as Ann and I did.

ANN: The only word that describes it, Sheriff, is — "monster."

SHER: Like them outlandish critters y' see sometimes in the movies ... them things that mad doctors make?

ANN: Yes ... a mad surgeon — in the movies — might have turned out the thing we saw.

SHER: (*PAUSE ... QUIETLY CASUAL*) Surgeons in real life can't make monsters, can they, Doc?

JAF: I have never known one who turned his knowledge to such an ignoble end, Sheriff. (*SLIGHT PAUSE*) I — I regret that I can be of no assistance to you. It's very late ... if you'll excuse me, I shall return home.

SHER: Sure, Doc.

JAF: Goodnight, Miss Williams.

ANN: Goodnight, Doctor.

JAF: Casey, I shall look forward to seeing you tomorrow ... will you join me at lunch —?

CASEY: Swell ... and I'll FIND your place tomorrow!

JAF: Uh — we'll dine here in town ... at the Palace Hotel. I'll meet you there at noon.

CASEY: (*PUZZLED & HURT*) Oh ... okay.

JAF: Goodnight, my boy.

CASEY: Goodnight.

JAF:	Goodnight, Sheriff —
SHER:	Just a second, Doc! Mr. Casey — you and Miss Williams haven't made any arrangements for rooms in the hotel yet, have y'?
CASEY:	No . . . We figured we might go back to the city on the one A.M. train. But there's no chance of that now.
SHER:	None at all . . . I'm keepin' you both here as material witnesses. My wife'll be glad to take care of Miss Williams in our spare room and, as you're such an old friend of the Doc's, he'll prob'ly wanta keep you at his house.
JAF:	(*A TRACE OF PANIC*) I'd love too have Casey at my house, Sheriff, but he wouldn't be comfortable . . . I live alone, Casey; the place is terribly untidy and — I'm sure you can still make arrangements at the hotel for tonight.
CASEY:	(*HURT . . . RATHER BRUSQUE*) Yeah . . . I'm sure I can.
JAF:	Now I — MUST run along. (*SLIGHT FADE*) Lunch, my boy — at the Palace, tomorrow at noon. (*) Goodnight all.
SOUND:	DOOR OPENED AT * ABOVE. CLOSE AT * BELOW
OMNES:	(*MURMURED*) Goodnight. (*)
SHER:	(*PAUSE . . . QUIETLY*) Hmm . . . looks like not even you are wanted in that house of Doc Jaffers', Mr. Casey.
ANN:	That's the old friend you wanted to surprise, Casey . . . guess he's surprised you.
CASEY:	(*PUZZLED & UNCOMFORTABLE*) Doc seemed terribly upset . . . there's some worry in his mind.
SHER:	I'm gonna find out what that worry is . . . and what's in that house he wants no one inside of.
CASEY:	What —?
SHER:	He gave me a <u>perty evasive answer</u> when I asked him if real-life surgeons could make monsters . . . and then he made a quick excuse to get outa here.
CASEY:	Sheriff, you don't seriously think —???
SHER:	I'm not sure yet what I think . . . but I've been connectin' up a lot of things. Them women who saw the monster last night saw it in the same vicinity you did . . . maybe they saw it in the self-same spot. And you say the house ye stopped in front of was surrounded by trees, had broken fence rails and that there was a big granite rock at the roadside. It's just occurred to me that that description fits Doc Jaffers' place . . . which is in a section where there's <u>red clay mud.</u>

MUSIC: BRIDGE

* * *

CASEY: (*VERY IRRITABLE*) What we're doing this morning is crazy, Sheriff. How can you believe a guy like Doc Jaffers is connected with that ape-thing??

SHER: I ain't believin' anything yet, Mr. Casey — I'm only investigatin'. Hank, you get the care we came here in well hidden?

HANK: (*A RURAL DEPUTY... FADING ON*) No one can see it from the house or from the road, Sheriff.

SHER: Then let's start walkin'. . . and everyone keep outa sight behind this line of trees.

CASEY: I don't know what you hope to gain by this.

SHER: If you and Miss Williams recognize the front of Doc's house as bein' the spot where you saw that monster, I may gain somethin'.

CASEY: What? — its victim's body wasn't found here!

SHER: I'll have located the starting point of a killing... that's somethin', ain't it?

ANN: Casey knows it's plenty, Sheriff... he simply won't let himself have any suspicion of Dr. Jaffers.

CASEY: (*ANGRILY*) What CAN I suspect, Ann... that Doc's a second Frankenstein, as Sheriff Frost hinted last night?? You've seen too many Boris Karloff movies, Sheriff.

SHER: (*CALMLY*) Maybe I have, young fella... but I've also read a few hist'ry books in my time, too. Haven't you ever heard that, only a couple hundred years ago, some surgeons made a regular business of turning normal people and normal animals into freaks?

CASEY: Humph.

SHER: And they tell me surgeons now know quite a little more than surgeons did then.

CASEY: Doc Jaffers spent most of his life making sick people well and crazy people sane, Sheriff... if ANY surgeon could create the bad dream we saw last night, it wouldn't be him.

ANN: It's been years since you've really known him, Casey.

CASEY: Don't start that again, Ann! — his kind of guy doesn't change.

ANN: I hope you're right.

SHER: (*PAUSE... LOW & CAUTIOUS NOW*) You can get a good view of the house from here, Miss Williams, and the busted fence and rock in front. Think it's the place you stopped last night?

ANN:	(*PAUSE*) Yes . . . definitely. I remember that rock.
SHER:	Mr. Casey?
CASEY:	(*RELUCTANTLY*) I — the rock and that fence looks like . . . what I recall.
SHER:	Doc said he'd meet you in town for noon lunch — it's about time he left here to keep that 'pointment. When he does, we'll step out in the open and look closer.
HANK:	(*LOW*) Doc's comin' outa the house now, Sheriff.
SHER:	I see. (*PAUSE*) and lockin' his door good and tight . . . few folks 'round here ever bother to lock a door.
CASEY:	He's different . . . and so what??
ANN:	Keep quiet, Casey.
CASEY:	(*GRUMBLES*) Okay.
HANK:	He's gettign' inta his car now.
SOUND:	CAR STARTED DURING FOLLOWING SPEECH ** DISTANT. AT * IT APPROACHES & FADES OUT
SHER:	Everybody keep outa sight 'til he drives out and around the bend in the road.
HANK:	Here he comes. (*)
SHER:	(*LONG PAUSE*) He's turned the bend. Come on, Miss Williams and Mr. Casey . . . show me exactly where you saw that Thing last night.
ANN:	First, it ran in front of our headlights from over there . . . and through that break in the fence — that's where it went after Herb.
SHER:	(*SLIGHT FADE*) It was off the hard road and in the soft mud most of the time, then . . . look for its bare foot tracks, fellers.
CASEY:	Why didn't you look for prints where you found Herb's body and trace the thing from there?
SHER:	(*PATIENTLY*) We looked there, Mr. Casey, but it's all rock where the body was discovered — there weren't any prints showin'.
HANK:	None here, either, Sheriff.
SHER:	Don't see any. (*PAUSE*) Hmm . . . see somethin' else, though — looks as if someone had smoothed off this ground since last night's rain with a shovel and a rake. See the marks, Mr. Casey?
CASEY:	(*GRUDGINGLY*) Yeah.
SHER:	Think the man who lives here might done it?
CASEY:	Not necessarily. He CAN'T have any connection with that Thing!
SOUND:	THE GIBBERING SNARLS — <u>VERY</u> DISTANT & MUFFLED . . . HOLD UNDER

ANN:	Casey —!
SHER:	What's that??
CASEY:	It — it's that gibbering, snarling sound, Ann.
ANN:	The sounds that monster made last night! — only it's far away now . . . and muffled.
SHER:	It's muffled 'cause the Thing is inside Doc Jaffers' house.
ANN:	He's right, Casey.
CASEY:	(*BEATEN*) Yes. I — I'm afraid he's right.
SHER:	Come on, you deppities — we're gonna bust inta that house. (*HALF FADE*) Have yer guns ready . . . we saw what it did to Herb.
CASEY:	(*MISERABLY*) You stay here, Ann . . . I've got to see —
ANN:	I'm going with you.
SHER:	(*FADING ON*) Them sounds seem to come from under the ground here. Hank, we'll bust in that cellar door . . . give it the axe.
SOUND:	A BLOW OF AXE ON HEAVY WOOD. AT * SEVERAL BLOWS ON WOOD & METAL . . . THE METAL SNAPS AND HEAVY DOOR FLIES OPEN . . . BRING IN GIBBERING SNARLS OFF BUT UNMUFFLED. FADE THEM ON FULL AT **
HANK:	It's solid oak, Sheriff _
SHER:	Don't hit the wood, y' chump — hit the LOCK! (*) that's got it! Hear that noise now, Casey?? — it's good and clear!
CASEY:	I hear it.
SHER:	Come on down and we'll see what makes it —
ANN:	It's dark as pitch down there —
SHER:	I brought a flashlight — here! Now we're all set.
SOUND:	FOOTSTEPS DESCEND STONE STEPS
HANK:	Them bars, Sheriff —!
CASEY:	A big cage —!
SHER:	A wild animal cage!
ANN:	The thing's inside it . . . there, in the far corner !! (**)
SHER:	So THAT'S the ape-thing!
CASEY:	(*BEATEN*) That's it.
HANK:	I can't believe it's real.
SHER:	It's real enough . . . and, from its looks, it'd like to come through them bars and at us.
HANK:	I hope them bars are good and strong.
ANN:	I don't see any lock on the cage door.

SHER:	It's one of them automatic doors that's locked by a lever outside.
HANK:	(*SLIGHT FADE*) Yeah . . . that is the lever right here — (*A CRY*)
SHER:	Hank —!!
CASEY:	The Thing reached through the bars and grabbed him!!!
HANK:	(*TERRIFIED*) It's pullin' me, Sheriff!!
SHER:	(*BIG*) And you're holdin' onta that level — you're pullin' IT!
SOUND:	CAGE DOOR CLANGS OPEN. A SNARLING ROAR OF TRIUMPH
CASEY:	The door's opened!!!
ANN:	(*BIG*) The Thing's coming out!!
HANK:	Shoot it, Sheriff!!!
SHER:	It knocked the flashlight from my hand . . . I CAN'T SEE!!
ANN:	SCREAMS
CASEY:	Ann —???
ANN:	(*STRUGGLING . . . FADING*) Help me, Casey . . . HELP **!!
CASEY:	It's GOT ANN!!
HANK:	It's goin' upstairs . . . I can see it now against the open door!!
CASEY:	You've got guns . . . shoot before it crushes her —!!
SOUND:	THREE HEAVY SHOTS . . . AND ANIMAL CRY OF PAIN. HEAVY BODY FALL *
CASEY:	You got the Thing . . . it's let her go!! (*)
HANK:	It's fallin' down the stairs!!
ANN:	(*A SOB*) Oh, Casey —!
CASEY:	Are you okay, kid . . . are you —??
ANN:	Yes . . . but hold onto me!
HANK:	You got the monster right between the eyes, Sheriff!
SHER:	I — I didn't get it . . . I didn't shoot!
CASEY:	You didn't shoot???
SHER:	No . . . I was afraid of hittin' the girl!
CASEY:	Who DID shoot???
JAF:	(*OFF . . . QUIETLY*) I did, Casey.
OMNES:	Doc Jaffers???
JAF:	(*SLOW FADE ON*) A — a premonition brought me back here after I'd started away . . . fortunately, I arrived in time to use this gun.
SHER:	What is this Thing you shot, Doctor . . . this thing you keep in a cage?
JAF:	That "Thing," Sheriff, is . . . my son.
OMNES:	Your <u>son</u>??

JAF:	(*SIMPLY ... NO PATHOS*) Yes. As you know, Casey, my — my wife left me a child when she died. You — and nobody — knew that the child lived and that it was a — monster. (*PAUSE*) Usually, frightfully malformed infants don't survive ... I made mine survive ... because it was all I had to care for. I brought him to this out of the way place where he — and I — could live unmolested, I thought. But his mind was as animal-like as his body ... as he grew strong, I was forced to confine him in that — cage. Two nights ago, in the first moment of forgetfulness I have had concerning him since his birth, I did not properly secure his prison and he escaped. You know the results. Last night, just before the Sheriff phoned me, I found my — my son and brought him back here. Now ... I have prevented him from ever causing further harm. (*VERY SOFTLY*) But a father must not kill his child and live himself.
CASEY:	(*ALARM*) Dr. Jaffers —!!
SHER:	Get that gun!!
SOUND:	A SINGLE PISTOL SHOT
ANN:	Oh —h —
SHER:	(*SOFTLY*) He's shot himself.
CASEY:	(*VERY SOFTLY*) Oh, Doc — what a guy you were ... what a guy.
MUSIC:	BRIDGE

* THE END *

---

* Cole's original copy of this script did not contain a Closing segment. See the Closing added to the end of the first script earlier in this chapter.

10
Casey at Alfred A. Knopf

The *Black Mask* Years

When George Harmon Coxe wrote his first novel about Casey, *Silent Are the Dead*, in 1941, he had already had nine novels published by Alfred A. Knopf. Six of them were about photographer Kent Murdock, two were about Max Hale and the last one, *No Time to Kill*, was not part of a series. So, Coxe was no novice at writing novels and *Silent Are the Dead* was not just a long short story about Casey, but also a complex crime novel.

Prior to its publication by Knopf in 1942, *Silent Are the Dead* had appeared as a three-part serial in *Black Mask*, and that appears to have been editor Ken White's idea. Coxe wrote it as a book and showed it to White who decided it should do double duty and appear in the magazine as well. It appeared in the September, October and November 1941 issues under the title "Killers Are Camera Shy." It should be noted this was not Coxe's original title. The title under which the book was published in 1942 came from a statement made by ex-newsman Jim Bishop and repeated by Casey in the denouement, that "only the dead are silent."

The magazine installments were divided into 18 chapters and given imaginative titles, the first five being "Endicott Skips Bail," "Casey Takes a Chance," "Checkmate," "A Quiet Evening," and "Slay-Ride." Some of these titles were apparently intended to be ironic: the first one referred to the fact that Stanford Endicott was the first murder victim. The final chapter was "Casey Gets the Picture," referring to his discovery of the identity of the killer as well as his taking pictures for the *Express*.

It wasn't Coxe's practice to give titles to the chapters in his books, so when Knopf published it in hardcover the following year it was divided into 24 chapters without titles. Later, when Dell reprinted it in paper covers, the 24 chapters were assigned new titles. Those first five were now: "The Camera Eye," "Heading for Trouble," "Close-up of a Corpse," "Casey gets Cooled Off," and "Pure Dynamite." The final chapter was "Only the Dead Are Silent."

Dell routinely added chapter titles to most of their books published before 1952, usually without the authors' knowledge. The publisher also abridged the texts, again usually without the authors' knowledge. The second or third page of most mysteries would be headed "Things This Mystery is About" or "What This Mystery is About." There were also character lists, their descriptions often taken verbatim from the books.

The description of Casey in the Dell edition of *Silent Are the Dead* read: "Flash Casey, powerful ace cameraman for the *Express* is outwardly hard and cynical, but he has a peculiar sentimental streak about his profession. The police trust him because they know he is out to get pictures and not to solve cases."

Despite some minor textual differences among the three versions: serial, hardcover book and paperback reprint, the story was the same. With its classic opening scene in the corridor outside the courtroom where five news-photographers were waiting for the announcement of the arraignment of Stanford Endicott, former Assistant District Attorney, for receiving stolen property, it echoed at least two other opening scenes in the fiction of journalism.

One was the vigil kept by the reporters in the opening scene of the 1928 drama *The Front Page*. The other was the opening chapter of Coxe's own 1935 novel, *Murder with Pictures*, with the newsmen waiting outside the courtroom for the verdict on Nate Girard's trial for murder. Among them was a young photographer named Kent Murdock.

The solution arrived at in *Silent Are the Dead* was not everything Casey wanted. In fact, the conclusion had a depressing effect on him and left him with a feeling of loneliness that only a little drinking could assuage. He expected a phone call that would end one of his relationships, but hoped he could get some sleep and wouldn't get that call until morning, so he put a silencer on the phone's bell.

Reviews were favorable. Isaac Anderson in the *New York Times Book Review* summarized the plot in a few sentences without giving away the solution. "The police reach one solution of the mystery, and Casey reaches another which he keeps to himself for reasons which become apparent before the last chapter is ended. It is an exciting, rapid-fire story of the sort for which George Harmon Coxe is well known." The anonymous reviewer in "The Criminal Record" column in *The Saturday Review of Literature* was more succinct. "Well worked out plot convincingly written and packed with action. Casey the news photographer is excellent addition to tough 'tec ranks." Apparently the reviewer was not a reader of *Black Mask*.

The second Casey novel had much the same publishing history as the first. *Murder for Two* was also written as a book, but turned into a serial for *Black Mask*. Coxe's manuscript was given the title "Blood On the Lens" and published in the January, February and March 1943 issues. It was divided into 19 chapters this time with titles as imaginative as those for the first serial. The first five were "Tell It to the Major," "Girl Reporter," "Appointment with Death," "Murder Takes the Stage," and "Tell It to the D.A." The final chapter was "Casey keeps It Quiet."

When Knopf published it later that same year, the text was divided into 24 chapters without titles. In 1949, Dell published it as a paperback, added their own chapter titles and made some changes in the text. The first five Dell chapters were "Casey Takes on a Dame," "A Broken Appointment," "That Would Be Murder," "Logan Asks Questions," and "A Lady Takes a Picture." The final chapter in the Dell edition was "A Deal in Rewards."

The description of Casey in the list of characters in the Dell edition of *Murder for Two* read: "Flash Casey, more than six feet of bone and muscle, plus brains, is the number-one cameraman for the *Express*. Underneath a shell of cynicism he has a wide sentimental streak for his profession—and for people who get pushed around."

The opening chapter of *Murder for Two* reflected the period in which it was written. Casey had gone to the Army recruitment center to enlist only to be turned down because he was "a little over thirty-five and had a trick knee that had been operated on three times." His colleagues at the *Express*, Wade and Finell, thought he could do better at home than overseas and would now have more time to teach photography to the young ladies of the American Women's Voluntary Services.

The differences between the texts of the three versions: serial, hardcover book and paperback were slight, principally in making it clear that this was a wartime story, but a few paragraphs were cut from the Dell edition. Those three versions exhibit some interesting variations in the final paragraphs. After winding up the case it was decided that Casey was eligible for the reward, something he didn't want. In his conversation with Logan he agreed to give some of it to the two cops who saved his bacon and the rest to the U.S.O. or the Army and Navy relief.

All three versions included the next scene as Casey began to examine the two pictures he had taken that morning, but which the engraver had cropped a little too much for his taste in making the layout in the paper.

The Knopf edition, which represented Coxe's original manuscript ended with the following three paragraphs:

> "To hell with it," he said softly. "It's still a lousy job."
>
> But by the time he reached the hall he knew he was lying. Taking pictures for a big city newspaper might be a headache, but for him it was the only job in the world and there was no other that could compare with it.
>
> Unless, he thought, those monkeys down at the recruiting station change their minds some day and give me a break.

The copy editor at Knopf set that final sentence in italics (except for the words "he thought") to give it more emphasis.

When *Black Mask* published the serial the editor cut the last two paragraphs, ending the story with Casey's down beat observation about what a lousy job he had.

And when Dell was working with the Knopf edition for the 1949 reprint, World War II had been over for four years and someone may have thought it sounded dated to refer once again to Casey's attempt to enlist in the Army, so the final sentence was cut. In fact, that final sentence made a perfectly good ending to the story.

In his review for the *New York Times Book Review* Isaac Anderson considered "Casey's best asset is neither his strength nor his toughness, but his ability to put two and two together and get the right answer. He uses strong-arm methods when they are necessary, as they frequently are, but he uses his head even more effectively. 'Murder for Two' deserves a high rating for puzzlement and for its sizzling narrative style." The reviewer in *The Saturday Review of Literature* concluded that the novel was "impeccably plotted, tersely and effectively told, believably characterized—with wind-up that boosts the blood-pressure."

How did the first two novels differ from the short stories and novelettes that preceded them? The plots were more complex and contained more incidents, there was room for the characters to reflect on their situations and there were more characters to keep track of. Coxe took Casey out of the newsroom and turned him loose in the city. He had only the briefest of encounters with his colleagues of the fourth estate. Tom Wade became an extra in the cast and Blaine was never mentioned. The city editor was replaced by managing editor MacGrath who was not nearly as colorful a character as Blaine. Only Lieutenant Logan remained constant, but even he wasn't described in detail, as he had been in the stories in *Black Mask*. However, he could still be depended on to come through a door with a gun in the nick of time.

Hardcover Cameraman

Casey Goes to Alfred A. Knopf

Casey "Pastiche" from Bell Publishing

The Revival Novels

Nearly twenty years later, Coxe returned to writing about Casey. As far as can be determined, there was no public explanation for the revival of the character. Perhaps letters from fans and comments from friends contained the suggestion they would like to read a new Casey story and Coxe obliged. The first result was *Error of Judgment*, published by Knopf in 1961. Unlike the first two Casey novels, the new book had no previous appearance as a magazine serial. Time had obviously passed for Casey since his earlier adventures, but he retained much of his old vigor. He was still the same burly, deep-chested man, only his hair had more silver in it and he kept forgetting to go to the barber until his colleagues at the *Express* needled him into it.

Casey's temper was not as short as in the old days, but things could happen that made him angry or resentful. He no longer answered to the name "Flash," although old-timers like Solly who ran the hole-in-the-wall shop next to the sandwich shop still called him by his old nickname. Most people called him Jack, or Casey, or even Mr. Casey, but it was usually only the young people with good manners who called him the latter.

The title of the novel was taken from Casey's belief that Jerry Burton was drunk so he left him alone to sleep it off, at which the unlucky Burton got up and walked out and got himself killed. Logan called it just an error of judgment and he seemed to know what he was talking about.

Logan had worked with the photographer so long he considered him one of his best friends, in spite of the numerous arguments they had had over the years. Logan thought he knew what made Casey tick and he remembered the old days well. He even remembered the old radio program that was supposed to have been based on Casey and his experiences. According to Logan's memory, a writer friend of Casey's had come up with the idea for a radio series about a newspaper photographer. He got Casey to agree to the program's using his real name and promised him some sort of royalty for the use of his name.

Crime Photographer, the radio show, had been an unexpected success, which had its advantages and disadvantages. The boys at the *Express* had kidded Casey about the show and even though Casey argued that the actor on the radio wasn't anything like him, the needling took a long time to die down. Once people took the show for granted, it did something for the photographer's reputation and those royalties, when they started coming in, provided him with a nest egg for his retirement.

Reviews of *Error of Judgment* were favorable and at least one of them referred to the revival of the character in glowing terms. Anthony Boucher's "Criminals at Large" column in the *New York Times Book Review* called the denouement "inimitably well constructed." Other reviews by James Sandoe in the *New York Herald Tribune* and Lenore Glen Offord in the *San Francisco Chronicle* were equally positive while Sergeant Cuff in the *Saturday Review* summed it up as "nice going, with crash finish."

Sales of the book were enough for Pyramid to add it to their line of Coxe paperback reprints six years later, though the publisher changed the title to the more vivid *One Murder Too Many*.

Encouraged by the reception of *Error of Judgment*, Coxe set to work to write another Casey novel, and *The Man Who Died Too Soon* appeared from Knopf in the spring of 1962. As with the first book, this one had no magazine publication beforehand.

The second book was largely a continuation of the pattern established by *Error of Judgment*. There were some additional pieces of lore about Casey's past, perhaps the most interesting was an explanation of the origin of his nickname. According to the new account, as a young man Casey had used too much magnesium powder in his flash-pan and had almost set a room on fire. Someone nicknamed him "Flash" as a result and the name stuck, shaken off only in later years when he was called Jack or Mr. Casey. In a reflective mood, Logan once again remembered the old radio show, supposedly based on Casey's exploits, but there was a new revelation: Casey had written a letter to the radio show's originator in which he complained that the radio character bore little resemblance to the real Casey.

The Man Who Died Too Soon contained two examples of Coxe's sense of humor: the story of Keeler's using a ferrotype to fry hamburgers (to the dismay of the photographer who tried to dry his prints on it later) and the character of Sam Delemater, a private detective and avid race track devotee.

Once again, Anthony Boucher gave Coxe a warm review in a section of his "Criminals at Large" column in the *New York Times Book Review* he called "New Adventures for Old-Pro Detectives." Boucher found the new novel "Coxe's tightest and strongest story in over three years, a model specimen of the medium-boiled action-whodunit." James Sandoe in the *New York Herald Tribune* thought that Coxe "keeps us concerned with and for Casey and does even better by a middle-aged private eye name of Sam Delemater, a dependable guy to have around." Sandoe thought the book was "ship-shape and speedy." Both Lenore Glen Offord in the *San Francisco Chronicle* and Sergeant Cuff in the *Saturday Review* wrote positive reviews.

Coxe published his last magazine fiction in the 1960s: a short story, "A Neat and Tidy Job," for *Ellery Queen's Mystery Magazine* in 1960 and two novelettes for *Cosmopolitan*. The first was "The Barbados Beach House" in

Cosmopolitan in 1961, the basis for the novel *Moment of Violence* the same year. His final story of all for a magazine was "The Girl in the Melody Lounge" which appeared in *Cosmopolitan* in 1963. *Cosmopolitan* had never been an important market for him and in a 1971 conversation with this writer he reflected that when the magazine changed its editorial policy in later years, he could no longer imagine what sort of story the editors might want.

"The Girl in the Melody Lounge" was a Casey story and Coxe's last Casey story as well. It was a fitting end for the cycle: as it was nearly thirty years since Casey had made his first appearance in a magazine, it was appropriate that his final magazine story should be about Casey. The next year, Alfred A. Knopf published a longer version of the story under the title *Deadly Image*.

The new novel was the same mixture as before with its story of incriminating photos that led to two murders. The novel included characters and subplots that weren't in the magazine version, such as the one involving mobster Tony Saxton. The novel didn't mention Casey's old nickname of "Flash" at all, as though time had moved on and there was no one to remember him by that name. There was only one oblique reference to the radio show when Casey paid a second visit to the Melody Lounge where he "listened to Duke Baker's easy piano, appreciating the good left hand and the occasional inverted tenths with the right hand that reminded him somehow of Herman Chittison."

The references to music and the appearance of band-leader Ralph Jackson as an important character were perhaps the closest Coxe ever came to writing a mystery with a jazz theme, something some critics occasionally suggested he ought to try.

The novels about Casey were all well received, with perhaps a hint of nostalgia from more than one reviewer. Anthony Boucher may have erred in his column by referring to *Deadly Image* as having been serialized, but he was on target when he wrote "the ingredients may be familiar, but they are deftly and assuredly mixed, with precisely the right amount of fresh variations on standard themes."

In the final trio of novels Casey was moved farther than ever from the old-time newspaper milieu and closer to the society he was covering for the *Express*. With the exception of private detective Sam Delemater, the usual rich supporting vast was reduced to Logan and Manahan with a brief reference to managing editor MacGrath. By now, the boisterous days of *Black Mask* were behind him, he had aged some, and was more mellow. Now, after a case, he felt at home in a piano bar, enjoying a good meal followed by a bourbon and water, listening to a rendition of "Memories of You."

Casey at Alfred A. Knopf 159

George Harmon Coxe's final magazine fiction becomes his last Casey novel.

The Pastiche

About 1949, someone in the offices of CBS had an idea for promoting the property of *Casey, Crime Photographer* which involved merchandising the title and characters and having them appear in media other than radio. Among the results were a series of comic books and a stage play, both of which are covered in other chapters in this book.

Another example was a pastiche using the characters and concept from the radio show, but not written by George Harmon Coxe. By 1971, in an interview conducted by this writer, Coxe no longer remembered whose idea it was to write and publish the book, but he felt it was probably someone at CBS. The book, *Dead Heat,* was copyrighted both by CBS and George Harmon Coxe and published by Bell of Drexel Hill, Pennsylvania. Today, such a publication might be referred to as a "novelization" or a "media tie-in" and published in paper covers.

As it was, the novel, which took its title from its racing theme, was published in hardcover, the only Casey novel not published by Knopf. It was a smoothly written work by 34-year-old Edward S. Aarons, writing under the pen name of Paul Ayres, apparently the only time he used that name. In later years, Aarons was known as the author of the long running Sam Durell paperback thrillers.

Perhaps "pastiche" is the wrong term for this novel, for no one familiar with either the Casey stories or with any of George Harmon Coxe's other works would ever mistake this novel for any part of the original saga. For one thing, it began with scenes involving other characters, including the man who would be the murder victim. Coxe almost always began a Casey story with a scene in which the photographer was the prominent figure. The use of such regular secondary characters as reporter Ann Williams and Blue Note bartender Ethelbert, as well as homicide detective Captain Logan, made it clear this was based on the radio show. However, none of these characters was given as prominent a role in the novel as they had been given in the radio show. In structure, it was as though a radio script had been expanded until it resembled a book length narrative.

Some questions arise, among them: did Aarons have access to any of the scripts to use for ideas? The answer is in the affirmative. The racetrack setting and many of the characters were based on "Pick-Up," written by Alonzo Deen Cole and broadcast on May 22, 1947. Then the clue of the two pictures, one of an open window and the other of a closed window, resembled an idea from an early Casey radio show. In addition, the sub-plot dealing with young Alan Forster, aspiring news photographer, resembled the plot of a 1935 *Black* Mask story, "Mr. Casey Flashguns Murder." While the overall plot of the novel moved quickly, with an element of excitement, many of the characters seemed flat as though they needed actors' voices to bring them to life.

From the way the novel was described on the jacket, *Dead Heat* was probably planned as the first of a series in the "Crime Photographer" series, but its success was not such that it merited even a sequel. It was another decade before the real Casey would appear again.

Of the six Casey novels described above, the first two were definitely the best, but the three revival novels from the 1960s were pleasant additions to the chronicles in which the author bid a fond farewell to a pulp icon who had helped him on the first rungs of the ladder to success in the world of crime fiction.

The Casey Novels

Silent Are the Dead

Alfred A. Knopf, 1942. Reprinted, Dell Publishing Co., 1948. (Dell mapback #225) Dedicated to Brewster Morgan. Originally published as "Killers Are Camera Shy" in *Black Mask*, September–November 1941.

Casey and society photographer Perry Austin find notorious attorney Stanford Endicott murdered in his own office. Casey manages to get a picture of the killer as well as a picture of a girl who had called on the dead man. When Lieutenant Logan joins the investigation, Casey explains what he knows and Logan begins to question people with connections to the dead man. Among these are Harry Nye, a private detective working for Endicott and the dead man's widow, Louise Endicott.

Others who come under scrutiny by the authorities are Lyda Hoyt, niece of Jim Bishop, former desk man on the *Express*, and Bernie Dixon, one-time racketeer and now owner of the swank Club Berkeley.

When Perry Austin is found murdered in his apartment, a new character is added to the mix: Nancy Jamison, a socialite whose brother Austin has been blackmailing over some incriminating photos. For the sake of the *Express*, Casey decides to keep Austin's criminal tendencies a secret.

Meanwhile, Logan's investigation of Harry Nye for handling stolen bonds and jewelry ends when Nye is found murdered. Casey continues to see what he can learn about Bernie Dixon, even to the extent of picking the lock to Dixon's apartment to learn what he can about the club owner's relationship to Louise Endicott. Casey and Logan compare notes and the photographer shows him a picture. Then Casey goes off to confront the person he suspects of being the killer, hoping that Logan will arrive in the nick of time the way he always did.

Murder for Two

Alfred A. Knopf, 1943. Reprinted, Dell, 1949 (Dell mapback #276). Dedicated to George III. Originally published as "Blood on the Lens" in *Black Mask,* January–March 1943.

After trying to enlist in the Army and being rejected, Casey is sent to interview Rosalind Taylor, crusading reporter. Rosalind plans to expose Matt Lawson who is promoting a new plastics formula he just may have stolen from young chemist John Perry. With Casey is Karen Harding, a student in the American Women's Voluntary Services photography class he has been teaching. Karen, it turns out, used to be engaged to Perry. Rosalind wants Casey to meet her at Perry's and accompany her to talk to her secretary, Helen MacKay, who was once Lawson's secretary as well, on the chance she will have evidence against the promoter. When Rosalind fails to make the appointment, Casey and Karen go to her apartment where they find Helen MacKay tied up.

Shortly afterwards, Rosalind's husband, Russell Gifford, arrives followed by two homicide detectives, Lt. Logan and Sgt. Manahan. The detectives tell them that Rosalind has been found in her car, shot in the back of the head. Further investigation reveals that Gifford and his wife were separated but his wife had refused to give him a divorce, that Gifford wants to marry Dinah King, a singer at the Club 17 with whom Rosalind Taylor had quarreled, that Helen MacKay is engaged to Rosalind's first husband, and that Rosalind owned a gun that was the same caliber as the murder weapon.

The case becomes even more complicated when it is discovered Karen has taken some revealing photographs and the gunmen who come after them find Casey in the way and knock him unconscious. Then there is the folder with evidence that Dinah King is in the country illegally. The local papers offer $5,000 reward for Rosalind's killer. Then Lawson's former secretary Henry Byrkman (alias Henry Byrnes) is found murdered and a lawyer named Morris Loeb is shot in his own office.

A mysterious envelope containing documents that prove Perry was to receive royalties for his plastics formula turns up. Casey is determined to uncover the whole story behind the murders and goes to Rosalind Taylor's apartment for some further investigation. There he finds the killer waiting for him and learns how murder for one became murder for two.

Error of Judgment
Alfred A, Knopf, 1961. Reprinted as *One Murder Too Many*, Pyramid Books, 1967 (R-1653). Dedicated to Wes Pullen.

Frank Ackerly is a shyster lawyer who offers Casey $50 for taking a photo of a business transaction on a downtown street corner. The job involves recording an exchange of manila envelopes between Ackerly and gambler Tony Calenda. Casey stops in a bar near his apartment where he encounters Jerry Burton an ex-newsman who is described as "adequate but not particularly ambitious." Burton has been drinking heavily and is suspected of carrying a gun in his coat pocket. Casey takes Burton home to his place and gives him enough to drink so that he falls asleep, but not before he learns that Burton's alcoholic wife has been seeing a psychiatrist under the delusion that he is a marriage counselor. Now someone has been blackmailing her over her private confessions to the psychiatrist, which have been recorded without her knowledge.

When Burton passes out, Casey finds his revolver and unloads it, then leaves the apartment to get something to eat. When he returns, Burton has gone, leaving a note confessing he was only pretending to have drunk enough to make him pass out. When next Casey sees Jerry Burton, the ex-newsman is dead in the front seat of a car and Casey knows the appointment he had kept was with his killer.

The characters and suspects are many: Max Decker, man Friday for Ackerly and a disbarred attorney; Betty Jarvis, free lance writer who once worked in the society department of the *Express*; George Needham, Betty's fiance; Alice Burton, Jerry's widow; Dr. Horvath, the psychiatrist who had been treating Mrs. Burton; Horvath's secretary Helen Tyler; John McCabe, a former bootlegger who now runs an electronics company; Brenda McCabe who poses as a "Mrs. Hanson" when she is in Dr. Horvath's office.

It is up to Casey to identify the person making recordings of confidential conversations in the psychiatrist's office and to sort everything out as only he can, but at the denouement still allow Logan to arrive in time to hear the killer's confession.

The Man Who Died Too Soon
Alfred A. Knopf, 1962. Dedicated to Ken Marks.

Casey has a wealth of sources so he is one of the first to hear of Johnny Keeler's illness and is on hand to realize the photographer has had a stroke. When Keeler dies, Casey learns he is not only one of the pallbearers at the funeral, but he is also in Keeler's will.

At the reading of the will, Casey is made executor of part of Keeler's estate: his collection of cameras and equipment, of which he is responsible for disposing, and two metal boxes of negatives and plates, which Keeler could never bring himself to destroy. The bulk of the estate goes to Alma Jensen, Keeler's companion, while Keeler's daughter, Sheila Garrett, receives a life trust. It appears that Keeler didn't approve of either his daughter or the man she married.

Word comes through Julius Levy, Keeler's lawyer, that someone has offered $5,000 for the two boxes of films. A letter from Keeler, written before his death, but addressed to Casey and delivered *post-mortem* suggests there are things on some of the films that certain people would like to have suppressed.

Casey goes to the Melody Club after dinner and encounters Fay Novak, a woman who supports herself as waitress, barmaid and hostess and is on the run from someone. Casey gives her some advice and puts her in a cab home. He then hears a police radio signal that directs him to a ransacked office and the body of Clem Alpert, a private detective who is also Fay Novak's former husband.

Logan and Manahan arrive and the investigation gets under way. Casey goes home to his apartment where he encounters two men looking for the films that Keeler willed to him. For once he lies and tells them he left the films in lawyer Levy's office, but as they take Casey's own file box of photos and leave, he snaps a picture of them.

Keeler's funeral is well attended and Casey sees nearly everyone involved in the case. Keeler's daughter asks Casey for the films, for sentimental reasons, she claims, but the photographer refuses to give them up. He doesn't tell her he has already retrieved the two boxes from Levy's office and put them in the storage area at his apartment.

Casey calls on private detective Sam Delemater, and after they spend a little time handicapping the horse races, he hires Sam to identify the two men who called on him, and retrieve his own photos, which they had taken from his apartment.

Casey calls on a trio of very important people: Congressman Frederick Babcock, broker Donald Caldwell and District Attorney T. J. Eagan. These are the people who have offered money for Keeler's film because some of the pictures show them at a party in their college days with a partly clad woman—a stripper hired by Johnny Keeler for the occasion. Even 20 years later, such a picture could be embarrassing to men of their station. For some reason, which he does not quite understand, Casey claims the film boxes are still in Levy's office. He leaves, feeling a little ashamed of himself for telling such a bald lie.

Casey looks for Logan, but he isn't in his office. He goes to Julius Levy's office and finds the lawyer with his head beaten in amid signs that someone was looking for something in the office. He talks with Logan when the detective arrives and then goes to see Alma Jensen. Something about the account of what happened the night Keeler died doesn't seem right to him. Meanwhile, Sam Delemater has found the men who took Casey's own box of photos and sets out to trail Fay Novak.

Eventually, the appropriate suspects are brought together, the incriminating photos are destroyed and the identity of the killer is revealed, and Casey makes a dinner date with Alma Jensen.

Deadly Image

Alfred A. Knopf, 1964. Reprinted, Pyramid Books, 1966 (R-1541). Dedicated to Bruce. Condensed version published as "The Girl in the Melody Lounge," *Cosmopolitan*, December 1963.

When Casey stops at the Melody Lounge for an after dinner drink and some music from Ralph Jackson's band he sees several people he knows. Among them are Donald Farrington and his wife, Shirley. As a partner in the brokerage firm of Farrington and Coe, he handles Casey's own account. Farrington is drinking more than usual. Another is Monty Bates, a freelance photographer, who has a tab with Casey at the bar running up to $70. During the course of the evening, Shirley Farrington asks Casey for a ride home.

The next morning two men call on Casey at his apartment: Donald Farrington and his brother-in-law Arthur Mayfield. Farrington has received an envelope by special delivery that contains three photos of himself in indiscrete poses with a blonde. If this is a form of blackmail, where is the note demanding money? The two men want Casey to sort things out and he suggests they hire private detective Sam Delemater to find the blonde. Casey then remembers there was another private detective, Earl Geiger, at the Melody Lounge the night before and decides he should go in search of him.

When Casey catches up with Geiger, their conversation gets nowhere so he goes to find Delemater. While Delemater has had no luck finding the blonde, there is evidence there may be more than the three photos that were sent to Farrington. Then Geiger is found dead and homicide, in the person of Lt. Logan, arrives.

Because Casey has found a check for $1,000, signed by Louise Mayfield, in Geiger's wallet, the photographer and Logan call on Louise Mayfield, the sister of Don Farrington and the wife of Arthur Mayfield. Mrs. Mayfield neatly evades their questions and they leave.

Casey then calls on Tom Quigley, the bartender at the Melody Lounge, to ask about the people who were there the same night he was. Mrs. Mayfield comes to his apartment to fill him in on some of the family background and they discuss possible suspects in the murders. Casey goes to police headquarters to see Logan and runs into Marty Bates on his way out. Casey calls on Farrington and Mayfield where he learns the blackmailer has made a demand. Casey then goes to see Marty Bates only to find Logan and Manahan there ahead of him because Bates has been found murdered. Casey and Logan call on Mrs. Bates to tell her that her husband is dead. After Logan leaves, she shows Casey two envelopes, both containing negatives, but one contains the negatives of the photos framing Don Farrington.

There are more conversations and more information about the characters in the drama comes to light. The denouement occurs at the Farrington home where the murderer is unmasked, but escapes, only to be found by the police—this time two airport cops. Casey leaves the Farrington home arm in arm with Sam Delemater on the way to sample the wares of three or four or five bars.

Dead Heat: A Crime Photographer Mystery
By Paul Ayres (Edward S. Aarons). Drexel Hill, PA: Bell Publishing Co., 1950. Copyrighted by Columbia Broadcasting System and George Harmon Coxe. (Based on "Pick-Up," broadcast May 22, 1947.)

Jockey Cass Marlin is in trouble. He is having trouble with Vera Ashley, who wants more of a relationship than he is prepared to allow. Even though she is engaged to socialite David Graham she is more than smitten with the jockey. Marlin needs to get away and drives off in the little roadster that Hugo Ashley, racehorse owner, gave him as a reward for riding Jackanapes to an upset victory. On the road he is aware of being followed by another car and he cracks up his roadster in an effort to escape. He emerges from the car unharmed, but now someone is after him with a gun. He manages to elude his pursuers, finds a phone and calls Casey at the *Morning Express*. He learns that Casey is away on assignment so he leaves a message that he wants to see him as soon as possible, but that he will call back. He takes refuge at the home of singer Edith Landal and tells her that someone wants to kill him.

When Casey does see Cass Marlin, it is at the racetrack and Marlin is dead, shot through the back of the head. A spent flash bulb near by tells the photographer that someone had actually taken a picture of the jockey just as he died.

Captain Logan arrives and begins his investigation of the murder. At first, there are those who think Casey must be implicated because he found the body. Then Britt Hutchins, the trainer for the Ashley stables, announces that he saw the murder being committed, but he didn't see the face of the killer.

Alan Forster, a young camera bug and aspiring news photographer who actually did take pictures of Marlin at the moment he was shot and as the body slumped to the ground, approaches Casey. Forster wants to sell his pictures to the *Express* and hopes that Casey can help him. Forster agrees to develop his film and meet Casey later at the *Express*.

Later, Forster tells Casey that someone from the *Globe* offered him $200 for his pictures. Casey takes him to see *Express* city editor, Hiram Burke, who offers him $100 and no more. Casey tells Forster to take the pictures to Curtis at the *Globe* and sell them for $200.

Edith Landal arranges to meet Casey at Gilligan's Bar where she offers to sell the story of Cass Marlin's murder along with the name of the killer to the *Express* for $10,000. When Casey refuses to accept the offer she finds an excuse to make a hasty exit through the cellar. Casey tries to follow and is slugged by someone who is handy with a two-by-four.

Meanwhile, Alan Forster has disappeared and someone has ransacked his personal darkroom looking for the negatives of the two pictures he took at the racetrack of Marlin's killing. It turns out that the offer of $200 was a phony and wasn't made by anyone at the *Globe* at all but by a pair of crooks. Casey may not have the negatives, but he does have a set of prints made from them and he can't see anything of significance about the killing in them.

Casey calls at the luxurious apartment of David Graham, but the only person he can see at first is Graham's great grandmother, the imperious Mrs. Amantha Worthington Graham. Then he finds the body of Edith Landal who had escaped by way of the cellar at Gilligan's after all. Captain Logan takes over the investigation of the new murder and the homicide department moves its equipment into the Graham house.

Casey finds the door to Edith Landal's house open, goes inside to search for clues to her murder and finds a recording of the conversation she had had with Cass Marlin when he called on her shortly before his death. Casey doesn't get very far with his investigation before someone slugs him from behind. When he wakes up he makes his way back to town.

The denouement is at the racetrack where the identity of the killer is revealed, Alan Forster is found safe and sound, and Logan arrives in time to make the arrest. The fadeout is at the Blue Note with Herman Chittison at the piano and Ethelbert at the bar buying Casey an ale to make up for not being able to give him a clue about whose activities he should have watched.

11
Casey on Television

Early CBS Television: 1931–1944

An early pioneer in television, CBS began broadcasting programs on July 21, 1931 when W2XAB (CBS, NY) aired the first regular seven day a week schedule in the country, offering viewers 28 hours per week of programming with live pick ups.

By 1932 there were estimated to be anywhere between 7,500 and 9,000 television receivers in the country.

On July 1, 1941, CBS changed its New York City call letters to WCBW, an identification that was to remain until November 1, 1946 when it was renamed WCBS.

While the advent of World War II brought what until then had been a steady growth in the new entertainment media to a crawl, by May 1944 the network resumed live programming and by the end of the war CBS was ready to renew its commitment to providing live television entertainment to the still small but gradually growing number of homes that owned receivers.

Crime Photographer: 1945

Although standard references have *Casey* making his debut on the home screen in 1951, the network actually introduced *Casey* to television audiences several years earlier, broadcasting four programs in late 1945.

Folks fortunate enough to own television receivers and live in the New York City metropolitan area were able to view the very first episode of *Crime Photographer* on Thursday, September 20, 1945 between 8:30 and 9:00pm EWT (Eastern War Time). The script, "Diary of Death," written by Charles Holden, manager of production at WCBW and adapted for television by Lela Swift, had been used earlier on an October 31, 1944 *Casey* radio broadcast.

Oliver Thorndike (1918–1954), was cast as Casey. A well known actor at the time, he appeared in *Little Foxes* and *Charlie's Aunt* on the stage and, under contract to Cecil B. DeMille in the movies, appeared in *The Story of Dr. Wassell* and *Unconquered*. To this day, Thorndike's alma mater, Yale University, honors a graduating actor "who best exemplifies the spirit of fellowship, cooperation and devotion to the theater" with an "Oliver Thorndike Acting Award."

Others in the cast were Ruth Ford as Ann Williams (falsely accused of a crime in this episode), John Gibson, repeating his radio role of Ethelbert, the Blue Note bartender, and Gregory Morton, Marilyn Erskine, Edith Tackna, Larry Frisch, Charles F. McClelland, and Bernard Hoffman. The production was directed by Frances Buss.

A review of *Casey's* debut in a New York City newspaper was decidedly mixed.[1] While the reviewer noted that television could play whodunits as well as radio, the writer warned against quickie adaptations of "airers" (radio programs) lest the video medium go to waste.

On a positive note, readers were told that the show had "earmarks of careful camera planning (which) showed up well in what otherwise might have been dull spots through constantly shifting camera and well-angled shots of no-action sets." Less complimentary, though, were the reviewer's observations that the "corny dialog betrayed little script-planning with a minimum of good writing, lack of exciting situations or suspense...Small talk at the beginning and end...was too long and had little to do with the main story and might just as well have been cut down or eliminated."

The review also expressed little enthusiasm for the acting which was described as "adequate with no one shining." The review concluded by calling attention to the program's novel ending which had all the actors taking a curtain call, clearly a practice not typical of television, even as early as 1945.

Three additional episodes of *Crime Photographer* are known to have been broadcast, one each in October, November and December, 1945. In the November and December broadcasts, Casey was played by Don Kohler, an actor about whom very little is known except that he later worked in Hollywood playing mostly uncredited roles from 1948–1956. Other cast changes included Shirley O'Hara taking over the role of Ann Williams and Harold Waldridge replacing John Gibson as Ethelbert. Frances Buss continued to direct the program.

Crime Photographer: 1951–1952

Casey returned to television some six years later on April 19, 1951, four months after CBS dropped the radio version of the program. As part of the its

---

1. The name of the newspaper was omitted from the clipping.

transition to television, the program also underwent some stylistic make-overs.

While the radio *Casey* could have taken place in almost any large American city, on television it was clear that *Casey* operated in New York City. The characterization of Casey also underwent some alterations. As described in an April 12, 1951 CBS press release announcing the new series, "Casey's essential character as (a) strong, tender-hearted, astute reporter will be preserved, but his appearance will be a departure from the slouch-hatted, trench-coated lensman of the 'front page' school. He'll dress, and for the most part behave, like other people. His camera will be not merely a symbol, but the instrument with which he earns his salt on the staff of the *Morning Express.*"

Still another change was that the television Casey had a new young male "pal" (shades of Batman and Robin), Frank Lipman, as Casey's almost constant companion and the character who wrote the stories that accompanied Casey's photos. In the July 25, 1951 press release that announced the new character, CBS described Frank as "...a timid Ivy League product drafted from the paper's stock market page to help Casey spell the words that go with his pictures."[2]

Ann Williams, Casey's radio sidekick, continued to appear in the television version, but her role was reduced. Also, at the Blue Note Café, the single jazz pianist of radio days was replaced by a trio.

The program was sponsored on alternate weeks by Carter Products (Arrid deodorant) beginning with the first broadcast and Prom Cosmetics (White Rain Shampoo and Prom and Toni Home Permanents) beginning September 27, 1951.

Cast and Crew

Richard Carlyle (1912–1977), was the first actor to play Casey but following the pattern set in the original radio series and the short lived 1945 television series, he was replaced two months into the series. A respected actor who continued to work in television until 1973, Carlyle may well have lost the role as a result of his age as he was ten years older than his successor, Darren McGavin (1922–), who was 23 at the time and who continued in the role until its final episode.[3]

John Gibson (1905–1986), radio's Ethelbert, left the television series at the same time as Carlyle and was replaced by Cliff Hall (1894–1972), whose

---

2. The press release may be the origin of the confusion over whether the character was a "Jack" or a "Frank." While the 7/25/51 release used "Jack," the error was quickly corrected and all future references to the character used the name "Frank."
3. McGavin was to return to television 23 years later as Kolchak in the *Night Stalker* series where he played a brash newspaper reporter who carried a camera and whose stories were too fantastic for his frustrated editor to believe or publish.

fame was gained by partnering with Jack Pearl in the Baron ("Wass you dere Charlie?") Munchausen skits. In later episodes, Hall's Ethelbert almost faded entirely from sight.

Jan Miner (1917–2004), radio's last Ann Williams, played the same role for the entire run of the television series and Archie King was cast in the role of Frank Lipman. The part of Captain Logan was played by Pat O'Malley for the first three months and Donald McClelland for the remainder of the run.

The music at the Blue Note Café was provided by the Tony Mottola Trio with additional music being supplied at different times by Archie Bleyer, who also composed some of the music for the radio version of *Casey*, and John Marion Gart. In addition, at least one reference lists Morton Gould as having also provided music for the program although the authors have not been able to verify that reference.

While several references cite well known Hollywood director Sidney Lumet as the director of the series, records in the CBS Archives indicate that Lumet was only associated with the program from April to June, 1951, after which Curt Conway took over the directing duties and continued in that role until the program's final broadcast in June 1952.[4]

The scripts for the television programs were similar to those of the radio series only in terms of identifying Casey as a crime photographer; the imaginative ideas of Alonzo Deen Cole were sadly missing. Of the 58 scripts used during the 1951–1952 season, 34 were written by three writers: Ben Radin wrote 13, James P. Cavanaugh wrote 11, and Alan Sapinsley wrote 10. Three other writers were responsible for 12 additional scripts and the remaining scripts were written by four freelance writers and two teams of writers.

Overview of the Program

From an historical perspective, it is interesting to compare the production costs for the radio and television *Caseys* during roughly the same time frame. According to Air Features, the cost of producing a radio episode of *Casey* was pegged at only $2,750 in 1950 while the cost of producing a half hour television episode of *Casey* ran to more than three times that sum, or $9,000 in 1951. By 1952, *The Ross Report on Television Programming* noted that the cost of producing a television episode had jumped to $11,500 per episode.

Several factors contributed to the higher television costs, beginning with

---

4. In a phone interview with the co-author in November 2004, Lumet said he had a "vague memory" of having worked as an assistant director on a couple of the early programs and that he recalled that each program featured a click of Casey's camera.

Casey on Television 173

The Four Television Caseys

Casey #1
Oliver Thorndike
October 1945

Casey #2
Don Kohler
November–December 1945

Casey #3
Richard Carlyle
April–June 1951

Casey #4
Darren McGavin
June 1951–June 1952

television scripts. Whereas CBS had been paying $200 for accepted freelance radio scripts in 1950, in 1951 they were paying $500 for television scripts. Also, while radio and television both needed the services of actors, writers, producers, directors, sound people, musicians, announcers and engineers, television had the added costs for make up, costumes, cameras, scenery and set design as well as graphics.

Airing on Thursday evening, potential *Casey* viewers had an interesting array of program choices. In addition to *Casey*, the CBS Thursday evening lineup included *The Allen Young Show, Garry Moore, Big Town*, another radio series trying to make the transition to television, and after the news that followed *Casey*, the innovative *Steve Allen Show*.

On the other networks, NBC offered *Martin Kane, Detective* at 10:00pm, just ahead of *Casey's* appearance, and for lighter entertainment earlier in the evening, the *Kate Smith* program and a variety show called *The Ford Festival*. Dumont, a regional network that might be thought of as the FOX of its time, offered still another detective mystery, *Ellery Queen*, while ABC offered little competition with a variety program called *Holiday Hotel*.

Competition for viewers during *Casey's* 10:30–11:00pm time spot in the New York viewing area included *Quick On The Draw* (a charade program), *The Paul Winchell-Jerry Mahoney Program* (the ventriloquist-dummy duo), a home gardening show and *Talent Search* featuring Skitch Henderson.

Promoting *Crime Photographer*

In a brief April 30, 1951 review of the new program shortly after its debut, *Time* magazine called attention to Richard Carlyle's new television Casey as "a devil with the ladies." Noting that the radio "cops & robbers show" has moved to television "without leaving a single clue or cliché behind," the magazine concluded that the only thing that "halted (Casey) in his headlong pursuit of justice was a hush-voiced announcer breathing: 'Don't be half-safe, use Arrid!'"

A lengthier review of *Crime Photographer* appeared in Fred Rayfield's September 17, 1951 column, "TV Or Not TV," in the long defunct New York tabloid, *The Daily Compass*. Devoting the entire column to the *Casey* series with a headline that read: "Casey Crime Photographer Does Almost Everything Well," Rayfield started out by describing Casey to his readers as a combination Hildy Johnson (the sharp reporter in the Ben Hecht/Charles MacArthur stage play, *The Front Page*) and Sherlock Holmes, minus the addictions to drink and cocaine. And, although he acknowledged that Casey occasionally had a slug at his favorite bar, Rayfield observed that Casey "never had enough to impair his semi-infallible insight into crime and demands of the newspaper business."

Rayfield went on to describe Casey as "dapper, cocky and unruffled," and "irresistible to girls, a sort of TV viewer's Errol Flynn with a camera in place of the movies' usual sword." He also called attention to the fact that "wherever the crime, the only photographer on hand to snap the corpse is Casey. 'Oh, it's you again,' the cops usually say when Casey shows up."

The column also shed additional insight into the characterizations of Casey and Frank Lipman, his sidekick reporter, including a comparison between the television characters and the real world of newspaper reporting.

> Casey, in addition to snapping a picture here and there...is way ahead of the managing editor in seeing the possible ramifications of a story and is usually two steps in front of the police. As for the reporter who usually tags along behind the dynamic Casey, the photographer leads him along like a big star trailed by an autograph seeker.
>
> Casey orders him around, tells him how to handle his stories, how to write his series and even does the interviewing of key people in most cases. As a member of the Newspaper Guild, I'm a bit weary of Casey's all-embracing activities. I figure that for the work he does he should be paid as photographer, reporter, managing editor and detective, which should come to about $650 a week. I'm sure Casey is not paid the salary he deserves.

Commenting further on the relationship between Casey and Lipman, Rayfield described Lipman as a "stumbling, wide-eyed, rather awe-struck youngster" who Casey refers to as "Y'see kid..." or "C'mon, baby, let's go," concluding that, "I'm sure Hildy Johnson or Steve Wilson of *Big Town*, upon being referred to as 'Kid' and 'Baby' would have thrown their notebooks at Casey."

On the promotional front, CBS recycled the same "pr" concept it had used two years earlier to promote the radio program. In October 1951, *Radio-TV Mirror,* a typical radio and television fan magazine of the day, carried a two page "puff piece" about the program with an eight photo spread highlighting the program's July 12, 1951 episode, "Case Of The Scowling Boy." In the article, the magazine "challenged" its readers (to steal an *Ellery Queen* quote): "After studying the first seven pictures of Casey's camera quiz, see if you can spot the clue that offers the simple key to the mystery and traps the guilty one. Then check with the upside down final picture for the solution." The photo spread is reproduced on the following two pages.

And in January 1952, CBS came up with an interesting (and inexpensive) scheme designed to gain publicity for the program, and hopefully to increase its ratings. The station announced a contest for the most exciting news picture of 1951 taken by a press photographer. The contest, according to the CBS public-

Casey, Crime Photographer

As seen in a typical "PR" photo spread.

1. When the $30,000 payroll of Baldwin Construction was stolen and the paymaster killed by a police .38, Casey first shot a picture, then a question, "Where was Foley, the cop assigned as payroll guard?"

2. That also was the question demanded by irate Mr. Baldwin, angry at the crime although the company is insured. Logan heatedly backs police integrity but reluctantly admits Foley hadn't shown up.

3. As Casey takes his last picture, a frightened boy peers over a pile of sandbags. Casey calls to him, but he runs away. Just then Officer Foley appears claiming he had overslept. His rooms are searched.

4. Logan jails Foley after finding packed suitcases hidden in his apartment. At headquarters, Casey hears Foley's brother, Nat, protesting that the arrest is a frame-up, even though lab tests have proved that Foley's gun fired the murder bullet.

Casey on Television 177

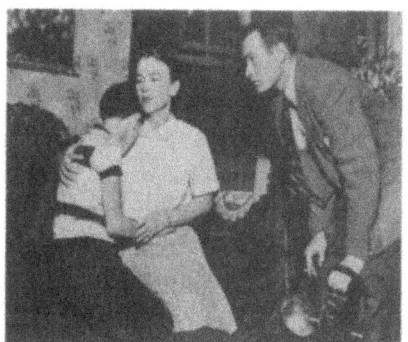

5. Casey agrees with Nat on Foley's innocence and uses picture to locate the scared boy, Jackie Adams. Elated when Jackie finally admits seeing the shooting, Casey then is stunned as the boy sobs that his idol, Officer Foley, had done it.

6. Casey shows the boy's photograph to bartender Ethelbert who sadly agrees the case in now airtight against their friend Foley. "Everything's sour," he mourns, "even the scowl on the poor kid." Casey gets an idea, returns to the Adams' home.

7. Unnoticed he places Foley's picture over a similar shot of the boy's dad, a dead police hero. Casey asks Jackie who the cop is in the photo. Jackie's startling reply is, "That's my father." STOP. What is the clue, who is the murderer?

8. The boy's scowl made Casey suspect nearsightedness, a secret kept to avoid "sissy" glasses. The photo test confirmed. Nat in a police suit could have resembled brother. Nat could have drugged him, taken gun. Nat comes after boy, is trapped.

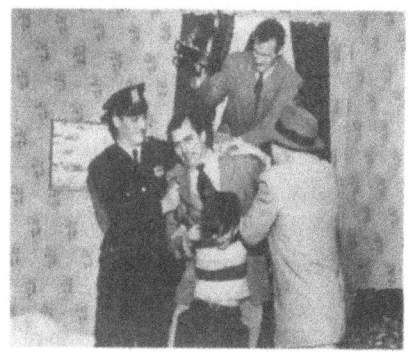

ity department, was designed to pay tribute to the work of the country's newspaper lensmen. The winner, in addition to receiving a $300 Savings Bond, would get a free trip to New York and appear on the *Crime Photographer* program. Ten runner up awards of $25 bonds would also be given. As spokesperson for the contest, McGavin explained: "It (the contest) will point out to the general public the excellent work being done by news photographers in accurately picturing every day news events in an interesting and exciting fashion."

William Vendetta of the *Chicago Tribune* won the contest with his photo of an ex-convict caught red-handed during a burglary and the ten runner up awards went to newsmen representing papers in Los Angeles, Denver, Binghamton, NY, Cleveland, and Norfolk, VA.

Crime Photographer's Final Days

The record of how many long running radio programs made the transition to television is mixed, with many notable successes but also many failures. Indeed one could certainly write a book on the subject, listing every radio program that attempted to make the transition and hypothesizing as to why the transition either succeeded or failed. This is not that book, however. Suffice to say that had such a book been in existence in 1951, the producers of *Crime Photographer* might have profited from its insights.

Among the radio programs that made a successful transition to television were *Dragnet*, 1952–1970, *Perry Mason*, 1957–1974, *Gunsmoke*, 1955–1975, *Suspense*, 1949–1964, *The Line Up*, 1954–1960, and on the lighter side, T*he Life of Riley*, 1949–1958, *Father Knows Best*, 1954–1968, *You Bet Your Life*, 1950–1961, *Candid Camera*, 1948–1967, *This Is Your Life*, 1952–1961, *Red Skelton*, 1951–1971 and, of course, *I Love Lucy*, 1951–1961.

In addition to *Casey*, other radio programs that just didn't quite click on the magic tube were *Dick Tracy*, 1950–1951, *Charlie Wild, Private Detective*, 1950–1952, *The Green Hornet*, 1966–1967, *Fibber McGee and Molly*, 1959–1960, and *Gang Busters*, March 1952–December 1952.

Alas, while the CBS promotional efforts may have generated interest in the program among the world of newspaper photographers, it did not draw in more viewers and *Casey* went off the air following its final broadcast on June 12, 1952 to be replaced the following week with a panel program that was far less costly to produce, *I've Got A Secret*, with Carter Products (Arrid deodorant) alternating sponsorship of the new program with Cavalier Cigarettes.

When *Casey* was not renewed, McGavin was quoted as having said: "The cast of *Crime Photographer* didn't go down fighting. They took off for the hills. It was so bad that it was never re-run and that's saying something when you consider the caliber of television programs in those days."[5]

Although there were likely several reasons why *Casey* failed, at least three factors contributed to the program's inability to catch on with viewers: its broadcast time, viewer dislike for kinescoped programs, and differences in taste between the east and west coasts.

When the program was broadcast live from New York at 10:30pm, it was shown simultaneously on 18 regional stations across the country and a week later as kinescopes on an additional 30 stations. For the live broadcasts, this created a three hour time gap between the two coasts and meant that *Casey* aired in the lucrative west coast market at 7:30pm, not a particularly appropriate time for what was supposed to be a gritty crime drama.

The other factors contributing to the program's cancellation were cited in the *Ross Reports* which noted: "Viewer hostility to kinescope and the market differences in tastes of Los Angeles fans have made the city a tough market for national sponsors."

Coxe also recalled some of the scheduling problems in his 1971 interview: "So they liked it and I liked it...It went on for a year. And then it went off because they couldn't clear the time...the programs were showing in Oshkosh or Arizona at half past 12 at night and the sponsors wouldn't go for it."

Still another factor that may have contributed to the show's demise after only one year was that viewers familiar with the radio program just didn't find its television counterpart up to the same standards of excitement that they had come to expect from the scripts of Alonzo Deen Cole.

Regardless of the reasons for the demise of *Casey* after a single season on the home screen, few tears seemed to be shed. And, since there is a good chance that had *Casey* remained on television for a second or third season he may not have returned to radio as he did in January of 1954, perhaps the adage "that all things turn out for the best" has some merit.

Never one to let disappointment interfere with his drive or imagination, Coxe spent many an hour following *Casey's* cancellation submitting proposals to CBS for at least two possible new series based on his other fictional characters, Kent Murdock, a newspaper reporter who first appeared in the pulps, and

---

5. When the author attempted to contact Mr. McGavin in late 2004, hoping that he might shed some additional light on the fate of the television run, he was advised that since suffering a stroke in 1999 and the loss of his beloved wife, it had become difficult for the actor to communicate. McGavin's loyal fans have set up a web site, www.darrenmcgavin.net, and eventually The College Of The Pacific which has McGavin's papers and memorabilia is expected to create a Darren McGavin Wing where scholars may unearth valuable information about the man who portrayed Casey, 1951–1952, Mike Hammer, 1957–1959 and Kolchak, 1975–1976.

Dr. Paul Standish, a physician in several of his 1940s short stories who doubled as the local medical examiner and tripled as a detective. If combining press photography and detection was fading in interest, perhaps, Coxe thought, combining medicine and detection would achieve greater success. While CBS did not pick up either series, Coxe may have been ahead of his time as the Standish idea was clearly a precursor to what later became the popular *Quincy, CSI* and *Crossing Jordan* television series.

In 1958, six years after *Casey* abandoned his television career and three years after he retired from radio, ABC introduced a new television series, *Man With A Camera*, featuring Charles Bronson as Mike Kovac, a World War II combat photographer who in civilian life used his photographic skills to enhance his private eye career taking assignments from the police, insurance companies and, of course, shades of Jack Casey, from newspapers. The almost *Casey* clone remained on the ABC schedule for 29 half hour episodes through 1960.

Over the next decade, other newspaper oriented television programs included *Night Stalker*, 1975–1976 with Darren McGavin and *Lou Grant*, 1977–1982, the last moderately successful television series dealing with the world of newspapers.

Two Contemporary Looks at *Crime Photographer*

While at least 81 episodes of the radio version of *Casey* have survived and can be heard today by Old Time Radio enthusiasts, *Casey* fans curious to see how their favorite detective fared on television have only limited choices.

As of April 2005, the Museum of Television and Radio in New York City listed one *Crime Photographer* program in its catalog. The Los Angeles branch of the museum had no copies on hand but a staff member there indicated that a visitor could request a duplicate copy of the episode in the New York collection. Also, as of April 2005, the Museum of Broadcast Communications in Chicago did not list *Crime Photographer* in its catalog of television holdings.

One contemporary viewer who posted a review of an episode on the Internet in June 2004 was science fiction writer and mystery fan F. Gwynplaine MacIntyre. In his review, MacIntyre described the series this way:

> The episodes were told in flashback format with Casey wearily narrating his latest exploit to the bartender, a standard tough guy type with the unlikely name of Ethelbert. The flashback format had its disadvantages, as we start off every episode knowing that Casey has come out alive. But this was a useful budget-saving device, as Casey's voice-over narration easily bridged gaps in the action...

Crime Reporter (note: the reviewer clearly meant "Photographer" here) was a bog-standard tough guy crime drama: the bartender's name 'Ethelbert' was the most unusual and imaginative aspect of the show. All of Casey's traits (his jaded attitude, his capacity for booze and cigarettes, his fondness for jazz, his antipathy for the police) were shared by several other fictional detectives. [6]

The reviewer also noted that with Casey frequently working at cross purposes with the police yet always solving the crime, it was understandable why Captain Logan disliked him.

In March 2005, this writer had the opportunity to view the December 6, 1951 episode of *Crime Photographer*, "Clay Pigeon," at the Museum of Television and Radio in New York City. Watching the video in a special viewing room filled with small cubicles, each with a monitor reminiscent of the tiny television screens of long ago and listening to the sound via earphones was almost akin to entering an H. G Wells time machine.

The black and white program began with the series title, followed by the episode title, followed by a smiling young Darren McGavin snapping a flash camera and entering the confines of his darkroom, followed by a pitch for White Rain Shampoo.

The plot, simple enough, involved the unsuccessful efforts of a crime syndicate to get rid of the meddling crime photographer whose efforts were exposing their various and nefarious rackets. The first attempt on Casey's life involved sending the photographer a bomb in the guise of a gift wrapped camera. The package was delivered to Casey while he was in the darkroom with his sidekick Frank but when Casey left the room to respond to a call Frank unwrapped the gift and was seriously injured when the bomb went off.

The second attempt involved planting an attractive "dame" (Maria Riva, the daughter and spitting image of Marlene Dietrich) at the Blue Note which Casey was known to frequent. Casey appeared to fall for the woman and for her tale of woe involving her dad's misfortunes as the owner of a local amusement park. Casey agreed to help the woman and made a date to meet her that night at the amusement park.

Unbeknownst to the woman, though, "clever" Casey, sensing a trap, checked out the park earlier in the day and that evening when the bullets started flying at the park's shooting gallery, the origin of the episode's title, "Clay

---

6. It is possible that when MacIntrye visited the Museum in 2004, more than one episode was available which would explain why some of his comments appear to refer to more than one program.

Pigeon," through nothing short of dumb luck and the clumsiness of the villain's assistant, the bad girl turned good, is killed, and Casey catches another evil doer.

After watching the concluding commercial with actress Anita Louise talking about the virtues of Prom Home Permanent, another of the sponsor's beauty products, Casey, once again busy in his darkroom, encouraged the audience to watch next week's episode entitled "Bill of Lading."

While it is admittedly risky to judge an entire year's worth of television programs based on viewing a single episode, for this writer, an acknowledged fan of the *Casey* radio program, the differences between the two versions were readily apparent: the pace of the television program was much slower and it lacked much of the wit and repartee that was an integral part of the radio scripts. Also, in making the transition to the home screen, the new writers changed what had been a winning formula, playing down, for example, the roles of Ethelbert and Ann and adding Frank Lipman as a new character.

Even after making allowances for the relative newness and lack of sophistication of television in 1951, the magic that made *Casey* such a popular radio program was not duplicated when the program moved to television in 1951. Sad to say, but the program probably deserved its early demise.

12
Television Log

1945 Series, WCBW (CBS), New York City
Broadcast 8:30-9:00pm

9/20 *The Diary of Death* by Charles Holden.
Story line: Based on the 10/31/44 radio program written by Alonzo Deen Cole. The daughter of Metho, the mind reader is murdered.
Cast: Oliver Thorndike as Casey, Ruth Ford as Ann Williams, John Gibson as Ethelbert, Marilyn Erskine as Eurice, Edith Teckna as Grace, Gregory Morton as Metho, Bernard Hoffman as a gangster. Others in the cast include Larry Frisch and Charles F. McClelland. Directed by Frances Buss.

10/19 *The Retired Camera*
Story line: Based on the 7/25/45 radio program written by B. Edgar Marvin. An image on an old camera helps Casey track down arsonists.
Cast: Not available.

11/9 *The Birthday Present*
Story line: Based on the 9/9/44 radio programwritten by Alonzo Deen Cole. Casey plays a trick on a crooked lawyer involved in a false arrest case.
Cast: Don Kohler as Casey and Shirley O'Hara as Ann Williams.

12/28 *Faked Suicide*
Story line: Based on the 2/13/45 radio program written by Alonzo Deen Cole. When a widow learns she won't get any money as a result of her husband's alleged suicide, she tries to make his death look like a murder.
Cast: Don Kohler as Casey, Shirley O'Hara as Ann Williams, Harold Waldrige as Ethelbert. Others in the cast include Bill Coleman, Charles Flynn, and Kermit Murdock. Directed by Frances Buss.

Flashgun Casey, Crime Photographer

1951–1952 Series

Basic Information

Network: CBS (New York City)
Schedule: Thursday, 10:30–11:00pm
Director: Sidney Lumet, 4/19/51–6/7/51
 Curt Conway, 6/21/51–6/12/52
Producer: Charles Russell, 4/19/51–6/7/51
 Martin Manulis, 6/21/51–6/12/52
Music: The Tony Mottola Trio (Tony Mottola, guitarist; George Wright, pianist; Stanley Webb, woodwind.)
Sponsor: Carter Products, on alternate weeks beginning with the first broadcast, and Prom Cosmetics, on alternate weeks beginning 9/27/51.

Major Cast

Casey: Richard Carlyle, 4/19/51–6/7/51
 Darren McGavin, 6/21/51–6/12/52
Ethelbert: John Gibson, 4/19/51–6/7/51
 Cliff Hall, 6/21/51–6/12/52
Ann Williams: Jan Miner, entire run
Capt. Logan: Pat O'Malley, 4/19/51–6/7/51
 Donald McClelland, 6/21/51–6/12/52
Frank Lipman: Archie King, beginning with 8/2/51
City editor: Robert Lieb, beginning with 8/30/51
Announcer: Stuart Metz
Others: Other cast members are listed with each program based on information from *The Ross Report on Television Programming*.
Settings: New York City, the *Morning Express*, the Blue Note Café.

1951

4/19 *Model Alibi* by Sheldon Reynolds.
   Cast: Shirley Ballard, Pat White, Bruce Gordon, Jay Barney, John Randolph, Ray Danton and Harry Mehaffrey.

4/26 Not scheduled

Television Log 185

5/3 *The Hunch* (Writer unknown).
Story line: Embittered innocent young man rescued from murder charge.
Cast: Leo Penn, Barbara Baxley, David Kerman, Jean Bartel and Ed Simmons.

5/10 Not scheduled

5/17 *Deadline Midnight* by Gail & Harry Ingram.
Cast: Miriam Goldina, Arthur Cassel, Harry Davis, Louise Larabee, Christopher Barbery and Salem Ludwig.

5/24 *The Gentle Strangler* by Alonzo Deen Cole, based on 4/27/47 radio broadcast and adapted by Alvin Sapinsley.
Cast: James Westerfield, Tom Gorman, George Mitchell, Virginia Robinson, Frieda Altman, Adelaide Bean and Paul Keyes.

5/31 *The Third Bridegroom* (Writer unknown).
Cast: Helen Gillette, Marta Linden, Stephen Elliot, and Peter Cookson.

6/7 *The Frightened Mouse* by Alvin Sapinsley.
Cast: Maria Riva, Ralph Theadore, Sylvia Field and Kurt Katch. (Final appearance for Richard Carlyle, John Gibson and Pat O'Malley.)

6/14 President Truman address. Program re-scheduled for following week.

6/21 *Double Negative* (Writer unknown).
Cast. First appearance of Darren McGavin, Cliff Hall and Donald McClelland. Also Meg Mundy, Leslie Neilsen, Brandon Peters and Don Kennedy.

6/28 *The Picture Of The Duchess* (a.k.a. *The Boarding House*) by Alvin Sapinsley.
Story line: A publicity hungry boarding house operator confesses to a murder she did not commit.
Cast: Blanche Yurka, Hildy Parks, Gordon Richards and Will Lee.

7/5 *Retirement Of Willie* by Alvin Sapinsley.
Cast: Cloris Leachman, E. G Marshall, Michael Strong, Ray Danton and Tom Gorman.

7/12   *The Case Of The Scowling Boy* by James P. Cavanaugh.
       Cast: Frances Fuller, John Baragrey, Bobby Nick, Bert Bertram and Lonnie Chapman.

7/19   *The Getaway* (a.k.a. *Charming Jewel Thieves*) by Marco Page.
       Cast: Solen Burry, Rita Fredericks and John Randolph.

7/26   *The Honest Jockey* by Carol Warner Gluck.
       Cast: Christina White, Leonard Barry, Robert Simon, Joseph Sweeney and Michael Kellin.

8/2   *The Sandhog Story* by Alvin Sapinsley.
       Story line: Workers who refuse protection face death in the underwater vehicle they must use.
       Cast: Archie King portraying Jack* Lipman, timid young reporter begins to work with Casey, plus Frank Tweddell, David Clarke, Natalie Priest, Virginia Downing, Salem Ludwig and Michael Gazzo.

8/9   *The Meeting Place* by James P. Cavanaugh.
       Story line: Loan sharks use violence to collect.
       Cast: Anne Seymour, Peggy McCay, Robert Pestene, Rusty Lane and Frank Tweddell.

8/16   *Murder On The Inside* by Robert J. Shaw.
       Cast: Lou Polan, Herbert Ratner, Don Kiefer, Julian Noa and Jill Kraft.

8/23   *The Payoff* by Max Ehrlich.
       Story line: Political corruption is exposed.
       Cast: Lawrence Fletcher, Leonard Barry, James O'Rear, Lorna Lynn, Jay Barney and Adnia Rice.

8/30   *The Road Back To Prison* by Alvin Sapinsley.
       Story line: Shady politician tempts ex-con.
       Cast: Paul Langton, Lois Wheeler, Jack Hartley, Floyd Ennis and Robert Lieb who portrays the city editor.

---

* The character was erroneously listed as "Jack" instead of "Frank" in an early CBS press release. The error was later corrected.

9/6 *The Judge Meets A Deadline* by Ben Radin.
Story line: Political cooperation between judge and gangster.
Cast: Suzanne Dalbert (French film star), Edmond Ryan, James Van Dyk, Robert Simon, Martin Balsam and Bettye Louise.

9/13 *Babies For Sale* by Carol Warner Gluck.
Story line: Black market babies.
Cast: Perry Fred Stewart, Georgianne Catal, Bernard Nadell, Lee Grant, Leslie Woods and Martin Green.

9/20 *Brains* by Raphael Hayes.
Story line: Washed up boxer encouraged to take a dive in comeback fight by a crooked promoter.
Cast: Maxwell Glenville, Jane White, Louis Soriin, Bert Conway, Lonny Chapman, Philip Leeds and Tiger Andrews.

9/27 *The Clean Up* by Ben Radin.
Story line: Struggle for control of waterfront union.
Cast: Gilbert Green, Lili Darvas, Mario Gallo, Wolfe Barzell, Joseph De Santis, Harry Clark and Carmen Costi.

10/4 *The Hero* by James P. Cavanaugh.
Story line: Gangster admired by neighborhood kids. (Similar to the play and film *Dead End.*)
Cast: Joseph Anthony, Lee Phillips, Madame Daykarhano, Joey Walsh and Bobby Santis.

10/11 *The Torch* by Carol Warner Gluck.
Story line: Arson for insurance.
Cast: Paul Ford, Peter Hobbs, Adnia Rice, Harry Davis, Ned Wertimer, Evelyn Shay, Doris Roberts and Pat O'Malley.

10/18 *The Long Shot* (a.k.a. *The Fix*) by Ben Radin.
Story line: Gamblers tempt hoop star to fix college basketball game.
Cast: Wright King, Ray Dantan, Henry Jones, Peggy Allenby, Jack Klugman, Myron Rubin and William Remick.

10/25 *The Blue Hand* by Alvin Sapinsley.
Story line: Murder and dope smuggling.
Cast: James Westerfield and Lonny Chapman.

11/1 *The Revolt* (a.k.a. *The Posse*) by James P. Cavanaugh.
Story line: Protection racketeers prey on small businessmen.
Cast: Will Kuluva, Miriam Goldina, Martin Newman, Peter Frye, Ruth Hammond, and Carmen Costi.

11/8 *Air Tight* by Raphael Hayes.
Story line: Gambler operates with help from crooked police.
Cast: Not available.

11/15 *Unlucky Number* by Ben Radin.
Story line: Numbers racketeer tries to stop exposé.
Cast: David Clark, Eleanore Wilson, Michael Demarais, Bernard Grant and Louis Charles.

11/22 *The Coward* by James P. Cavanaugh.
Story line: Seasoned criminal tutors young gang.
Cast: Carmen Mathews, Joey Walsh, Robert Emhardt, Gene Steiner and Mary Michael.

11/29 *The Juror* by Ben Radin.
Cast: Katherine Bard, Constance Dowling, Kem Dibbs, Stephen Elliot, Gene Lee and Jason Robards Jr.

12/6 *Clay Pigeon* by Alvin Sapinsley.
Story line: Crime syndicate targets Casey.
Cast: Maria Riva, Rick Jason, Philips Leeds and James Kaye.

12/13 *Bill Of Lading* by Ben Radin.
Story line: Dope smuggling.
Cast: Edward Binns, Russell Dennis, Phyllis Love, Jack Carron, Philip Kenneally, Mario Gallo and Joe Sullivan.

12/20 *Till Death Do Us Part* by Ben Radin.
Story line: Phony marriage notice in newspaper is used to lure a confession from a killer.
Cast: Edward Binns, John Buroff, David Kerman, Ann Lincoln, Adelaide Bean, Lee Phillips and Phil Kramer.

12/27 *The Victim* by Thomas Coley and William Roerick.
Story line: Jewel thefts.
Cast: Robert Lieb, Edward Binns, Irya Jensen, Jane Rose, Rita Lynn and William Watts.

1952

1/3 *The Warning* by James P. Cavanaugh.
Story line: Fur thefts.
Cast: Robert Lieb, Lois Wheeler, Gloria McGhee, Joseph Sweeney, Frank Fenton, John Marley, Lorenzo Fuller, Leroi Operti, Betty Morrissy and Elizabeth Jackson.

1/10 *Blueprint For Danger* by Harry W. Junkin.
Story line: Shady construction deal and murder.
Cast: Gilbert Greene, Don Henmer, Raymond Bramley, Edward Binns, Jane Huszach and G. Albert Smith.

1/17 *The Long Fall* (Writer unknown).
Story line: Life of small boy weighed against safety of entire community.
Cast: Not available.

1/24 *A Little Extra Income* by Ben Radin.
Story line: Jewel robberies and murder.
Cast: Russell Collins, Beverly Dennis, Don Dickenson, Janet Fox, Paul Andor, Arthur Batamides and Vilma Kurer.

1/31 *The Fall Guy* by James P. Cavanaugh.
Story line: Old army buddy framed as fall guy in insurance racket pay off.
Cast: Will Hare, Kim Stanley, Robert Middleton and Alan Mason.

2/7 *Key Witness* by Harry W. Junkin.
Story line: Plot against life of key witness in trial against notorious racketeer.
Cast: Bramwell Fletcher, Nova Patterson, Carl Don and Harry Bellaver.

190   Flashgun Casey, Crime Photographer

2/14   *A Tax On Decency* by Ben Radin.
Story line: Tax official blackmailed.
Cast: Henry Jones, Constance Dowling, Nancy Franklin, Alan Shayne and Gene Reynolds.

2/21   *The Dirt Peddler* by Carol Warner Gluck.
Story line: Rival newspaper specializes in malicious gossip.
Cast: Louis Kirby, John Hildebrand, Leonard Yorr and Michael Brown.

2/28   *The Easy Way* by James P. Cavanaugh.
Cast: Joan Copeland, Fred Wayne, Howard Freeman, Carmen Costi, Norma Connelly, Al Geto and Merle Anderson.

3/6   *Invitation To The Dance* by Ben Radin.
Cast: Steve Gravers, Ruth Hall, Joan Morgan, William Beach, Michael Howard, Al Silvanti, Gordon Stern, Joan Sincere and Charles Welch.
Note: The program may have been pre-empted by an address by President Truman.

3/13   *Black Widow* by Alvin Sapinsley.
Story line: Con game based on false report about soldier overseas.
Cast: Elizabeth Yorke, Lydia Clark, Dorothy Paterson, Nicholas Joy, Erik Rhodes, Ruth Chandler and Doreen Lang.

3/20   *Long Shore* by Ben Radin.
Story line: Brave dockhand tries to break up kickback racket.
Cast: Michael Howard, Mario Gallo, Logan Ramsey, Salem Ludwig, Amelia Romano, Bobb Nick, Victor Rendina and Peter Frey.

3/27   *Second Chance* by Ben Radin.
Story line: Check forgers try to frame innocent girl.
Cast: Katherine Bard, Johnny Kane, Sylvia Field, Virginia Downing, Andy Duggan and Joe Sullivan.

4/3   *Old Dog, New Tricks* by Nelson Gidding.
Story line: Friendly bulldog leads Casey to dope smugglers.
Cast: Thomas Palmer, Jock MacGregor, Victor Thorley, Martin Kosleck, Leonard Barry, Doris Dowling and Whitford Kane.

4/10 *Double Entry* by Edmund Morris.
Story line: Tax evasion and murder.
Cast: Si Oakland, Jody Drew, Roxanne, Frederick O'Neal, Ed Packer, Nikki Green, Nance Robbins, James McMahon, Bruce Gordon and Whit Bissell.

4/17 *The Good Turn* by John T. Chapman.
Story line: Girlfriend of escaped convict assists in his capture.
Cast: Lee Grant, Fred Sadoff, Ann Verneer and Burton Mallory.

4/24 *Agency Of Death* by James P. Cavanaugh.
Story line: Building racketeers deal in defective construction material.
Cast: Ann Seymour, Arthur Cassell, Beverly Whitney, David Clark and Earl George.

5/1 *The Last Mobster* by Alvin Sapinsley.
(1st Anniversary of TV series)
Cast: Maria Riva, Robert Middleton and Harrison Dowd.

5/8 *Blackmail* by Harry Junkin.
Cast: Rita Gam, Frances Starr and Joshua Shelley.

5/15 *A Score To Settle* by James P. Cavanaugh.
Story line: Innocent man accused of murder.
Cast: Joseph Sullivan, Robert Lieb, Florence Beresford, Melville Ruick, Oliver Thorndike and Alan Devitt. (Note: Thorndike played Casey in the 9/20/45 television program, Ruick's was the voice of the *Lux Radio Theater* and Devitt was a regular on *The Witch's Tale*.)

5/22 *A Hero Comes Home* by Carol Warner Gluck.
Story line: Gambling syndicate tries to cash in on award given to national hero.
Cast: Phyllis Hill, Michael Higgins, Stacey Graham and Phil Kenneally.

5/29 *The Tall Steel Nightmare* by Edmund Morris.
Story line: Casey works as a riveter to probe building racket.
Cast: Michael Strong, Allen Nourse, Jock McGregor, Mike Silvera, David Stewart and Anne Lincoln.

Flashgun Casey, Crime Photographer

6/5 *Letter Of The Law* by James P. Cavanaugh.
Story line: Young lawyer with underworld clients.
Cast: Walter Brooke, Peter Virgo, Bert Conway, Melanie York, Klock Rider, Philip Pine, Jacob Sandler and Floyd Ennis.

6/12 *Reward* by Ben Radin.
Story line: Death of key witness to underworld crime.
Cast: Joe Sullivan, Anne Hegira, Edwin Cooper, Bobby Fanton, Joey Walsh and Richard Robbins.

FINAL PROGRAM. Series replaced 6/19 by *I've Got A Secret*.

13
Casey in the Comics

While turning a successful radio show into a series of comic books or a newspaper strip wasn't a regular procedure, it happened often enough so that the appearance on the newsstand in late 1949 of the first issue of *Casey Crime Photographer*[1] wasn't really that unique. A survey of the titles in the *Official Overstreet Comic Book Price Guide* for 2005 reveals nearly twenty comic books based on radio shows.

Apart from such obvious titles as *The Lone Ranger* and *The Green Hornet* may be found *The Adventures of Ozzie and Harriet*[2], *Big Jon and Sparkie, Big Town, Bobby Benson's B-Bar-B Riders, Charlie McCarthy, A Date with Judy, Fibber McGee and Molly, Gang Busters, Jack Armstrong, Meet Corliss Archer, Mr. District Attorney, My Friend Irma, The Mysterious Traveler, The Sea Hound, Shadow Comics, Straight Arrow,* and *Suspense.* A few, like *Jack Armstrong, The Shadow,* and *Straight Arrow*, also appeared as syndicated newspaper strips.

What was the advantage of creating a comic book based on a radio series? Like basing a comic book on a current movie, it served as an advertising and promotion device, presenting the stories and characters to a different market in a new medium. Perhaps it would encourage readers of comics to tune in and listen to the radio program. As an aid to this, many of the comic books provided a list of the radio stations on which the program could be heard.[3] How successful this was cannot really be determined. Many of the comic books were short-lived. For every *Mr. District Attorney* which ran for 67 issues over a decade there were those like *Fibber McGee and Molly* which was a one-shot or *The Adventures of Ozzie and Harriet* which lasted only five issues.

---

1. Unlike the radio program, there was no punctuation in the title of the comic books.
2. *Ozzie and Harriet* was definitely based on the radio series and had no connection with the later TV series. The comic book was published from October–November 1949 to June–July 1950. The TV series began in 1952.
3. As of February 15, 1949, 159 CBS affiliates in 46 states and the District of Columbia were listed in the first issue of *Casey Crime Photographer.*

Casey Crime Photographer published only four issues from August, 1949 to February, 1950. The publisher was listed on the magazine as Broadcast Features Publications, Inc., 350 Fifth Avenue, New York City. The words "Marvel Comic" appeared in a circle on the cover and a label across the lower portion of the cover proclaimed the contents to be "From the Files of the Famous C.B.S. Radio Thriller." The splash page of the first issue indicated the editorial consultant on the magazine to be Jean Thompson, M.D., Psychiatrist, Child Guidance Bureau, Board of Education, New York City. It also included a credit line similar to the one used on many of the radio scripts which declared that the stories were "based upon the character Flashgun Casey created by George Harmon Coxe."

Each issue contained three stories about Casey, a "True to Life" police case (also in comic format, but without Casey) and the obligatory two or three-page text story (most without Casey). The Post Office required a certain amount of text for a comic book to qualify as a magazine. This was the part of the comic that no one ever read. The stories had more complicated plots than most of those in the comics and there was a great deal of dialogue, again more than was usual. Even the "True to Life" crime thriller had more text to the page than was common in a story told in pictures.

None of the features was signed by either the name of the writer or the artist but according to Mike Benton's *The Illustrated History of Crime Comics* (Taylor Publishing Co., 1993), the artist was Vernon Henkel who worked for Quality Comics and Timely Comics as well as other companies. As both a writer and artist for Quality in the 1940s, Henkel was responsible for the features "Chic Carter (The Sword)" in *Smash Comics* and *Police Comics*, "Don Q" in *Crack Comics* and "Whistler" in *National Comics*. He was also one of the artists on the original true crime comic *Crime Does Not Pay*.

In an interview with Jim Amash for *Alter Ego* (#48, May 2005), Henkel discussed his work on *Casey* and revealed the pressure he was under to produce each issue as quickly as possible. He admitted he didn't base his version of the characters on the radio actors, but used faces he had drawn for other comics. Each of the issues had photo-covers, but only two used photos of actor Staats Cotsworth.

Casey and Ann Williams appeared in each story as did Captain Logan, while Ethelbert was only in a few of the stories. Casey was almost invariably drawn wearing a blue trench coat, a fedora on his head with his press pass tucked in the hat band. He had a square jaw, dark hair and a grim look. He wore a necktie in some stories, a vest and bow tie in others. He often appeared with a pipe clenched between his teeth. A pipe? The Casey of the pulps and radio smoked cigarettes, but never a pipe.

Ann Williams was an attractive blonde, often referred to as Casey's assistant or as part of the news team. Ethelbert, the Blue Note bartender, was always depicted in his shirt sleeves, a neat black bow tie at his collar. His activity on the comic page was largely limited to answering the telephone and occasionally telling a story that supplied Casey with a clue. The famous bar and restaurant was readily identified by a menu placed on a table with the name of the establishment clearly showing. There was a piano player pictured in one panel in one of the stories. Captain Logan was drawn as a stocky older man in a blue police uniform. In the pulps Logan was a snappy dresser in his pin stripe suit. On the radio, Logan appeared to the imagination to be in plain clothes. Perhaps the uniform gave more of a touch of reality and the suits a touch of distinction and some literary license. City editor Burke was overweight, had untidy white hair and could be recognized by his white shirt, necktie askew and shirt collar undone, his dark vest unbuttoned and with a cigar in his mouth.

Some of the stories were based on actual radio scripts from two years prior to the date of publication. Thus, there was little likelihood that a reader might remember having heard the same story on the air. In the last years of Street & Smith's *Shadow Comics* (1948–1949) some of the stories about *The Shadow* were also taken from radio scripts, but the source was clearly identified.

A comparison between the broadcast version and the comic book version of the same Casey story indicates that the scripts were not reprinted verbatim. Character names were retained and some of the dialogue was transferred intact; other speeches were cut or even assigned to a different character in the same panel. Some scenes in the broadcast version were eliminated for the sake of advancing the story. For the most part the graphic version did not contain as smooth storytelling as the radio broadcast.

One may reconstruct the creative process here to some extent. It is likely that CBS supplied copies of the scripts to be used, perhaps selected at random from the files. The publisher, editor, or even the writer chose stories that had potential to be adapted to the new medium.

The final issue of the *Casey Crime Photographer* comic book was dated February 1950. No doubt prepared a month or more in advance of the cover date, it was still ahead of the radio show which left the air for awhile in November 1950. Apparently the experiment in cross-media promotion was not as successful as either CBS or Broadcast Features Publications had hoped.

Casey in Four Colors

CBS and Marvel Comics produced a comic book based on the radio show, 1949–1950

Casey Crime Photographer Comics
(The radio script source for each story is given where known.)

Vol. 1 No. 1: August 1949
1. "The Monkey Murder Mystery." Based on "King of the Apes," broadcast May 1, 1947. Casey and Ann go to the circus to interview Charles King who does a wild animal act with six orangutans and is billed as the King of the Apes. When King is murdered by one of his own apes, Casey must discover who encouraged the animal to turn killer and also to identify the members of a love triangle.

2. "The Girl on the Docks." Based on "The Girl on the Dock," broadcast April 3, 1947. When a terrified young woman collapses on the deck of Houseboat Kate's floating home, the first person Kate calls is Casey. Shortly after the photographer arrives, two masked men show up and kidnap the mystery woman. One of Ethelbert's anecdotes and more than a whiff of cheap perfume hold the clues to the location of the woman and the solution to the mystery.

3. "Death and the Daredevils." An assignment covering a group of auto stunt drivers leads Casey and Ann to a ring of professional car thieves. Casey substitutes as a stunt driver to get the goods on the gang.

4. Plus "Justice Has a Heart," a True to Life police case and "Too Many Mistakes!" a three-page text story. Neither of these features is about Casey.

Vol. 1 No. 2: October 1949
1. "The Sinister Carnival." Based on "In the Sweet Name of Charity," broadcast June 12, 1947. Burke gives Casey an assignment to uncover a phony charity racket. The carnival of the title has been organized to benefit charity, but is revealed as a scam when one of the partners in charge is murdered by the other.

2. "Face-to-Face with the Strangler." Based on "The Gentle Strangler," broadcast April 24, 1947. A lisping man is eliminating the people involved in an old murder case: the judge, the assistant district attorney and a photographic supplies salesman. Casey is next on the list and becomes the bait to catch the strangler.

3. "Trapped by the Penny Plunderers." Casey and Ann go undercover and pose as crooks to learn the identity of the ringleader of the petty racketeers fleecing the citizens. The racket boss is revealed as someone no one would have suspected and holds the two at gun-point. Ann turns the tables on him with a pistol hidden in her turban-like hat.

4. Plus "The Crime of Vicky Roberts," a crime thriller. This feature is not about Casey.

Vol. 1 No. 3: December 1949

1. "The Mystery of the Glowing Ghost." Based on "The Case of the Glowing Ghost," broadcast April 1, 1944 and repeated as "The Haunted House," June 5, 1947. Casey and Ann are on assignment to Tuckertown for a story on the town's famous haunted house. A shining ghost that walks only when it rains, a hidden treasure and a fall down an old well are just some of the elements along the trail to the revelation of the mystery.

2. "Damsel in Distress!" Based on "Lady in Distress," broadcast October 23, 1947. When Casey and Ann are on their annual assignment to cover the rodeo, they are faced with a case which involves a missing girl singer who worked at Pink Bannister's, a protection racket and a little case of blackmail.

3. "The Machine That Predicted Murder!" Casey and Ann, on their way to cover a swimming pool opening, visit eccentric inventor Philo Rennick who claims his "time machine" has a hot lead on a story for the cameraman. When the machine shows a man being murdered in the future, Casey is determined to catch the killer.

4. "A Murder a Day," a two-page text story featuring Casey. The clue to a series of murders is in an artist's sketch of the jury in a decade-old criminal trial. Casey sets a trap for the killer and catches him before the cameraman becomes the next victim.

5. Plus "They Walked with Danger!" a crime thriller. The story does not feature Casey and the art style appears to differ from that on the Casey stories in the issue.

Vol. 1 No. 4: February 1950

1. "Lend Me Your Life!" Casey and Ann save a man from being murdered and expose a scheme to loot a company's payroll and collect on an insurance policy as well. It's Ann who captures the evidence on film with a movie camera.

2. "'Ma' Jenkins, Gang Boss!" When "Nails" Jenkins dies, he leaves his business to his aged mother. Little does she know the business is a gang of truck hijackers and the gang is using her as a front. Casey works undercover as "Speed Perry" and teams up with "Ma" Jenkins to put her son's gang out of business.

3. "The Mystery of the Dead Man's Hands." After eccentric artist Emil Lanz dies in a plane crash, his manager, Otto Frey, begins to paint in the manner of the master, supposedly because he had the hands of Lanz grafted onto his own wrists. When the hands begin to commit murder Casey uncovers as bizarre a situation as he has ever encountered.

4. Plus "Three were Strangers!" a crime thriller and "Black Horror," a two-page text story. Neither of these features is about Casey.

13
Casey on the Stage

The popularity of our crime fighting press photographer was such that there were few media outlets that did not, at one time or another, focus a major project on the hero of this book. Thus, it is not surprising that *Casey* eventually found his way to the stage.

With *Casey* earning income for his creator on the radio and in the several other venues outlined elsewhere in this volume, Coxe, with the support of CBS, managed to arrange to have a play written based on his famous hero. The man selected to write the play was a little known playwright named Wilbur Braun (1896–1968)* who, having written several other adaptations for publication by Samuel French, Inc. for the amateur market, seemed a natural. Braun, used the pseudonym "Stephen Bristol" to pen a three act mystery-comedy around *Crime Photographer.*

It should be noted that the practice of adapting radio programs for amateur stage performances was not unique to *Casey*. Similar efforts were undertaken for programs like *My Friend Irma* and *Archie Andrews*. Far more common, however, was the reverse practice of adapting certain Broadway successes to long running radio series: *The Aldrich Family* had its birth in the Clifford Goldsmith play, *What A Life,* and *Meet Corliss Archer* had its inception in the F. Hugh Herbert play, *Kiss And Tell,* to name just two Broadway to radio successes.

Samuel French published *Crime Photographer: A Thrilling Mystery Comedy In Three Acts* in 1950, the last full year of Philip Morris's sponsorship of the radio *Casey* and just a year before the start of the program's second television run. The text of the play runs some 102 pages and calls for cast of six males and seven females.

---

* Alan Hubin, in his respected book, *The Bibliography of Crime Fiction, 1749–1975,* shows Braun's birth year as 1894. The Library of Congress records give the year of his birth as 1896.

In the play, Casey, Ann Williams and Captain Logan are the only radio personalities to appear on stage, which consists of a single set representing the drawing room of the Powdrell mansion situated in the suburbs of a great city.

As the play opens, the audience learns that Mrs. Langdon, the Powdrell housekeeper, has recently passed away, having died in her sleep. At this point in the play it is assumed that her death was of natural causes. The wealthy owner of the mansion, Sumner Powdrell, is engaged in conversation with a good looking young fellow, Hoyt Lawrence, who clearly is interested in Powdrell's niece, Glory.

As the scene develops, both Glory and Tony Marchant, the young man who Glory clearly favors, arrive and get into a bitter dispute with Uncle Sumner who finds Tony an unsuitable match for his niece. The action here is hardly new, creative or unique. Indeed, seconds before the curtain falls on the first act, the audience is treated to what is described as a "ghost" covered in a white sheet entering the room through French windows, causing Glory who is alone in the room to faint. Shades of 1920s melodramas like *The Bat* or *The Cat and the Canary*, but hardly suitable even for a play written some 55 years ago.

When the play continues the audience learns that Sumner Powdrell has disappeared and that Captain Logan is now on the scene. And, with Logan there, can Casey and Ann Williams be far behind? Not likely. Not only must the disappearance of Sumner Powdrell be cleared up, but now the audience begins to hear speculation about the actual cause of death of housekeeper Langdon. Could she have been murdered, and if so, for what motive?

No more will be said about the plot except to add that in the Introduction to the published play, the publisher states that: "The finish of the play is a honey and the solution to the many intricate problems is really a killer-diller." It should surprise no one to learn that Casey works the clues to their logical outcome.

Curious readers (or die-hard *Casey* fans) wishing to read the play are advised to contact Samuel French which had a few copies left as this book went to press. Other less compulsive readers may be able to satisfy their appetite for more *Casey* material by reading the *Casey* short story and radio scripts found in earlier chapters.

Crime Photographer

A THRILLING MYSTERY COMEDY IN THREE ACTS

Based upon the character "Flash Gun Casey," created by George Harmon Coxe

by Stephen Bristol

Samuel French

About the Authors

J. Randolph Cox and David S. Siegel first became acquainted with one another in the 1970s when Cox, a Reference and Government Documents Librarian at St. Olaf College in Northfield, Minnesota and an active detective mystery fan frequently contributed scholarly articles to the now legendary *The Armchair Detective* magazine. Siegel, a Superintendent of Schools in New York State, was also an avid fan of detective mystery stories and subscriber to *The Armchair Detective*. Based on their mutual interests, the two exchanged correspondence and remained in touch.

In the ensuing years Randy (as he is known to his friends) kept busy editing and publishing *The Dime Novel Roundup,* a bi-monthly journal and other volumes including *The Dime Novel Companion, Masters of Mystery and Detective Fiction* and *Man of Magic & Mystery*. Retirement in 1996 hasn't slowed him down.

David, who following a 37 year career as an educator and administrator, co-authored a series of seven regional guides to used book dealers which allowed him, along with his wife and partner, to travel across the continent visiting used book stores (and, in the process, add numerous volumes to his already impressive library). His travels also allowed him to finally meet his old pen pal in person. He also edited and published *The Witch's Tale*, a book about the classic golden age of radio horror program, has written about other radio detectives such as Ellery Queen and is currently working on *A Resource Guide to the Golden Age of Radio*.

Randy's print mystery expertise matched with David's media mystery know-how make the two an ideal team to produce a volume focusing on the many lives of Flashgun Casey.

Other Old Time Radio books available from Book Hunter Press

The Witch's Tale by Alonzo Deen Cole. Thirteen original scripts from the landmark 1930s program, plus a biography of Alonzo Deen Cole, a complete Program Log and cast photographs. (Dunwich Press imprint).

A Resource Guide to the Golden Age of Radio (November, 2005). A comprehensive guide to special collections, Internet sites and a select bibliography.

And to locate used book dealers specializing in out-of-print books about radio, check the *Used Book Lover's Guides*

For more information, please visit
www.bookhunterpress.com/radio